HOW SUCCESSFUL LAW FIRMS REALLY WORK

DAVID L. GINSBERG and ROBERT A. FEISEE

AMERICAN BAR ASSOCIATION
Law Practice Division

Cover design by Elmarie Jara/ABA Design

Printed in the United States of America.
26 25 5 4 3

A catalog record for this book is available from the Library of Congress.

Discounts are available for books ordered in bulk. Special consideration is given to state bars, CLE programs, and other bar-related organizations. Inquire at Book Publishing, ABA Publishing, American Bar Association, 321 N. Clark Street, Chicago, Illinois 60654-7598.

www.ShopABA.org

David dedicates this book to his wife, Caryn, and their daughters, Tess and Eve; his brother, Steven, and his family; and his parents, Gary and Diane. "A special thanks to my father, who showed me the path as he built his accounting firm and made it clear to me that anything was possible. I cannot put into words how grateful I am for each of you, and I will always treasure our time together."

Bobby dedicates this book to his parents, Jalalodin and Seddigheh Feisee. "As immigrants who came to the United States with a few hundred dollars in their pockets and a vision of a better life, they have showed me that any obstacle can be overcome with belief in yourself and knowledge. As my mom always says, 'Knowledge is power.' To my daughter, Nava, who has her whole life ahead of her, you can create and build anything if you want it badly enough. Never forget where you came from, and always keep your head up and dream big."

Contents

About the Authors

David L. Ginsberg, Esquire

Professional

David L. Ginsberg and his partners, Heather A. Cooper and Daniel L. Gray, founded Cooper Ginsberg Gray in 2004. Cooper Ginsberg Gray has grown from a small family law firm to a medium-sized firm under their leadership.

After beginning his legal career as a legal aid attorney in Danville, Virginia, David moved to Fairfax, Virginia, in 1998. Since moving to Northern Virginia, his practice has focused exclusively on family law. David's legal skills have been recognized on numerous occasions.

David actively participates in the Virginia State Bar and Fairfax Bar Association. He serves on the board for Shelter House, which is a nonprofit that assists the homeless and victims of domestic violence. David and his co-author, Robert A. Feisee, have co-taught a law practice management course at their alma mater since 2012.

Education

David earned his law degree from the Antonin Scalia Law School at George Mason University in 1996. He earned an undergraduate degree from the McIntire School of Commerce at the University of Virginia in 1992.

Personal

David and his family live in Northern Virginia. David enjoys watching and playing basketball and is an avid photographer.

Robert ("Bobby") A. Feisee, Esquire

Professional

Bobby founded InSight Law, PLLC in 2008. InSight Law has grown from a solo law firm to a firm of 12 consisting of attorneys and support team members.

Bobby started his career at a small litigation law firm in 1996 and left law to become a financial advisor in 1999. As a result of issues with his own family's estate plan, Bobby decided to return to the practice of law in 2002. He initially opened the business as a solo "general" law firm until eventually creating InSight Law focusing solely on estate and business planning.

Bobby is an instructor for the National Network of Estate Planning Attorneys (NNEPA) and is active in various organizations in the field of estate and business planning. He has been teaching law practice management with his co-author, David L. Ginsberg, at their alma mater since 2012.

Education

Bobby earned his law degree from the Antonin Scalia Law School at George Mason University in 1996. He earned an undergraduate degree from the School of Management at Syracuse University in 1993.

Personal

Bobby and his family live in Northern Virginia. Bobby earned two National Championships playing lacrosse at Syracuse University. He enjoys coaching lacrosse at Paul VI High School and mountain biking.

Acknowledgments

We could not have written this book without a great deal of support.

Our families encouraged us and provided invaluable assistance. David wants to thank his wife, Caryn, who read and re-read the manuscript and offered many valuable tips.

Both of us owe a huge thank you to our colleagues at Cooper Ginsberg Gray and Insight Law. David's partners, Heather Cooper and Daniel Gray, graciously volunteered their time to review and offer pointers on the manuscript.

We have had many mentors and colleagues who have helped us throughout our careers. We cannot possibly name everyone here, but we wanted to acknowledge a few by name: Greg Hairston, Dennis Hottell, Robert Shoun, Robert Kotwicki, Joan Macleod, Newsha Nazmi Ansary, Edward S. Clay, Curt R. Ferguson, Michael A. Dolan, and J. David Kerr.

Special thanks to Bobby's colleagues at National Network of Estate Planning Attorneys (NNEPA) Richard L. Randall, Esq. and Scott A. Williams, Esq. who have been his mentors and introduced him to the world of law practice management; Syracuse University Men's Lacrosse Coach Roy Simmons, Jr. who took a chance on a walk-on; and Strategic Coach® and Bobby's business coaches, Adrienne Duffy, Barb Da Costa, and Stephanie Song.

Thank you as well to the Antonin Scalia Law School, specifically Annamaria Nields, Victoria M. Huber, and Mary Schifferli.

We will be forever indebted to Sharon Nelson, who suggested that we write this book, led us through the publishing steps, and encouraged us throughout.

We thank our friends at ABA Publishing and the ABA Publishing Board, who have been with us from the first word to the last. In particular, we want to thank our editor, Sarah Craig.

1

Overview: How to Use This Book

The purpose of this book is to help you manage and run a successful law practice. Law schools do a great job teaching attorneys about contracts, property, torts, and so on, but rarely do they teach attorneys how to operate a law firm.

The success or failure of a law firm is based as much (or more) on knowing how to run a business as knowing the law. You cannot have a successful law firm without knowing how to run a business. We wrote this book after seeing too many law firms filled with brilliant lawyers fail because they lacked basic business skills.

Your Law Firm Is a Business

We encourage you to use common business practices to operate your law firm. These business practices and strategies have been proven to be effective and can be applied without compromising your ethics or professionalism. We know that you can run a successful law firm while providing the highest level of legal work.

Many lawyers simply have never learned these practices, and therefore they are not applied in many law firms. This book is designed to help lawyers at all levels of law firm management create and implement business strategies. We believe that business strategies can and should be applied by all attorneys regardless of their role within a firm.

Creating a Business Plan

Every law firm ranging from solo practitioners to international firms should have a business plan. This book is designed to help you write a business plan for your firm one building block at a time. Each chapter covers a different section that should be included in your business plan.

A comprehensive business plan will be invaluable for those who are planning to open their own firm or attorneys who are looking for ways to improve their existing firm.

If you are a partner or an associate at an existing firm, we encourage you to develop a business plan for your part of the practice. Partners should view themselves as having a mini-practice within their firm, and a business plan will help you build and enhance that practice. Associates can use a business plan to develop strategies that will improve their practice and help them become partners.

Our goal is to give every attorney the tools necessary to develop a business plan that will help you create or improve your firm or your portion of the practice. A business plan will provide you with a foundation that will help you through the ups and downs of running a law firm. We guarantee you there will be both peaks and valleys!

Reading This Book

Of course, we would love for you to read this book from cover to cover. If you read the entire book, you will understand all the concepts associated with running a law firm and how those concepts fit together. Each chapter addresses one segment of law firm management. From our perspective, each segment is important, and therefore, all the chapters require your attention. However, because the chapters are designed to cover individual issues, it is possible to pick and choose specific topics to review. Moreover, the index can help you identify where specific issues are discussed.

How to Use This Book

At the end of each chapter, we have outlined issues that we believe should be considered for that section of your business plan. Our intent is to create a means for you to draft a business plan in manageable steps. If you address the issues raised in these outlines chapter by chapter, you will have a complete business plan by the time you reach the end of this book. We cannot emphasize strongly enough how important we believe a written business plan is to your success.

What to Expect When You Read This Book

This book focuses on the operations of small to medium-sized law firms. Certain chapters will describe a firm's operations as if there is a team member or multiple team members to fulfill certain responsibilities. We purposefully outlined the responsibilities separately to give a clear picture of how the roles and responsibilities would be handled in an ideal situation.

We understand that very few law firms operate in the ideal situation. Very few of you will have the luxury of having enough time to complete every task outlined in this book, much less to hire multiple team members to complete tasks that you delegate. This book will show you how all the roles and responsibilities within a firm fit together and allow you to make educated decisions about what you prioritize and how you allocate your limited resources.

Overview

We start by taking a look at ownership structures and discussing the pros and cons of adding partners in the ownership chapter. A firm's ownership structure will serve as the foundation for how your firm is managed and operated.

After deciding who will own and manage your firm, it is time to determine how your resources will be allocated. While some resources should be allocated to all the major firm departments (human resources, marketing, legal services, finance, technology, management, and office environment) discussed throughout this book, every firm may allocate its resources differently.

The allocating resources chapter discusses how law firms can use their resources during different phases of operation beginning with the start-up phase. As the book progresses, it will take you through all the firm departments in detail so that you can determine which departments in your firm should be prioritized.

We start with human resources. The team members, human resources, and training chapters outline how you can build a productive team, manage them effectively, and train them to work efficiently. For those of you who do not plan to hire any team members, these chapters will help you identify what roles you must fill and how to train yourself to do them efficiently, and they will help you schedule time to fill each role.

Time is one of a lawyer's most valuable resources. We cannot overemphasize the need to properly manage your time to ensure that you are using it efficiently. Our managing your time chapter will help you design a plan to finish your work within your work week and leave your personal time free for your pleasure.

All law firms need clients. The ideal client, marketing, and managing clients chapters will help you define who you want as a client, how to attract those clients to your firm, and how to work with those clients.

All law firms provide legal services—the product that your business provides. The legal services and ethics chapters describe ways in which you can develop, expand, and maintain quality control over your legal services.

As a business owner, management of your finances is critical. Our billing and collection chapter will demonstrate how you can ensure that you are paid for the legal services you perform. Once you have collected the fees that you deserve, the finance chapter will show you how you can manage your finances.

Technology has always been important, but it plays a critical role in modern firms. Clients and team members expect top-notch technology, and often it is necessary to produce quality legal services. Our technology chapter outlines the technology issues that you should consider and how you can use technology to improve your firm.

We urge you to create systems and procedures for your firm. These will make your firm operate more efficiently and productively. Our systems and procedures chapters outline when a system or procedure is appropriate, what to consider when developing one, and examples of effective systems and procedures.

As explored in our office environment chapter, your office environment should be carefully considered whether you have a traditional physical office or a virtual one. Your office environment says a lot about you to not only your clients but also your team members.

This book encourages you to look at your law firm as a business, but we recognize that a law firm is not a run-of-the-mill business. There are special considerations to running a law firm that other businesses do not have to contend with. We take a look at these in our business versus profession chapter.

We strongly encourage you to plan for the future of your firm. Our strategic planning and emergency chapters outline how to create and implement short-term, long-term, and emergency plans.

All businesses depend on the performance of their team members, and no team member is more important than you. Our wellness chapter outlines how you can take care of yourself and your team members.

Reference Materials

Throughout the book, we reference key forms and templates that are often used in successful law firms. You should develop customized forms for your specific practice. The appendix to this book contains general forms that you can use as a starting point.

We have also provided guidance on where you can obtain more specific information about a topic or how a specific issue is handled in a particular practice area.

Our Goal

We know that opening a law firm or running one is always challenging and can be downright terrifying. Our goal is to give you the tools to overcome those challenges and fears so that you can run a successful law firm. This book provides real-world options to deal with the real-world challenges you face.

We wish all of you the best in your firms!

2

Ownership: Should You Have a Partner?

Do You Want a Partner?

You will not face a more difficult or critical decision than determining who else, if anyone, will own part of your business. Partners come in all shapes and sizes, but all of them will have a significant impact on the management and operation of your firm. The first question is whether you want or need a partner.

Many of you may be thrilled about the prospect of being the only owner since that would not only allow you to do everything "your way" but also allow you to be sole beneficiary. Others may not want the responsibility of making all the decisions and being solely responsible if things do not go as well as hoped.

Characteristics of an Ideal Partner

We recommend starting this decision process by making an honest assessment of your strengths and weaknesses. In your honest assessment of yourself, you need to determine if you have the ability and willingness to work collaboratively with someone else. Can you go from making all the decisions to allowing someone else to have input in decisions or even make some decisions?

If you have to be in total control or you will not be able to listen to and discuss your partner's position in good faith when he or she disagrees with you, you may be better off without a partner. Of course, if you decide that you are capable of this, you will want to find a partner who is also capable of sharing control and working collaboratively with you.

Regardless of how wonderful your potential new partner may be, a partnership will not work well if you cannot get along with your partner and you do not set clear expectations at the outset. We realize that this sounds simplistic, and many of you are thinking that, as individuals with advanced degrees, either we will be mature enough to focus on business issues rather than personalities or we can figure out a way to overcome any personality issues.

We disagree. A law firm may survive with partners who do not like each other and/or do not get along well with each other, but it will not thrive.

Pro Tip: Never underestimate the value of having a partner that you genuinely enjoy as a person. Your ability to get along with your partner(s) will have a significant impact on your bottom line and your overall happiness.

Ideally, you and your partner(s) will get along well. When you have a solid relationship, it is much easier to discuss sensitive issues when they arise. Do not delude yourself into thinking that there will never be a sensitive issue. Eventually, there will be discussions about compensation, how hard someone is working, whether to hire or fire someone, and so on that one or both of you feel strongly about.

Pro Tip: We spoke with an attorney who has been in practice for more than 50 years. During his career, he was a partner in several law firms that provided excellent legal services, but nevertheless the firms broke apart. When we asked him why the firms kept splitting, he told us that the one common denominator in the implosion of each firm was a disagreement over money.

If you cannot agree on the color of the sky before you start the discussion, it is not likely that you will agree on the important business decision that needs to be made. Even if you have a tie-breaking system in place, the partner who did not get his or her way will not be satisfied with the outcome if he or she feels that you reached this point because you were unwilling to listen because of your underlying dislike of one another. That dissatisfaction can manifest itself in many ways, none of which are positive.

One very important issue that you and your potential partner need to see eye to eye on is your firm's spending practices. If you cannot agree in principle on how the firm's resources will be spent, you will have at least two distinct issues. On the one hand, you will always be arguing about the firm's strategies and how the firm can be most successful. On the other hand, distributions and expenses cut into the firm's profits. When one partner thinks that his or her profit share is too low because the other partner spent firm resources recklessly or inefficiently, problems will arise.

While you do not have to agree on every single budget line item, you and your potential partner need to agree on the philosophy regarding major aspects of the budget. In a modern firm, the major aspects include human resources (Will you pay your team members top dollar, as little as you can, or market rate?), technology (What role will it play in the firm's operations, and how many resources will be allocated to it?), and marketing (How much time and effort will be put into generating revenue?).

Firms should take diversity into consideration when choosing a partner. More clients may be willing to consider hiring firms that are diverse or firms that have partners who more closely resemble them. In addition, diverse firms can also open the door to a wider range of potential team members.

An ideal partner will share your philosophy toward practicing law and managing a business, and your goals for both. The ideal partner will also compliment your strengths and/or provide a strength in an area where you have a weakness.

As this book progresses, we will describe the roles that must be filled in a successful firm in much more detail. It is highly unlikely that you will find a partner who excels at everything that must be accomplished. When choosing a partner, the most important starting point is to determine what you expect of your new partner. Are you looking for someone to lead the firm? Someone to fill a specific role within the firm?

Before you start looking for a partner, outline your expectations of one. Before you form a partnership with someone, make sure your expectations are communicated clearly and that your potential new partner agrees with them. The most successful partnerships are ones in which the partners know what to expect of each other, and those expectations are reasonable.

Invest Time and Effort to Choose the Right Partner

For those of you who want a partner, a significant investment in time and effort to find the right partner will be well worth it. Take the time to identify the qualities you are looking for in a partner and what role you expect the partner to fulfil.

When you find a good candidate, make certain that you and the prospective partner have the same or at least similar goals, philosophies, and expectations, and then memorialize them in a partnership agreement. Finding partners who fit your vision for the firm will lead to a very productive and efficient firm.

As you develop your vision for the firm, you should also be developing a vision for the role that a new partner will have within the firm. There is no single correct definition or description for a partner. As the leader(s) of your firm, you have the responsibility of defining and describing what a partner means to you.

The old-fashioned image of a partner is someone who leads the firm by having decision-making authority in all major firm policies and issues. We encourage you to shape the role of a potential partner to meet the needs of your firm rather than a traditional image.

You may want a partner who is deeply involved and invested in every meaningful firm decision, but you may also want a partner who focuses on one area of expertise, such as bringing in cases or managing a new practice area.

Choosing a Partner in a Small or Medium-Sized Firm

If you or your firm are inclined to hire a new partner, you need to determine how you will choose the partner. Most sole proprietors make the decision whether to add a partner and who that partner should be on their own. This is too big a decision to make on a whim, and as much as you may trust your own judgment, we strongly advise you to get input from others.

You can obtain valuable input from a variety of sources. If you prefer a structured process to search for and hire a partner, you should look to a recruiting company or business coach. Recruiting companies and coaches are easy to access but will be more costly in terms of dollars than less formal approaches.

Less formal options will depend more on your diligence and persistence. Therefore, they may be harder to access and costly in terms of time but less costly in terms of dollars. The simplest approach is to seek feedback about your potential partner from other members of the legal community you trust and respect. Another option is to create a group of lawyers who meet periodically to discuss and strategize about management issues. Many larger bar organizations will have law practice management groups that can provide a ready-made group.

Pro Tip: An attorney's personal life can have a huge impact on the attorney's professional goals. The fact that all of the founding partners in David's law firm had small children and shared the same work/life goals gave them a common philosophy upon which to build the firm's business.

The selection process for small to medium-sized firms presents a complex scenario. A new partner in this size firm will impact all the existing partners personally, legally, and financially. Because there will be a significant impact on everyone, should everyone have input into whether a partnership is offered to someone?

The more people who are involved in the decision-making process, the more likely someone will object to the potential partner candidate. Nevertheless, we encourage small and medium-sized firms to involve everyone in the search and decision-making process. Your selection process should be robust, and it may well be difficult and time-consuming for the potential partner and for the firm. But it will be worth it, as you do not want just anyone to become partner.

Including everyone in the decision-making process will enable all of your partners to understand the decision to make someone partner or to reject an application. This will minimize the fallout that could ensue if someone is named a partner without unanimous support from the existing partners. The objecting partner(s) will have an opportunity to hear the positives about the candidate that led the other partners to approve the new partner, and while they may not have placed the same value on those positives, they can at least see the logic behind the decision.

Factors to Consider When Adding a Partner to a Solo or Small Firm

The smaller the firm, the greater the risk when adding a partner. As a solo practitioner, you were responsible for everything related to your firm until you added a partner. With a partner, someone else may suddenly control 50 percent of the firm for better or worse.

It may feel as if the firm you created either no longer exists or has morphed overnight into something that you do not recognize. Before you add partners, it is important that you visualize what the new partnership will look like.

Most partners in small firms expect to have a significant voice in how the firm is run. Decisions that you made unilaterally as a solo practitioner now must be discussed and agreed upon with your partner(s). Inevitably, there will be some decisions that your partner(s) want to handle differently, and you will need to be prepared to accept that you will no longer have complete control.

Pro Tip: Partners can add value without increasing your income. A partner can reduce your stress levels, make your work environment more enjoyable, and provide a sounding board. The emotional benefits of adding a partner should not be ignored.

Many solo practitioners appreciate adding a partner because it gives them backup coverage for their cases. Even if a new partner does not add a dime of income, a new partner adds value because you as a solo practitioner no longer have to scramble to cover court dates or client emergencies when you want to take a vacation or a sick day.

In addition to having coverage for your cases, there may be other aspects of adding a partner that you find valuable. These benefits can range from personal ones such as having a companion to professional ones such as having a colleague available to discuss case strategies. While valuable to some lawyers, these benefits may not have a direct impact on the bottom line.

We encourage you not to ignore these "soft" benefits because money is not the only measure of happiness. However, the financial impact of a new partner cannot and should not be ignored.

For solo and smaller firms, the most likely benefit of adding a partner will result from an efficiency of scale. The number of calls or amount of outgoing mail generated by a solo practitioner typically does not keep an administrative team member busy all day, but most solo practitioners want to have someone full time to be available whenever the need arises. Adding one partner will not generate enough administrative work to necessitate a second administrative team member.

Therefore, the solo practitioner immediately reduced the cost of his or her administrative team member. There are numerous examples of how adding a partner can lower your expenses including, but not limited to, the following; lower overall rent because you can share a conference room, lower copier/scanner fees because you can share one machine, lower utilities bills, less time spent on non-billable work because you can share it with your partner, and so on.

The reduction in costs will enable partners in small firms to increase their income without increasing the amount of legal work they generate. It should not be too difficult for you to identify expenses that would take less out of your pocket if a partner was sharing them.

Choosing a Partner in a Large Firm

Larger firms have more resources at their disposal than small and medium-sized firms. As a result, they have the luxury of conducting a longer and more thorough search and hiring process than smaller firms. These firms can afford to have human resources teams conduct the initial screening, and their partners have enough support that they can afford to take more time away from their law practice to evaluate the partner candidates.

While we encourage you to involve as many partners as possible in significant firm decisions, there reaches a point at which it becomes impractical to involve every partner in every decision. When there are too many decision makers, it will become too difficult to reach a consensus on any issue. For this reason, the partner selection process is typically delegated to a recruiting committee or a smaller subset of the partners.

Since choosing partners is such an important decision, all partners should have input into the system or process that the firm implements to choose a partner even if they are not directly involved in each partner decision. The partners must have faith that the system or people in place are going to choose partners that they will want to work with.

Larger firms can pursue two general approaches to choosing a new partner. One option is for the firm to establish a firm-wide committee to select partners. The advantage of a firm-wide committee is that it can develop an expertise in recruiting and selecting partners, and if the committee is a fair representation of the entire firm, it will select partners that will advance the interests of the firm as a whole. The downside of a firm-wide committee is that it may not obtain as much information from the actual department where the partner will work as to whether he or she will be a good fit. As a result, the department may end up with a partner who looks good on paper but does not work well with the existing team.

Key Characteristics of a Good Partner

- Leadership skills
- Loyalty to the firm
- Ability to manage not only a legal team but also a business team
- Shared goals for the firm
- Strong work ethic
- Ability to generate financial benefits for the firm

The alternative to a firm-wide committee is to let each department operate like a small or medium-sized firm and make their own decisions as to who becomes partner. While this may lead to finding partners who fit well into each working group, it could also lead to a fragmented firm. The departments may start developing their own philosophies that are not aligned with other departments, and they may start operating independently from the other departments.

Ideally, the firm will be able to balance the needs of the firm as a whole with the department where the new partner will be working on a daily basis. We favor models that establish a standing firm-wide committee to select partners that is required to involve and obtain feedback from the department where the partner will work as part of the process.

Promoting an Associate to Partner

It is not uncommon to hear that a firm has made an associate a partner to reward the associate's loyalty. Many partners feel an obligation to promote associates to partner who have been with the firm for many years.

Certainly, there is something to be said for showing loyalty to your team members. However, we strongly recommend against making someone a partner solely because he or she has been with your firm for a number of years. Partners have a great deal of responsibility to their other partners and the firm as a whole, and longevity on its own should not determine whether someone can handle such responsibility. There are several other key characteristics that a good partner should have besides just loyalty.

You should evaluate an associate seeking partnership on the same criteria as you would use when evaluating someone outside of your firm. The associate should have several advantages over a potential lateral hire, and if all things are otherwise equal, you should promote the associate. Making a tenured team member a partner allows younger and less experienced team members see how their hard work and sticking with the firm can pay off. Seeing the prospect of partnership at the end of the rainbow is infinitely more powerful than hearing stories that there may be a partnership there.

In terms of evaluating an existing firm associate, you have a lengthy track record to measure the associate's legal ability and his or her ability to fit into the firm's team and culture (see Chapter 5 regarding reviews). Presumably, if the associate did not meet these standards, your firm would have cut its ties with the associate earlier. Legal ability and a "good fit" are prerequisites, but a good partner must also have quality management skills.

When we talk about management skills, we are referring to not only the ability to make decisions about the firm's operations but also an ability to transition from an associate role to a management role. When it comes to decision-making skills, you need to determine if the associate shares your goals for the firm and has the ability to analyze business decisions in the same way that he or she analyzes legal issues.

In many respects, the hardest part of transitioning from associate to partner is the team dynamic. Yesterday, the associate was on one level within the team, and today that same person is on a higher level that requires him or her to make decisions about colleagues' day-to-day work and their futures. The flip side is that the nonpartner team members must be able to respect and follow the lead of a partner who was in their shoes the day before. The associate should have been working toward this transition for a long period leading up to the partner decision since this is not a transition that will occur overnight.

Pro Tip: When an associate first becomes a partner, provide opportunities for the new partner to manage situations that appear to be a natural extension of what the new partner had been doing as an associate. For example, the new partner should be managing team members on case-related issues. The new partner should not be conducting the annual reviews for associates.

Hiring a Lateral Partner

A lateral partner may offer your firm a wider range of options than an internal associate. Presumably, your associate's strengths will lie in the practice areas that your firm has established. A lateral hire may be able to open doors in practice areas or with clients that your firm has not been able to reach previously. If you are going to hire a lateral partner, it is important that you and the lateral partner agree on what each of you expect out of the partnership. Will this partner bolster an existing practice area, create a new one, or provide some other benefit?

Pro Tip: Associates who do not generate business are not likely to start generating business just because they become a partner. The title does not generate business by itself. Lateral partners who do not generate business at their current firm are not likely to magically start generating business at your firm. When deciding whether to make someone a partner in your firm, be honest with yourself as to how much business the potential partner can really generate.

The easiest type of partner to incorporate into your firm is one who has the same skillset you do. This type of partner can allow you to expand your capacity or market share in product lines that you have already established, and this partner will be able to support your existing partners.

Aside from personality questions as to how the prospective new partner will coexist with you and your partners, the next biggest question is whether there is or will be enough work in the existing product lines to keep your new partner busy.

The logical starting point to determine if there is enough work for a new partner is to take a look at the partner's historical workload. Of course, there is no guarantee that the new partner can bring his or her entire book of business to your firm. However, if the new partner has a long track record, it is reasonable to assume that the new partner will be able to maintain a comparable amount of work at your firm. The caveat to this is that you need to ensure that the new partner was generating his or her own cases and that the new partner's caseload was not the benefit of overflow work from other partners at the previous firm.

If the lateral partner candidate does not have a long track record, you have to gauge whether the new partner will be able to generate enough business to justify a partnership. The two best indicators regarding an individual's ability to generate business are the candidate's willingness to generate business and whether you trust the candidate's plan.

Pro Tip: If you are hiring a lateral partner to start a new product line, the benefits and costs should be analyzed as if you are starting a new business. Project the additional revenue the new partner/produce line will generate in the early years and what it will cost to produce those legal services.

A lateral partner may be willing to base his or her income on the profits the new product line generates. This is one way to reduce your firm's financial risk.

Certain individuals simply do not want to be responsible for obtaining clients. They only want to perform the legal work. Perhaps the candidate's legal skill and talent will be enough to attract business on its own, but very few people are likely to have that skill level.

For those who are willing to try to generate work, you need to evaluate the likelihood that the candidate's plan will succeed. No lawyer walks into a courtroom without a plan; one should not walk into a partnership without a plan either.

When you are considering a lateral partner whose goal will be to generate new business for the firm, not only do you need to evaluate the potential partner's plan to obtain business, but also you need to determine if a market demand exists. We have observed firms measure market demand with approaches that range from informal word of mouth to formal analytical studies. Smaller firms tend to gauge the need for another attorney on whether they are getting requests for more legal services than the existing team can handle. Larger firms or ones with larger marketing budgets often conduct more formal and analytical market research to determine whether a new partner will be profitable.

You have to balance your need to know whether there is enough work to support a new partner against the costs of getting the most detailed information. Not everyone can afford the most sophisticated market research, but everyone can and absolutely should investigate whether there is enough market demand to support a new partner.

Market research becomes even more important if you expect your new partner to expand your practice to cover new product lines. While you can use the same techniques to measure the demand for legal services as when you are hiring a partner to help with an existing product line, it is critical to accurately gauge whether your prospective partner can generate enough business in the new product line.

Even if you can overcome the challenges associated with hiring a lateral partner and creating a demand for a new product line, there are other costs associated with this plan that need to be considered. A new product line will require changes to your systems, team structure, and potentially team members. All of these changes come with a cost. You need to evaluate whether the benefits of the lateral partner and new product line outweigh the costs.

Most lawyers anticipate that a new partner means more money. From a business perspective, adding revenue is typically a good thing. However, lawyers are notoriously bad at measuring whether the added revenue actually means more profits. More revenue sounds great, but not if it requires an even greater investment in human resources in terms of new salaries and/or management. Old-fashioned lawyers and/or managers tend to discount the cost of asking existing employees to work with new people or to take on new responsibilities. (See Chapter 14 for a more detailed discussion of profit analysis.)

In addition to bolstering existing product lines or developing new ones, a new partner can attract new clients and team members. Certain lawyers have excellent networks and connections that enable them to generate business. These lawyers are often referred to as rainmakers, and on the surface, they appear to be very attractive lateral hires.

Rainmakers may bring in the most revenue, but they also tend to cause the most disruption—both good and bad. When they bring in more work, someone has to do the work, but it is not always the rainmaker. This means that you need to either prepare your team for the extra burden or enlarge your team to accommodate the extra work.

In addition, rainmakers often play fast and loose with office rules and procedures, and therefore, they may be less likely to adhere as closely to your systems as others. This is especially true of a rainmaker who is used to a different system or no system at all. This partner may have difficulty adhering to your established workflow process. Not only will this impact the efficiency of your systems, but also it could cause friction with the rest of your team if the rainmaker is allowed to follow a different set of rules.

Role in Firm Decisions

One aspect of partnership that is often overlooked is what, if any, role a new partner will have in firm decisions. It is important to have clearly defined parameters on the role of a new partner with regard to firm decisions. If your new partner is going to have a say in firm management, you need to know what his or her management philosophies are. Of course, the smaller the firm, the more important this is because each partner's vote carries more weight.

We find that it is incredibly rare for an equity partner not to have any input or voting rights in firm decisions. That said, the voting rights may range from nominal to a controlling interest. Before making someone a partner, everyone must be on the same page with regard to the authority that will come with the partnership.

When you plan for the new partner to have input into management decisions, it is critical that you and the new partner review expectations and short- and long-term plans to ensure that you are on the same page. In-depth discussions with your potential partner regarding his or her philosophies can increase the likelihood that decisions will fall within a range that you will find acceptable even if you and your new partner do not see exactly eye to eye on every decision.

Furthermore, an individual's general philosophies and strategies are less likely to undergo wholesale changes over time. Getting to know a potential partner's general philosophies and approaches to issues will be a more reliable predictor of future behavior than taking a snapshot as to how your potential partner will decide a pending question or issue.

Pro Tip: How do you decide whether it makes financial sense to make someone a partner? For a moment, ignoring the nonmonetary considerations, what variables should go into the decision as to whether to make someone a partner?

- How much revenue will the partner generate for him- or herself and the rest of the firm?
- How much will the partner be paid?
- Will paying an additional partner result in a decrease in income for the existing partner(s)?
- What support will a new partner require, and what will it cost?
- If an associate is being considered for partner, how much will it cost to replace the attorney if he or she leaves if not made partner?

Succession Plan

A critical benefit of having partners is that they function as a succession plan. Firms do not close up shop when one partner leaves as long as there are partners in place to take the departing partner's place. For this reason, you should seriously consider incorporating partners who have different experience levels. While it may feel more comfortable to hire partners who are your age and have similar experience levels, the firm will not survive if you and your partners all retire at the same time.

Making younger attorneys into partners can also serve as a quasi-retirement plan. When firms require new partners to buy their way into the partnership, the new partners are buying a piece of your ownership in the firm. On the other end, as your career winds down, you can continue to earn a significant salary as your younger partners hit their prime billing years.

Pro Tip: Absolutely make reasonable efforts to make your partnership work. But once you determine that the partnership cannot be salvaged, put your efforts into terminating it amicably and moving in a different direction. Do not prolong the agony.

Terminating a Bad Partnership

The question that no one wants to address, but that absolutely must be addressed, is how do you get out of a partnership that is not working? We are regularly amazed by how many attorneys ignore this issue when they enter into a partnership. Lawyers routinely advise clients and draft contracts that address how issues will be handled when the two sides do not agree, but they do not take their own advice when it comes to their partnerships.

Despite everyone's best efforts and no matter how much analysis and research you do before entering into a partnership, not all partnerships will work. You must have an exit strategy. The best time to develop the exit strategy is when you are forming the partnership and everyone is optimistic and working cooperatively.

You will have to decide how easy or difficult you want to make it for a partner to leave the firm or for you to expel someone from the partnership. Regardless of the criteria that would allow you or your partners to dissolve the partnership, your partnership agreement should set forth a clear path that will allow you to break up the partnership as easily as it was put together. One colleague of ours suggests that a firm should be put together as if you were going to take it apart.

The exit strategy must address how you would vote someone out of the partnership and/or what would trigger an automatic expulsion (see Chapter 5 for other termination considerations). When a partner is forced to leave, at a minimum the following issues should be addressed: how the partner's case load and clients will be handled, how accounts receivables will be shared, what the buyout amount will be for the partner's ownership interest in the firm, what responsibility the departing partner will have for firm liabilities, and how the departure will be communicated to other team members and the legal community.

If you do not realize that there are significant differences until you have a new partner, at best those differences will be a drag on the firm's efficiency and at worst they will create major divides within the firm. Even if you have the means to expel a partner from the partnership, that process will be much harder and costlier than if you had never entered into the partnership.

Furthermore, accepting and then expelling a partner will not give your team members much confidence in your decision-making ability, and your team members will wonder how temporary their status within the firm may be. If a partner can be expelled, no one is safe.

The Importance of a Partnership Agreement

All firms should have a written partnership agreement. No lawyer would advise two people who operate a business together to rely solely on a handshake deal, and no lawyer should enter into a partnership without a written agreement.

The partnership agreement should discuss how additional partners may be added, how partners can be terminated, how firm decisions will be made, work and/or revenue requirements for partners, and how partners will be compensated. To the extent that your firm has special circumstances, those should be addressed in the partnership agreement as well.

The best partnership agreements set forth the expectations that you have for a new partner and what the new partner can expect from you in terms of work load and management responsibilities. You and your new partner need to know how much revenue you must generate each year and how much new business you need to bring into the firm. Just as importantly, both of you need to know which firm decisions each of you will make individually and which ones will be made jointly.

The negotiation and/or review of a partnership agreement will help you and the prospective new partner identify any differences in expectations and/or philosophies. Even if exploration of these differences results in the prospective partner declining the partnership offer or you withdrawing the offer, this is a far better result than the alternative.

Ownership Section of Business Plan

We anticipate that your answers to the questions below will serve as an outline for the ownership section of your business plan. These answers will form the foundation for how your firm is managed and operated.

1. Do you want a partner, and if so, why?
2. Characteristics of an ideal partner
    a. What are your strengths?
    b. What are your weaknesses?
    c. What priorities or issues do you and your partner need to agree upon?
3. Choosing a partner
    a. Who will be the decision makers in selecting a partner?
    b. Who will you seek advice or guidance from about potential partners?
4. Expectations of a lateral partner
    a. Is there enough work for another partner?
        i. *How will you measure whether there is enough work?*

   b. Do you expect a new partner to bring in additional work for the firm?
      i. *What support will the new partner need to generate more work?*
      ii. *What support will the new partner need to perform the legal work?*
   c. Do you expect a new partner to develop a new practice area?
      i. *What additional systems will your firm need to accommodate the new practice area?*
      ii. *What impact will a new practice area have on your firm?*
5. Promoting an associate to partner
   a. How will you know when your associate is ready to become a partner?
   b. What steps will you have to take to help the associate and your team adjust to the new role as partner?
6. Role in firm decisions
   a. What firm decisions will your partner have a say in making?
   b. How much say will your partner have in each of these decisions?
7. Succession plan
   a. Will the new partner have to buy into the partnership?
   b. Will the new partner have the ability to increase his or her ownership level?
8. Terminating a bad partnership
   a. What actions would a partner have to take to trigger his or her removal?
   b. What steps would you have to take to terminate a partner?

See the Appendix of this book for a sample Partnership/Operating Agreement that you can customize for your firm's needs.

3

Allocating Resources: What Is the Best Use of Your Limited Resources?

Every firm we have encountered has limited resources. The goal is to allocate those limited resources in the most efficient and effective manner possible.

Pro Tip: Allocation of resources is a key aspect of your strategic planning (see Chapter 20). Allocations should be made in the context of your long-term plans, not solely on what seems best for today.

Resources

The two most important resources are time and money. Time is arguably your most valuable asset because it is limited. There are only so many hours in the day. The only way to increase the time available to you is to add team members and leverage technology.

If time is your most valuable resource, money is a close second. It never feels as if there is enough money to go around. Money is necessary to compensate your team members and to pay for all of your plans.

Allocations in General

Very few firms allocate an equal amount of resources to all their plans or projects, and we do not recommend that you try to allocate your resources equally. We encourage you to determine what your priorities are and to allocate more resources to your priorities.

The allocation of your resources will change as your firm matures and its goals change. We encourage you to project what resources you will have and how they will be allocated not only in the present but also in the future.

We find it helpful to create pie charts for each resource. The visual of a pie chart is often more memorable than simply looking at numbers in a spreadsheet.

Adjusting Allocations

We recommend analyzing this issue with a close eye on the business development stage of your firm. The needs, and therefore allocation of resources, for your firm will differ significantly depending on where the firm falls in the business development life cycle.

At each stage, you can choose to devote your time to any of the core business departments discussed previously such as marketing, legal services, finance/accounting, human resources, and technology. You cannot ignore any of these departments, but you also cannot devote your full time and attention to each area. The key is to determine what your firm needs and allocate your resources accordingly.

Since every firm's needs will change over time, it is important to review and adjust your allocations periodically. An established firm should review its allocations at least annually. Newer firms should review their allocations more frequently because their needs are likely to change more quickly.

Pro Tip: There is no required time period for your pre-opening phase. We know firms who have opened their doors three weeks after they decided to break off from another firm, and others who have taken close to a year. It all depends on how quickly you can accomplish everything that is necessary to open your business.

Pre-Opening Phase

Before you open your doors, you need to purchase and establish the basic infrastructure required to operate. Unless you are purchasing another firm and all of its assets, you will need to set up your workspace and determine how you will run your firm.

When your first potential clients contact you, you will likely need a workspace to meet with them and the ability to handle their legal matter. In addition to a place (whether physical or electronic) to meet with your client, you will need to purchase the technology—for example, word processing, document formation, and/or presentation programs—that you will need to represent them.

Other technology tools, such as billing, accounting, and customer service software—will also be necessary to run your firm. We will address these in greater detail in later chapters. We strongly encourage you to have all of these tools operational before you open your doors. You likely will not have the capacity to work out technology bugs while you are servicing your initial clients.

You will have to determine whether you should purchase or lease equipment, technology tools, furniture, and so on. If you decide to purchase, you will then need to decide if you want to invest the bare minimum at the start or purchase something that will not need to be replaced anytime soon. The functional timeline of these items will dictate how quickly you will need to invest financial resources into them again.

We anticipate that you will allocate your time to establishing your systems and procedures. The more thought you put into developing these systems and procedures, the more smoothly your office will run once it is opened. Of course, there will be some trial and error, but hopefully you will have anticipated most of the issues that will arise.

You are not required to do everything yourself. In fact, we strongly recommend against trying to do it all yourself. You are a lawyer, not a technology or accounting professional. Spend some of your time finding vendors you are comfortable working with, and spend some of your financial resources on them.

We recommend that you get referrals from other colleagues. However, you should recognize that you may have different needs than some of your referral sources. Even after obtaining referrals, it is important to interview the recommended vendors to ensure that they can provide what you need.

Pro Tip: Remember that workspace does not necessarily mean more office space. Technology allows you to have workspaces in your team members' homes, favorite coffeehouse, and so on.

New Firms

You are open!

Many attorneys envision being overrun with clients the minute they open their doors, but that rarely happens. Most attorneys must really work to attract clients to a new firm. For this reason, we recommend that you allocate a significant portion of your time and money to marketing (see Chapter 9 regarding marketing).

Once you attract clients, your largest financial expenses and use of time will be associated with ongoing operations. You will certainly need time to perform the legal work you have been hired to handle.

Depending on the type of case, you may need significant financial resources to fund the case. For example, personal injury lawyers often have to advance the costs of expert witnesses.

In addition to the legal work, you will need to spend money to operate the firm. You will have to maintain your workspace, update the technology licenses, and most importantly, pay your team members and yourself.

While many attorneys feel that their human resources obligations are complete when the payroll checks are issued, this could not be further from the truth. This is the end of the financial aspect, but it is often just the beginning of the time you need to invest in human resources.

In order to operate an efficient firm, you need to invest time in managing your team members and your third-party vendors. Everyone needs to work as a cohesive unit. Without leadership and guidance, that will not happen.

Whether you have clients or not, you will have operating expenses. You will need to budget to pay for your workspace, utilities, and most importantly your team members and yourself.

Growing Firms

Firms that have been operating for a few years but are still growing tend to spend more on their workspace and marketing than firms in other phases. These firms will need more workspace (or even new offices) for their new team members, and they will need to bring in more and more clients to justify expanding.

The largest expense increase for a growing firm will be human resources. Very few firms can grow without adding team members, and quality team members are expensive. Of course, additional team members can pay huge dividends either by producing revenue themselves or by freeing up another team member to focus solely on revenue-producing projects.

Established Firms

These firms have gone through growth spurts and are more stable in terms of clients, team members, revenue, and expenses. Given this stability, the allocation of resources is less likely to change significantly year to year.

If they are comfortable with their current status, these firms have the luxury of maintaining the allocation that works. These firms still need to monitor market conditions to determine if any allocation changes are necessary to maintain their comfort level.

Well-established firms are more likely to have surpluses, particularly financial, that they will need to allocate. Of course, the firm can allocate them to team members in the form of bonuses, but they can also choose to invest in improving their infrastructure and operations or to expand into new fields.

Budgeting

Budgeting and allocation of resources go hand in hand. You must take the time to budget accurately to understand what resources are or will be available to you.

Once you make certain decisions, such as office space and software licenses, you will be locked into certain financial obligations. These recurring expenses will limit the discretionary amount of money available to you and, therefore, limit your flexibility in reallocating resources until those obligations expire.

The same principle applies to your time. If your team members are already working at capacity to represent your existing clients, they will not have additional time to take on new projects.

Future Allocation of Resources

Making predictions years into the future is always challenging and is certainly not an exact science. Nevertheless, you need to do your best to predict what you will need so you can put yourself in position to meet those needs.

These predictions must be based on your business plans and your long-term goals (see Chapter 20 regarding strategic planning). For example, if your goal is to hire an associate in year three, you need to plan ahead. The allocation decisions related to the new associate may start a year or more before the associate arrives.

Solo Practitioners

Just because you are not adding associates to you firm does not mean that you can ignore the question of how your resources will be allocated in the future. You will likely be faced with decisions regarding upgrades to hardware, software, and so on to increase the efficiency and profit of your firm.

Prior to the associate's arrival, you will need to increase your marketing budget to ensure that there is enough work to allow the associate to hit the ground running. As the associate's start date approaches, you will need to allocate resources to equip the associate's workstation. At a minimum, the associate will need a computer; and if you expect the associate to work at a physical office, you may need to purchase furniture and other accessories for the office space.

Pro Tip: Review and revise your projections regularly. Do not be dismayed if every projection is not accurate. They are projections, and no one is 100 percent accurate. As you gather more information, incorporate it into your projections and adjust them accordingly.

Once the associate starts working, you will need to allocate human resources to train and manage him or her. Also, of course, you will need to spend money to compensate the new team member.

Some allocations will follow consistent patterns. For example, technology, furniture, and equipment will have lifespans that can be reliably predicted. Other allocations will be harder or impossible to predict, such as the resources necessary to operate the firm through natural disasters, health issues, and malpractice claims.

Projections

We recommend that you attempt to project your firm's resources and needs for at least several years into the future. By looking several years ahead, you will be able to change the trajectory of your firm if necessary. Reviewing and revising your written business plan will provide you with a solid foundation for making projections.

For most firms, changing directions or allocation of resources looks more like turning an aircraft carrier than turning a speedboat. Firms need time to prepare for and to adjust to new directions. The only way to do this is to project your future need to determine what direction you want to go, and to project your future resources to determine how quickly you can make the turn.

Allocating Resources Section of Your Business Plan

We anticipate that your answers to the questions below will serve as an outline for the allocating resources section of your business plan. These answers will form the foundation for how your firm's resources will be allocated.

1. What resources do you have
   a. When you open?
   b. In three years?
   c. In ten years?
2. How will you allocate your time?
3. How will you allocate your money?
4. Who will you hire?
   a. Your first hire
   b. Your next hire
5. What is most important for your ideal client?
6. What is most important for your ideal team member?

4

Team Members: Who Should Be on Your Team?

Solo and Small Firms

Even solo practitioners have secretaries, assistants, paralegals, and so on. Very few law firms consist of only one person, and those firms often hire contractors or vendors to help them complete certain tasks.

If you are a solo practitioner or lead a small firm, we urge you to read this chapter even if you never plan to add any team members. This chapter can be read from two different perspectives: (1) the chapter outlines how to add team members and who those team members should be, or (2) the chapter outlines the roles and responsibilities that you will have to fill yourself.

We understand that many small firms cannot afford to hire all the team members contemplated in this chapter. As a manager of your firm, you need to be aware of the different roles that need to be filled so that you can allocate sufficient resources, namely your time, to address them.

The Right Team Members

Selecting the right team members is the decision that will have the greatest impact on the success of your firm. Your team members are your most valuable asset, not technology or any other tool you have purchased to set up your firm.

Some of you may dispute the statements above and argue that your team members can be replaced. On its face, this statement is true. All team members can be replaced, but then again, so can every computer, website, and desk.

We strongly believe the most successful law firms are those whose team members develop good relationships with clients, colleagues, and vendors. No matter how much you use technology to provide legal services, your team members are the ones who develop positive relationships.

Pro Tip: Every team member must have a role. That role must be one that you can define and that you believe will add value to your firm.

Human Resources Investment

You will spend significant financial resources on each team member. The costs extend well beyond the team member's salary. You will spend money on benefits, taxes, office space, equipment, and training for each team member.

When you select a team member, you are making a significant investment for your firm. For this reason, we strongly recommend that you put real time and effort into the hiring process to put yourself in the best possible position to make good selections.

How to Assemble Your Team

Throughout this book, we refer to everyone employed by your law firm as team members rather than employees. We urge you to think of your colleagues as team members.

When you think of someone as a teammate, you think of someone who has significant value. Teammates work together and help each other out. Employees and subordinates take instructions and execute orders; they work *for* someone, not *with* them.

Every team member has a role to play. Teams have superstars, grinders, cheerleaders, and other roles. The best teams have someone in all the important roles.

Your job as the owner is to build an effective and efficient team. The first step is to select the best possible person to become your team member, and the second step is to put each team member in the best possible position to succeed.

Unfortunately, no firm, especially smaller firms, has unlimited resources. This means that part of deciding how to assemble your team is deciding how many team members you can afford and which roles must be filled first.

Selection Process

Contrary to popular belief, an interview is not the first step in the selection process. In fact, this is almost the last step you should take.

Identify Positions You Need to Fill

As set forth in more detail when we discuss your human resources plan in Chapter 5, the first step is to determine how you want your firm to be structured. While there may be similarities between some firms, no two firms are exactly the same.

Just because another firm has a certain position does not mean that you need or should have that position. Furthermore, your idea of the responsibilities that come with a certain position may be radically different than what another firm expects from that position.

Smaller firms may prioritize their hiring needs based on what skills the current team members have. For example, one solo practitioner with an accounting background may be perfectly comfortable balancing and reconciling the firm's accounts while another cannot add two plus two but is a wiz on social media. The first solo practitioner has a greater need for marketing assistance while the second needs a bookkeeper.

As you decide which positions to fill, your firm structure will start to look different from the firm down the street. This is a positive, not a negative. Your firm should be structured around its needs, not someone else's needs.

If your goal is for your firm to grow, it is truly important to look at your projected organizational charts. Knowing your ideal team structure will help you make choices in the present that are designed to accomplish your long-term goals.

Think about your long-term strategy as you progress through the hiring process. When you make hiring decisions based solely on today's needs, you may box yourself into a corner. Each hiring decision on its own may not seem significant, but a series of hiring decisions based solely on a snapshot of what today looks like may lead you far from your ultimate goal.

Once you have started down a path, backtracking will be difficult. Eventually, you will reach a point on the path at which backtracking is no longer possible. You may be forced to develop new goals because the combination of individual decisions you have made may make it impossible to achieve your original goals.

Define Responsibilities of Each Position

Even more important than the title of the position you need to fill is the definition of the responsibilities that need to be handled. Listing a job title, such as receptionist or attorney, is helpful in identifying general categories that a potential team member will fall within, but a job title does not really say what you want the team member to do at your firm.

For example, different firms likely will have very different expectations of a second-year associate. A job listing that seeks a second-year associate could attract a wide range of applicants, many of whom are not good fits for your firm.

Your definition must include specific tasks you want your team members to perform. When you list the responsibilities, you should also include an estimate of how much time will be devoted to each task. This definition should form the foundation of your job listing.

For solo and small firms, it will be valuable to define the responsibilities of potential positions even if you do not anticipate hiring anyone to fill the position. The definitions will provide you with a clear outline of the tasks you need to accomplish to run your firm. That task list will enable you to either develop systems to perform the tasks efficiently or identify specific tasks to outsource.

Pro Tip: Sports fans can think of plenty of teams who added a player with more talent than the team had the previous season only to watch the team with the more talented player end up with a worse record. Those teams learned the hard way that chemistry matters. Do not make the same mistake that those teams made—learn from them.

Who Will Be the Best Fit?

We suggest that the candidate who has the best objective skill set is not always the best person for the job. We urge you to consider how the job applicant will get along with your existing team members. Regardless of how much talent the job applicant has, your firm will suffer if a new team member cannot work well with your team.

An important, and often overlooked, factor to consider is whether you want someone in the position who is looking for opportunities to advance or is content to remain in the position indefinitely. If the job applicant is looking at the position as a stepping stone, he or she will not be happy once the realization sets in that you do not intend to promote him or her.

When gauging who will be a good fit, we suggest that you consider using personality tests. The following companies have developed personality and strength tests for employees: Kolbe (Kolbe.com), StrengthsFinder (gallup.com), and Myers Briggs (myersbriggs.org). If you know that a certain job requires someone with certain characteristics, a personality test may be able to point you toward candidates with those traits.

Pro Tip: Use whatever tools are at your disposal to evaluate who will be a good fit on your team. Those tools include the judgment of the team members you already have and trust. They include references, writing samples, test projects, personality tests, background checks, and so on. Be creative when considering what is the best measure of whether the candidate can handle the responsibilities of the position and will mesh well with your team. Do not rely solely on a 30-minute interview.

Some basic personality characteristics these tests are geared toward measuring are follow-through, ability to adapt to new situations, if the candidate is more extroverted or introverted, communication style, learning preferences, and ability to implement given tasks. A properly applied personality test may be a more accurate measure than your observations in a 30-minute interview.

We must note that many personality tests are not designed for hiring purposes. Furthermore, if the evaluator does not have the skill set to evaluate the results or the test is not properly applied, the results can be misleading.

List of Potential Candidates

You likely will not be able to hire everyone you want at the same time. Very few law firms have the financial resources to hire all the candidates they like. Also, very few law firms have the capacity to integrate multiple new hires simultaneously.

Keep a running list of individuals you believe would make good team members. When you are ready to add a new team member, you should first reach out to these individuals when you initiate a search.

You should not place any restrictions on how or where you find individuals to put on the list. We suggest that the list should include individuals who impressed you through their work on the other side of a case, participation in committees or boards, or other situations in which they demonstrated skills you find valuable.

The list may also include individuals who interviewed well, but you could not afford to hire or did not have an opening for at that time. This might mean that the individual was your second choice at the time he or she interviewed.

We encourage you to interview candidates who show potential and interest in your firm whether or not you have an opening when they indicate their interest. The candidates may be so impressive that you find a place for them, or you may develop a relationship with the candidates so that you are first in line to recruit them when an opening arises. Other than the loss of an hour or so of your time, there is no downside to getting to know a potential candidate.

Recruiting

If no one on your list is available, how will you find good candidates?

You should maintain a good relationship with the career services office of your alma mater and/or any law schools located near your office. A law school's career services office should be in the best position to connect you with an entry-level attorney who may be interested in working at your firm.

The same principle applies with regard to your undergraduate college and/or local schools. Schools are highly motivated to place their students in jobs, and at the same time, career counselors will want to place their best students to develop a good reputation.

When you are looking to fill a particular job, we encourage you to let your contacts know what type of person you are looking for. Your network may know of someone that is not a great fit for them (whether because of timing, firm structure, or any number of other reasons) but is perfect for you.

If you cannot find a good candidate through any of your networks, it is time to post a job listing. The cost range for postings varies significantly. There are many sites that will allow you to post your job description for no charge, such as LinkedIn, Indeed, Monster, ZipRecruiter, Craigslist, and others.

Often, the downside of these listings is that you will be overwhelmed with applicants, very few of whom will meet your criteria. This has been our experience regardless of how concise or specific the job description, salary range, and other details are. You will end up spending resources to weed through all of them in the hopes of finding the diamond in the rough.

Listing your job opening on a site that charges a fee is by no means guaranteed to lead you to a good candidate. However, because these options usually target narrower audiences, the candidates are more likely to meet your criteria.

Another option is to hire a recruiter to identify candidates for you. The recruiter will handle the initial vetting of potential candidates, and as a result, the ones you actually meet are far more likely to be good candidates.

The biggest disadvantage of using a recruiter is the cost. Most recruiters will charge a percentage of the team member's first-year salary. This percentage typically ranges from 10 to 25 percent. Although this can be expensive, the cost is well worth it if you find a solid, long-term team member.

You should encourage your existing team members to be on the lookout for potential additions to the firm. Team members will only recommend someone as a potential work colleague if they respect them and believe they will be a good fit in the office. These candidates should be strongly considered.

Pro Tip: Consider offering financial incentives to your team members to recruit new team members. A financial incentive may make the team member biased in his or her evaluation of the candidate, but this potential cost is outweighed by the benefit of having a team member make a direct referral.

Recruiting from Rival Firms

Solo and small firms frequently face a dilemma when looking to add team members. Most of the individuals who make it onto their lists of potential candidates or who surface as applicants during your recruiting process work for a rival small firm.

In our experience, solo and small firms form their own communities within their practice areas. They help each other out with advice and recommendations regarding all aspects of their firms. Even in large urban markets, these communities tend to become tight-knit, and many firm leaders consider themselves friends.

Pro Tip: Interview candidates who appear genuinely interested in the job. If you are looking for a family law attorney, interview the candidates who have shown some interest in family law through their internships, course selection, and so on.

Hiring a rival firm's valued team member for your own firm could create friction between the two firms, and it may also have an impact on your reputation within the small firm community. Even if the candidate is a perfect fit for your team, you should take into consideration the reverberations it will have within the community you depend on.

Interview

Now that you have found several candidates with the potential to handle the tasks you need to be done, you are finally ready for the interview stage. The interview process is an interesting exercise when you think about it. You are trying to determine, in a short period of time, if the person in front of you will add value to your organization.

Because each position you are trying to fill is different in nature, the interview process can and should be different. Whatever process you follow should be designed to measure the applicant's skills for the specific position you need, not a generic law firm job.

There is no question that an extensive interview process is time-consuming and, therefore, costly. For this reason, you should find a way to limit the number of interviews.

You should be able to screen applicants by reviewing a written submission, such as a resume, writing sample, or cover letter, or by conducting telephone interviews. The goal is to narrow the number of in-person interviews to three to five candidates.

Remember that you have complete control over the interview format. This means that you do not have to limit the interview to the traditional 20- to 30-minute meeting.

These meetings often follow the same general script, and their predictability makes it possible for candidates to prepare for the interview. As a result, you meet someone who is very skilled at answering interview questions, but you have no idea if he or she will meet your needs.

If you can test your candidates during the interview process, then the likelihood of selecting the right candidate increases. For example, one test for an administrative position could be correcting grammatical errors in a writing sample. Another test could be completing sample financial forms. Another tip is to provide particular instructions for the candidates and review if they actually followed the directions.

Depending on the position, you should consider multiple meetings with the candidates. This will serve the dual purpose of giving you a better chance to evaluate the candidate and involving more team members in the interview process. Certainly, the team members who will work closely with the candidate should have an opportunity to weigh in on which candidate they believe will fit in the best.

During the interview process, you must at a minimum cover the following topics: (1) what the firm does and its mission, (2) the candidate's role in the firm, (3) your expectations for them for the short and long term, and (4) compensation.

Everyone who is going to participate in the interview process must understand the questions you can and cannot ask. Federal and state laws prohibit you from asking certain questions.

We suggest that you take notes during the interview session. If you are interviewing multiple candidates, notes will be a valuable tool to help sort through the candidates after you have met with everyone. Also, multiple interviewers may hear answers differently, and reviewing your notes together can allow you to explore the different reactions.

Give the person being interviewed an opportunity to ask questions. We expect at least several questions from a potential candidate. From our perspective, candidates who do not ask any questions either are not that interested in the job or have not done enough research about the job to know what to ask.

Pro Tip: Do not ask candidates about the following: age, religion, political preferences, marital status, intentions regarding children, sexual orientation, or disabilities. As a general rule, stick to questions that are directly related to the applicant's ability to perform the job you are looking to fill.

After the Interview

Always, always ask the candidate for references and take the time to follow up with them. So many employers assume that references provided by a candidate will provide limited value because candidates will only provide references who will provide favorable reviews.

Time after time, we have found that this is not true. Candidates often provide references who do not think as highly of them as they thought, or the references are more willing to provide a candid assessment when they are not speaking to the individual. At a minimum, references will provide a more complete picture of the candidate.

Offer Letter

We encourage you to memorialize any employment offer in writing. Certainly, you can share an offer and its terms orally, but it should be confirmed in writing. This will reinforce and/or clarify everyone's expectations, which is always a good thing.

The offer letter should spell out all aspects of the team member's compensation and at least the core requirements of what you expect from the team member.

Roles

From our perspective, every firm should have someone in the following roles: (1) legal, (2) human resources, (3) finance, (4) technology/IT, and (5) marketing. These are vital roles.

As you design your firm, you may determine that there are other roles that must be filled in addition to these. However, we would argue that you cannot operate a successful law firm without these five roles.

We understand that the same person may fill multiples roles, particularly for a new or smaller firm. Even if you anticipate that one team member will fill multiple roles, it is helpful to identify the job description and ideal characteristics of the team member filling that role for the time when each role will be filled by a different team member.

For a solo practitioner or very small firm, spending time describing the different roles and ideal characteristics for each will help you identify which roles you are qualified to fill—if you are honest with yourself. Certain roles will require skills or qualities you do not possess. As a solo or small firm, you must decide if you can succeed without those roles being filled or if you should outsource them.

Furthermore, solo and small firm members should designate specific times to handle each of these roles to ensure that they all receive proper and undivided attention. When we discuss time management in Chapter 7, allocating time for each role should be a critical consideration in how you arrange your calendar.

Legal Department

Legal services are the product your business produces. The specific product (type of legal services) a firm provides will depend on its practice areas and product lines.

Different products will require different skill sets. For example, the product produced by a trusts and estates firm will likely consist entirely of estate planning services and related documents, whereas, a business litigation firm's product will be its trial performance.

Given the wide range of products and skills necessary, it is important that you carefully consider your firm's product when building an organizational chart and determining the skills you want each team member to have.

Traditionally, most law firms employ some variation of the structure in Figure 1.

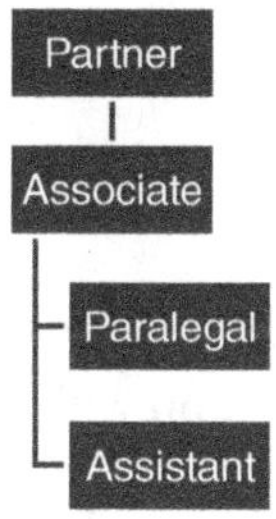

Figure 1

Before you lock yourself into this model, we encourage you to look at this structure from the perspective of what tasks must be accomplished to provide your legal services. Figure 2 is a general production line.

Figure 2

Of course, your production line should be customized to your products, and it should be far more detailed. Once you have customized your production line, the next step is to identify the skills and characteristics your team member will need for each stage.

For a trusts and estates law firm, the skills and characteristics necessary for each stage may look like the following:

Initial Client/Meeting/Retention

1. Knowledge of the law
2. Knowledge of the process
3. Ability to convey information to client

Discovery

1. Ability to identify client goals
2. Knowledge of what information will be needed
3. Persistence to obtain information regardless of obstacles
4. Ability to organize information
5. Ability to understand information

Strategy

1. Knowledge of law
2. Understanding of how law and practical aspects for client intersect
3. Ability to see big picture and long term

Legal Work Product

1. Legal skill
2. Attention to detail
3. Ability to draft documents
4. Ability to research and analyze legal questions
5. Follow-up and communication with client

Now consider the same production line for a litigation law firm:

Initial Client/Meeting/Retention

1. Knowledge of the law
2. Knowledge of the process
3. Personable enough to gain client's trust

Discovery

1. Knowledge of what information will be needed
2. Persistence to obtain information regardless of obstacles
3. Ability to organize information
4. Ability to understand information
5. Ability to work with other side or third parties to obtain information
6. Ability to obtain court rulings to gather information

Strategy

1. Knowledge of law
2. Understanding of how law and practical aspects for client intersect
3. Ability to see big picture and long term

Legal Work Product

1. Legal skill
2. Ability to present case to a judge or jury
3. Ability to adjust and adapt to changes without advance notice

While many of the skills are the same or similar for both practices, there are critical differences. The trusts and estates attorney must be proficient in drafting documents and provide critical follow-up, whereas the litigation attorney must be able to present a case to a jury. The trusts and estates attorney will have few time constraints and can analyze legal issues in his or her own office. On the other hand, the litigation attorney will need to be able to make snap decision on his or her feet while a jury is watching.

Human Resources

Your human resources department will handle a wide variety of issues related to your team members. Human resources will be involved even before a team member is hired, through every step of his or her employment, and closing out the relationship of any team member who leaves the firm.

This department is responsible for managing the issues relating to existing employees, recruiting, hiring and firing; onboarding new hires (employee and procedure manuals), making sure all required paperwork is processed, employee training, reviewing employee performance, compensation, and benefits. Common tasks for a human resources team member are explaining how benefits will be transitioned, obtaining keys and keycards, determining how files will be handled/transitioned, documenting reasons for termination, and securing the computer and IT technology provided to the employee.

The human resources department is focused on your personnel development. On one end of the spectrum, human resources may be responsible for outlining the path from associate to partner. On the other end of the spectrum, human resources may be either educating team members about sexual harassment, cybersecurity, confidentiality, work place attire, and dispute resolution procedures or handling a violation of these procedures.

The number of tasks your human resources department will handle is far too long to try to list here. However, the overarching goals of any human resources department are to recruit good team members, build a strong team, and develop strong working relationships. Key characteristics for team members in this role are as follows:

1. Strong interpersonal skills—the ability to get along with people with all types of personalities and idiosyncrasies is critical in this role.
2. Ability to be clear and direct—this person must convey the firm's expectations of each team member clearly and be willing to address any issues that arise.
3. Objective—human resources must provide objective feedback when employee issues arise and during reviews and performance evaluations. The person in this role cannot play favorites and must have the utmost discretion.

Finance

All of the money that comes into or leaves the firm is handled by the finance department. This involves everything from collecting and organizing payments and paying bills to handling payroll and producing financial statements. In addition, the finance department will be responsible for planning how money will be earned or spent in the future.

Key characteristics for team members in this role are as follows:

1. Detail and accuracy—anyone handling the firm's or the client's money must pay careful attention to each detail.
2. Honesty and integrity—you must be able to trust the person handling your and your client's money.
3. Ability to work with technology—billing and budgeting projections will rely heavily on software that your financial team must be able to use.
4. Organized—there is no room for disorganization in this department.

Many small law firms outsource some of the finance department's responsibilities. We have no objection to this approach, provided that there is a point of contact within the firm who can work effectively with the vendor. Also, someone within your firm must be able to determine what the financial goals of the firm are and to direct the outside vendor toward those goals.

Technology/IT

The technology department is responsible for all your firm's technology needs, which expand every day.

This department must determine what technology (computers, phones, software, security systems, etc.) you need, when it will be purchased, and how it will be used. Your technology department will need to order and set everything up and maintain subscriptions, service plans, passwords, and so on. Not only does the technology department need to maintain everything the firm already has, but also it must keep up with trends and recommend improvements.

The key characteristics for team members in this role are as follows:

1. Detailed oriented—they should understand what your firm needs and what the technology needs to do for your firm.
2. Knowledge of relevant technology—technology is ever-changing, and you need someone to stay abreast of the latest technology and how it applies to the legal field.
3. Good communication skills—the technology department will be responsible for training the team on the technology and fixing any issues that arise.

Marketing

The marketing department is responsible for communicating your firm's message to the world in a clear, consistent, and efficient manner. The marketing department is in charge of attracting your ideal potential clients and converting enough of them into actual clients to provide sufficient revenues for the firm to continue operations and provide you with the amount of money you need to support your goals and lifestyle.

Attracting potential clients and converting them into actual clients can be done in countless different ways. The approach you take will play a huge role in the skill set your marketing team members need.

For example, if networking with other individuals and public speaking engagements are important components of your marketing strategy, you will need team members who are comfortable giving presentations. However, if you plan to attract clients through online advertising, your marketing team needs to be filled with individuals who are fluent in technology, websites, search engines, and so on.

The following are some key characteristics for team members in the marketing department:

1. Strong communication skills—they must be good on the phone or video conference and able to articulate and believe in the firm's mission.
2. Follow-up/follow-through—team members must be consistent following up on leads, quantifying results, reviewing results, and targeting leads.
3. Personable—they have strong interpersonal skills and the ability to make friends quickly.
4. Positive attitude—they must be able to take rejection and go on to the next lead.

5. Ability to understand and utilize your marketing technology—customer relations management (CRM) software is critical to sales, and your marketing people need to be able to get the most out of the software.
6. Knowledgeable about marketing platforms including social media.

An effective marketing department will be able to quantify the success ratio for each of its marketing campaigns. The skills necessary to measure success are very different from those that will be needed to attract clients. This team member will likely have skills that more closely resemble those of the team members in the finance department.

Team Member Section of Your Business Plan

We anticipate that your answers to the questions below will serve as an outline for the team member section of your business plan. These answers will form the foundation for how you will build a productive team for your firm.

1. How will you find team members?
2. What team members do you need for each department of your firm?
   a. Law
   b. Finance
   c. Technology/IT
   d. Human resources
   e. Marketing
3. What type of team member do you want in each position?
   a. Management
   b. Worker bee
   c. Visionary
4. What skills does the ideal team member have for each position?
   a. Work-related skills
   b. Personality traits
5. What team members can you afford financially?
6. What does your organizational chart look like
   a. Today or on opening day?
   b. Three years from now?
   c. Ten years from now?

See the Appendix of this book for a sample Job Offer Form Letter and Job Description Form that you can customize for your firm's needs.

5

Human Resources: Handling Your Most Valuable Asset—Your Team Members

While your systems, procedures, technology, and other aspects of your law firm are important, your team members are far and away the most valuable aspect of your firm. We cannot emphasize this enough—nothing else is close.

For those of you who are thinking that technology has become or soon will become more important than your team members, remember that someone needs to decide what technology you need, develop a plan for the technology, and implement the plan. Your team members are the ones who will put all your strategies and systems in motion. To get the best results out of your team, you have to find qualified team members and put them in position to succeed.

Human Resources Plan

The foundation for any human resources plan is an organizational chart. We recommend building an organizational chart based on the tasks your firm must accomplish rather than making one based on the existing team members. By using this method, your chart will emphasize those tasks that you believe will make the firm most productive.

Even if you are the only team member when you start your firm or you plan to remain a small firm or solo practitioner, it is helpful to have an organizational chart that outlines the tasks that must be accomplished. A basic organizational chart could look like Figure 3.

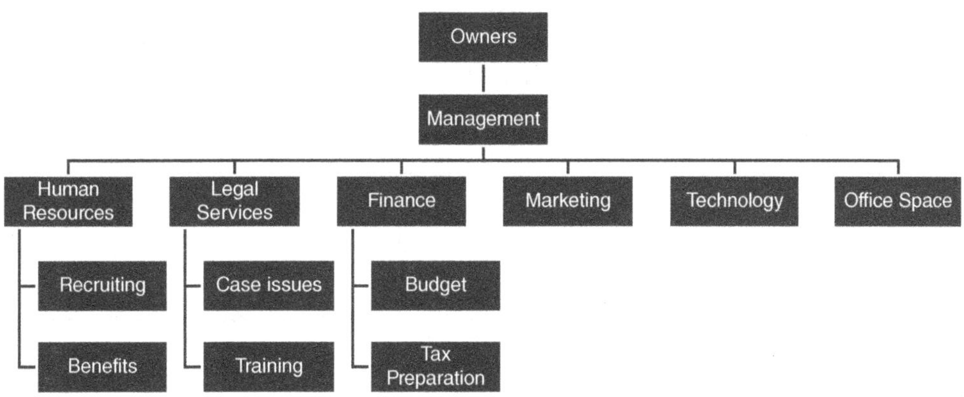

Figure 3

This organizational chart is not intended to be complete, but it is intended to give you a starting point. For example, some person or group of people needs to set the agenda or direction of the firm, and they fall in the management section. Under management are typical departments in a modern law firm. We have found that merely identifying the departments has forced some (generally smaller) firms to develop plans for departments that may have been overlooked otherwise.

Pro Tip: Preparing an organizational chart will force you to think through your process and system from start to finish. Just going through this exercise will help you find ways to make your process more efficient.

As you work your way down the organizational chart, the boxes should identify more specific tasks. We purposely did not fill in many of these categories because this is where you need to develop plans that will work best for your firm and determine which tasks must be accomplished to carry out those plans.

After identifying the tasks that need to be done, the next step is to identify which team member will perform the task. When you are the only team member, your name will be inserted in virtually every box of the organizational chart. The only exception would be if you outsource or hire a third-party vendor to handle certain tasks, such as tax preparation or training.

Task List and Living Document

At first, the organizational chart may serve as a task list for you. It will help ensure that you do not ignore the tasks that you know should be done but that you do not enjoy doing. As your firm grows and can afford to hire team members, the organizational chart will help you identify what skills the team member should have and where the new team member will fit within your firm.

The organizational chart should be a living document that you update regularly. As the legal marketplace, technology, and other aspects of law practice change, you should revise your organizational chart to keep current. As your firm gains some experience, you will also be able to more accurately predict who should perform certain tasks—for example, how many team members will be necessary to accomplish a certain task, whether one team member can competently handle multiple tasks, or whether an outside vendor should be hired because your team does not have either the capacity or the competency to accomplish the task.

Pro Tip: Remember that human beings with strengths and weaknesses are going to fill in the boxes on your organizational chart. There will need to be a balance between the reality of what someone can do and the organizational chart that looks perfect on paper.

As you start to insert team members into your organizational chart, you need to be realistic about each of your team member's capabilities. It is unrealistic to expect someone with less experience or education to perform a task that you have been doing for years as quickly or efficiently. If you are reasonable in assessing expectations of your team members, you will have a better sense of how many team members you will need for each task.

After you build the first task-focused organizational chart, you should build organizational charts that project your future organizational structure. The charts that project three, five, and ten years into the future should estimate how many team members you will have in future years. Of course, these charts are more important if you anticipate that your firm will grow in size.

Fostering Productive Growth

The organizational chart will help you grow productively rather than haphazardly. Consider the two most common forms of growth. First, many firms grow when they want to improve upon something they are already doing. For example, the firm may want to offer more training or market in different ways but is waiting until the resources are available. By inserting these concepts into your organizational chart, you can see what skills the next hires should have.

Second, firms often grow to expand into different practice areas or new product lines. By outlining what that growth will look like on an organizational chart, you will see what new team members you will need to support the new product line in the standard you believe is appropriate.

Pro Tip: Preparing an organizational chart for a new product line will make it easier for you to project what an expansion will cost in human resources.

The most rewarding part of assigning tasks to team members in the projected charts is when you get a chance to insert someone else in your place. The smaller your firm is, the greater chance that you are performing tasks that you do not like. Really, who went to law school to create a website or a budget? We went to law school because these were not things we wanted to do or things we were not very good at doing. They have to be done, but they do not have to be done by you. An organizational chart will remind you to make sure to do them and inspire you to a time when you will have the luxury of assigning the task to someone else.

If our preferred philosophy about hiring is not apparent already, let's be clear—we do not recommend hiring a team member you believe is talented and then figuring out what to do with him or her. No matter how talented the new team member may be, he or she will reduce your firm's efficiency if you do not have a role for him or her to fill.

We often see firms hire new attorneys because the attorney is a "great lawyer." This may be true, but hiring a great lawyer and figuring out how the new lawyer will fit in later is not an efficient strategy. Even lawyers who will provide legal services your firm already provides will need support—paralegals, assistants, billing, and other administrative personnel—to be successful.

A new lawyer providing different legal services needs exponentially more administrative help. Before hiring a new lawyer, your firm must determine whether it can provide (or afford to provide) the needed support to reach the "great lawyer" potential you thought you were hiring.

A well thought out organizational chart will help you identify what team members are necessary to make the firm run efficiently and effectively in the present. It will also help you plan for the future by outlining the role(s) your next hire should fill and enable that team member to fit into the firm operations seamlessly.

Firm Culture

Businesses and business books always talk about firm culture, yet most businesses seem to adopt a culture by default instead of developing one.

The first step in developing a firm culture is to determine what culture you want. Take some time to sit down and think about what you want your firm to feel like to you and your team members. The easiest time to develop the concepts for the firm culture you want is before you open your firm.

The hard part is dedicating the time and energy necessary to implement your culture once the doors have opened and you start practicing law. There is no question that there will be countless tasks (initiated by clients, judges, case deadlines, and payroll, to name a few) pulling you in different directions once you open your firm, and many of those tasks will feel far more urgent and important than setting aside time to develop or cultivate a firm culture.

We urge you to reconsider. Fight the temptation to set aside firm culture decisions even when you are stressed and overwhelmed with the day-to-day operations of a new business. Yes, those tasks are urgent, but they are also temporary in nature, whereas your firm culture will endure.

Your culture will permeate every aspect of your firm, and it will be incredibly difficult to change it if you head down the wrong path or head down an unguided path. We cannot emphasize enough how much your culture will have an impact on all firm decisions including topics such as ethics, compensation, and office space that you may not anticipate.

If you want a particular culture, you will have to assign time (an individual's most valuable resource) and energy to make it happen. We urge you to do this, as it will pay huge long-term dividends. When you are developing your firm culture, we encourage you to do so in conjunction with your definition of success. This will help you avoid having conflicting policies. For example, it is hard to have a firm culture based on a good work/life balance if your definition of success is solely based on how much money you earn. The firm culture should help push you and your team members toward your definition of success.

After writing down what you want your firm culture to be, you cannot file it away and hope it magically comes to fruition. The next step is to make sure all of your team members know what you want the firm culture to be. If your team members know what the goals are, they will be predisposed to seek out ways to fit in the firm culture and to make decisions aligned with the firm culture.

One way to develop firm culture is to have a unifying mission the entire team understands and can get behind. Your mission statement from your business plan should be communicated to your team members, and your goal should be for the mission statement to inspire a sense of pride for the team.

Aside from sharing the culture goals with your team members, establish and implement firm policies and procedures that are aligned with the firm culture. For example, if you want to establish a reasonable work/life balance, do not set billable hour goals that are through the roof. If you want your team members to be collaborative, reward them for working together. In short, whenever you establish an incentive, make sure that it is driving the team member to do something that is aligned with the culture you want.

The easiest incentives to control are compensation incentives, but they are not the only ones. Many team members value recognition, praise, time off, and other benefits as much or more than compensation. If you want your firm culture to be one of teamwork and collaboration, you should take the time to tell a team member how much you appreciate the quality of the work done no matter how preoccupied you are with your own tasks. Failing to appreciate effort in this manner may foster a culture of every person for him- or herself.

Some extreme firm cultures we have encountered:

1. All work and no play: The sole focus of the firm is the legal work. The billable hour expectation is very high, and there are very few firm functions.
2. The almighty dollar: Nothing matters unless it leads to more revenue.
3. The buddy system: It is more important for everyone to get along and to enjoy spending time together than it is to bill hours.

You have probably observed a number of different work cultures and know that the range of potential cultures is endless, and there is no right or wrong culture. The value of a firm culture is that it attracts team members who will thrive in your culture and keeps away those would do better elsewhere. As you can imagine, different personalities will thrive in different cultures.

Expectations of Your Team Members

As discussed previously, before you can find qualified team members, you have to identify what you need from them. You must plan ahead to understand how your processes should work and what must be done to implement them. Then you can design job positions that will accomplish *your* goals, not the goals of your competitors or the goals of firms of yesteryear.

Job descriptions need to be specific and detailed. It is not enough to describe the job opening as a "paralegal" or "associate attorney." Those job titles can encompass a wide variety of tasks and duties because different firms will use these team members in different ways. Taking the time to describe the tasks you want the team member to perform will be far more valuable than listing the job title.

As we emphasize throughout this book, setting reasonable expectations will go a long way in pretty much everything you do. The primary benefit of setting expectations for your team members, particularly new ones, is to ensure that they are actually taking on the responsibilities you have in mind for them.

If you do not set clear expectations, your team members will develop their own job descriptions, which will likely exclude the tasks they like the least. You start setting expectations with the job listing, continue to emphasize them in the interview process, reinforce them during the team member's probationary period, and remind your team member of them in reviews. This process never ends.

We strongly recommend against entering into the hiring process with the mindset that you will hold back information from the potential hires and then after they are hired you will convince the new hires to do more or something different than what was described in the interview phase. Nothing good will come from misleading someone to get him or her to take a job. In this scenario, your best case is that the new hire does not meet your expectations (the ones you did not share) and the worst case is that the new hire tears apart the morale and production of your entire team.

We hear attorneys say that they do not want to tell potential hires all of the stresses and demands of the job during the recruiting or interviewing phases because they are afraid that it will scare off some potential hires. But that is exactly what you should do! If they cannot handle the pressures of the job, better that they say no before they join your team. Be willing to take longer in the interview process to find the right person. The extra investment in finding the right person will pay off in the long run in terms of less turnover, higher production, and better morale.

Pro Tip: Calculate the back end costs of a poor hire before taking a chance on a questionable candidate. The costs include

1. Time spent by a team member training the new person;
2. Costs of setting up everything for the new team member, such as enrollment in firm programs, setting up payroll, business cards, phone and computer access, and so on;
3. Backlash from your team members if they have to train new hires repeatedly because your choices do not work out; and
4. Negative impressions your clients will have of you if they interact with a different team member every time they contact you.

If you are not confident about the candidate, decide if you are willing to incur these costs if the candidate does not work out.

Recruiting Process

On the front end during the hiring process, spending more time looking for the right person will be more costly. Not only will your human resources department spend more time on the hiring process, but also the remainder of your team members will have to pick up the slack for the empty position for a longer time.

You should not be afraid to keep looking for a good candidate even if you have already conducted multiple interviews. As long as you are being reasonable with regard to your expectations, a great (not necessarily perfect) prospect is out there. Do not settle: a team member who cannot complete the tasks you have assigned to him or her will either create a negative drag on the efficiency of your systems or break them, and a team member who will not fit into your firm's culture will harm morale.

From our perspective, the back end costs of a poor hire are the reason to keep looking for a good candidate. However, not all positions are created equally. As you design job descriptions, one factor to consider carefully is how easy or difficult will it be find someone with the skills this team member needs. Although we strongly recommend that you invest the time and effort to find the best person for every position, there are arguments for spending less time on positions that do not require specialized skills. You must conduct a cost-benefit and risk-reward analysis on the time and money you put into your recruiting efforts.

Pro Tip: Encourage your team members to look for potential team members. Entry-level associates are more likely to be familiar with entry-level associates at other firms than the senior partner. The same principle will apply to paralegals and other positions.

Consider offering incentives, such as bonuses or more personal time, to motivate team members to engage in this process.

We encourage you to establish systems that will allow multiple members of your team to meet prospective hires you are taking seriously. Get several perspectives on a potential team member, and if possible, those perspectives should come not just from a supervisor but also from team members who will be subordinates or on equal footing. The interaction between your team members and the potential hires does not have to be in a formal interview setting to be productive. For example, we always ask our receptionist for her impressions of job candidates based on their interaction when she greets them and when they are waiting to be interviewed.

Regardless of how your interviews are structured or who conducts them, it is critical that the interviewers know what skills the potential hire needs to perform the job applied for. This sounds obvious, but we have seen far too many law firms hire team members because the interviewers "liked" the applicant without gauging whether the applicant could handle the job responsibilities.

Although not feasible for most positions, you should explore "trial runs." For example, consider hiring law school students as interns or summer clerks if you anticipate hiring young attorneys. There is no better way to gauge how a young attorney will fit in your firm than to have that candidate work at your firm for a semester or summer.

Expectations after Hiring

Let's turn our attention to the candidates you hire. Just because you found a good prospect does not mean that your human resources job is complete. In fact, your work is just beginning. As mentioned above, you need to set expectations for all your team members.

These should be explained both in writing and orally, and they should be repeated regularly. You do not want any misunderstandings or confusion as to what the team member's role is.

Examples of common law firm positions:

1. Receptionist: Answers the phone before it rings twice; greets all clients who enter the office within 30 seconds.
2. Paralegal: Files all incoming correspondence within 24 hours of arrival; files case materials pursuant to the filing system.
3. Associate: Bills X hours per day/month; conducts x networking functions per week.
4. Partner: Collects X dollars per year; brings in x number of new clients per quarter.

Wherever possible, establish objective measures for each team member. It is much easier to encourage team members to meet objective measures than subjective ones. Furthermore, the more objective the measures, the less likely a team member will feel that his or her job performance is tied to the whims of his or her manager. You may not be able to eliminate subjective measures for each position, but you can certainly identify objective ones for every position.

The quantitative goals must be reasonable and achievable, and they need to incentivize your team members to do the tasks you believe will lead to the best results for the firm. Remember to exercise caution when determining objective measures to avoid creating the wrong incentive. For example, an objective measure such as billable hours sounds fine, but it will have little value if none of those hours billed results in payments collected. You must put real time and effort into your strategic plans so that you can be in a position to tell your team members what they need to accomplish to fulfill their role in the strategic plan.

Office Manual

In addition to individual goals, every law firm should have an office manual that sets forth your policies. You can obtain models from the ABA to use as a starting point for your firm, or you can consult with an employment lawyer to draft your manual. This manual should be given to each team member on his or her first day of employment, and the team member should be reminded of his or her obligation to comply with it at least annually.

The policy manual should set forth as many firm-wide policies as possible. At a minimum, the policy should include some basics such as hours of operation, vacation policies, review policies, and IT security policies. Regarding the last point, cybersecurity threats pose one of the greatest risks to your firm (see Chapter 15 on technology). You need to have a solid data storage and security plan for your firm that is memorialized and known by your team and communicated to your clients. There is no hard and fast limit as to what the manual contains. It should be tailored to your firm and how you want it to operate.

Compensation and Benefits for Team Members

In short, what are you going to pay your team members, and how are you going to pay it? The first thing everyone thinks about is salary. This makes sense since salary is usually the biggest part of compensation (at least in terms of dollars), but it should not be the end of the discussion.

From a firm perspective, it is important to establish compensation ranges for each position before recruiting or interviewing potential team members. You need to know not only what you can afford to pay but even more importantly how much monetary value you place on each position. No matter how much you love the person interviewing for the receptionist position, you are not going to pay him or her more than a senior associate because the receptionist position does not add as much value to the firm as a senior associate.

Pro Tip: Be very careful in the financial incentives you create for your team members. Consider an example of one firm's incentive structure that has a very negative unintended consequence. The firm pays its attorneys 50 percent of all fees collected on work performed by the attorney and 25 percent of all fees collected on a case that the attorney originates whether he or she does the work or refers the case to someone else within the firm. The firm has multiple practice areas, and the 25 percent origination fee is intended to encourage attorneys to send the work they cannot perform to someone within the firm who can do it.

This compensation structure gives an attorney the incentive to work on cases that he or she originated first. The unintended consequence of this is that attorneys put the cases referred by their colleagues at the bottom of their to-do list. The attorneys originating work at this firm became so frustrated with the lack of attention their cases were receiving that they started referring the cases to lawyers at other firms. The 25 percent origination fee was not worth the negativity resulting from the poor referral.

Your firm needs to be careful to keep its compensation in alignment. This means that the compensation you pay to team members matches their value. In addition, issues will arise if team members with the same job description are compensated differently. There should be a good and easily explainable reason as to why their compensations are different.

The compensation for each team member should be designed to encourage him or her to complete the tasks you believe will make the firm the most efficient and successful. There are many ways to incentivize an attorney team member. If your goal is for associates to bill a certain number of hours, you can tie a portion of their salary and/or bonus to meeting this goal. If you want your associates to generate business, you can reward them based on how many new cases they generate.

It is harder, but not impossible, to create incentives for non-revenue-generating team members. The metrics you are measuring for these team members are not likely to be as objective as billable hours or the number of new clients. Nevertheless, each position has metrics you can use to measure success. The prospect of a raise or bonus based on your evaluation of whether the team member has met his or her performance goals can and should motivate your team member to meet or exceed the expectations you have set.

Once you get beyond the base salary and bonuses, there is a wide assortment of compensation options. Although all of the options outlined below will cost the firm money, you have to consider whether the team member will consider the firm's payment to be a benefit that could be characterized as a form of compensation. For example, most lawyers expect their firms to provide malpractice insurance and to pay for their continuing legal education requirements. While expected, it does not change the fact that the firm is paying these expenses and that they are attributable to those team members.

Legal Education

There probably will not be a huge variance between malpractice insurance options, but there could be a huge amount of discretion when it comes to continuing legal education. The two biggest decisions will be whether you will pay for more credits than the bare minimum and where the team member can obtain the credits. Inevitably, you will have a team member who finds great courses, but he or she does not need any additional credits to remain licensed. If you are going to let that team member go to extra classes, you need to let the team member know if the cost is being provided by the firm or if you are planning to reduce the team member's bonus by the cost of the courses.

Bar organizations are looking for more and more exotic locations for their courses to entice more attendees. Of course, the transportation to and lodging at these locations are far more expensive than a course being offered at the local courthouse. The question becomes whether you are willing to subsidize a portion of your team member's vacation, and if so, if this falls under what the team member expects as a basic term of employment or a portion of his or her compensation.

Pro Tip: Encourage your team members to use their leave time. They will come back energized and refreshed.

Even if you cannot bring yourself to encourage a team member to take time off, do not discourage ones who wants to use the leave time that you granted to them as part of their compensation package.

Insurance

Aside from malpractice insurance, there are a wide variety of other insurances you may want to offer your team members. We have seen a number of firms that offer some combination of health, dental, vision, life, and disability insurances. Simply setting up one of these policies as a group policy may save your team member money even if the firm does not pay a portion of the premium. Of course, if the firm pays a portion of the premium, there will be savings for the team member. If you are going to pay a portion of these costs, it is important to ensure that your team member recognizes the benefit you are providing.

Leave

All team members expect to receive time off. Whether you call it vacation time, personal days, or sick days, the bottom line is that these are days when your firm is open but your team member is not working. You may view time off differently for revenue-generating team members as opposed to non-revenue-generating team members.

For revenue-generating team members, it may not matter as much how much time they take off so long as they meet their revenue goals, such as billable hours or new clients. For non-revenue-generating team members, their presence may be essential to perform their jobs. For example, a receptionist cannot perform his or her job without being at the office. Your firm needs a receptionist every day the office is open, and therefore, when your receptionist takes time off, someone else has to fill in. Either you are paying a temp to cover this time off or another team member is taking time away from his or her primary responsibilities. In either scenario, there is a cost associated with the receptionist's time off that needs to be factored into how much of your limited resources you are willing to allocate to this position.

Other Forms of Benefits

Firms and businesses can get creative in the benefits they provide. We have seen firms offer gym memberships, transportation reimbursements, flex time, trips, volunteer opportunities, massages, casual days, meals, snacks, coffee/drinks, birthday or anniversary celebrations, award ceremonies, and more. There really is no limit to the creative options available. The only limits you should apply are to stay within the range of benefits you believe your team members will appreciate and to stay within your budget.

Management and Enforcement of Human Resources Policies

Once you establish expectations for your team members, you must be prepared to enforce them. Having a policy or stating expectations is meaningless if you are not going to require your team members to comply with the policy or meet the expectations. It would be great if every team member was self-motivated; however, we have yet to find the firm in which every team member was perfect.

Inevitably, a team member will violate a policy term or fail to meet an expectation. We urge you to develop a consistent method for addressing these issues. If human resources or a particular employee is going to address the issue, the same process and procedure must be followed each time so it does not appear as if one team member is getting favorable treatment over another.

Unmet Expectations

If possible, when you are disciplining a team member, two people should be present. One person can be the primary spokesperson, and the other can take notes. Any time that you are disciplining a team member, there must be a written record that states what the expectation was, how the team member failed to meet the expectation, the steps the team member will take to correct his or her behavior, and the time period in which the correction must occur. This approach is fairly straightforward when you have given the team member clear and objective expectations. When there is an unmet expectation, you are managing the policy, not the individual.

Pro Tip: Although it can be inconvenient, solo practitioners should make arrangements for a second person to be present at a significant human resources meeting. You want to avoid situations that can turn into your word against your team member's word. Depending on the complexity of the human resources issue, the person who accompanies you could range from your firm's employment lawyer to an independent witness who is simply there as a witness.

When there is no clear or objective expectation but you are unhappy with a team member's performance, you are essentially left with telling that team member that he or she needs to do better. Well, what does that mean? Neither you nor the team member will be satisfied with a general directive to "do better." When the expectations are not spelled out, you and the team member could have very different ideas of what "doing better" means.

Reporting Concerns

Ideally, you will have your finger on the pulse of your firm and be able to recognize when things are not working as they should. However, this is often not the case, particularly as the firm grows. Many owners are too busy or preoccupied to notice when someone who does not work directly with them is not meeting expectations until the annual review.

Pro Tip: Every team member needs to know that there is safe place for him or her to report concerns. If you are a one-attorney firm, find an attorney in another firm who will serve as the sounding board for your team member to report sensitive information about you.

For this reason, we encourage you to ensure that your team members have a safe (and potentially anonymous) way to report concerns they may have about other team members. Otherwise, you may be unaware of an underperforming team member for the better part of a year. Not only will you have lost the work that this team member could have performed, but also you will have to address the team members who are frustrated by management's failure to address the issue and/or having to do extra work to cover for the underperforming team member.

No one likes to discipline a team member. As a result, many firms let noncompliant behavior slide. Resist this temptation. It is far easier to correct deviances when they first occur or when they are minor than it is to correct behavior after it becomes entrenched. We encourage you to stay engaged with your team members and to routinely (more than annually) ensure that they are on the path you outlined for them.

Reviews

We strongly recommend that you establish a formal review process for both team members and your firm. Most people assume that reviews consist of management or a supervisor giving feedback about performance to another team member. While this is one important aspect of reviews, the part that is often ignored is the team member's review of the firm and/or management or supervisor. Both aspects of a review are very valuable.

Every firm should have a policy regarding how it will review team members. At a minimum, this policy should set forth how often the reviews will take place, who will conduct the reviews, and how the team member's performance will be measured.

Most firms tend to have annual reviews for their team members. We recommend having a review at least once a year; however, there must be an avenue to provide feedback to a team member more often if a work performance problem arises. You do not want an issue to go unresolved for a long period of time. On the flip side, if a team member far exceeds expectations, you should not wait until the annual review to recognize his or her performance.

Pro Tip: Take the probationary period seriously. No interview process is perfect. If handled properly, a two- to three-month probationary period should let you know whether the new team member is cut out for the role you planned for him or her. Use the probationary period to test the new team member's skills in practical scenarios and monitor his or her ability to fit into your team.

Whenever possible, there should be at least two people presenting the review. Ideally, one will be the direct supervisor and the other will be a human resources manager or office manager. The direct supervisor will have in-depth knowledge of the team member's responsibilities and will be able to clearly outline the team member's successes, failures, and where he or she can improve.

Pro Tip: Reviews are a great opportunity for your team members to review their job description and for you and your team members to confirm that they understand their roles and responsibilities.

The human resources manager can help facilitate the communication between the supervisor and team member, particularly when talking about areas that need to be improved, in a productive way. From our perspective, the reviews should be used to recognize successes and to outline areas for improvement. The reviews should not be intended to criticize or cut down team members but instead to show them how they can advance their career.

You should enter every review with a written summary of what you are going to discuss. You should be prepared to share that written summary with your team member. Having a written summary is even more critical when you are conducting a review by yourself to avoid situations in which you and/or the team member are confused or uncertain about what was said.

Pro Tip: You should always be looking for ways to improve. Frequently, the best way to do this is to hear (really hear) criticisms. As tough as it is to hear, the criticisms are incredibly valuable. Find a way to give your team members the confidence to give you honest feedback.

When you are conducting reviews, please remember that many team members are nervous and anxious about them. The team members being reviewed often feels as if they are being judged (they are), and often their compensation, which is very important to them, is at risk.

You can reduce, but probably not eliminate, this anxiety by making it clear in advance who will be present at the review, the logistics of the review, and how they will be measured. Nervous and anxious individuals are not likely to remember much of the discussion. This is another reason you should be prepared to provide a written summary to your team members.

Probationary Period

For new team members, you should establish a probationary period and conduct a review at its conclusion. The probationary period needs to be long enough to get a feel for the team member's strengths and weaknesses but should not be too long. Most probationary periods are 90 days, but you can adjust this depending on whether you believe that length of time will be sufficient to determine if the team member will be a good fit.

Even though you will have set forth your expectations of the team member when you initially hired him or her, the review at the end of the probationary period is the perfect opportunity to reinforce the expectations and evaluate whether the team member is meeting them or on track to do so. If not, you have to determine whether to terminate the team member or to provide him or her with guidance and/or assistance to get on track.

If the new team member is not meeting your expectations but you still believe he or she has potential, you can extend the probationary period. However, you need to be specific regarding the terms and length of the probationary period.

Review of the Firm

A team member's review of the firm can be as valuable as or more valuable than your review of a team member. We do not recommend conducting the team member's review of the firm at the same time you are reviewing the team member's performance. Such an arrangement is not likely to lead to the most candid or productive feedback from the team member.

Perhaps the most important determinant of whether you will get candid feedback is to whom or how the team member provides his or her feedback. Most people lack the direct and blunt personality it takes to criticize a direct supervisor to his or her face. A review of the firm will not be particularly valuable if the team member providing the review holds back his or her thoughts because the team member fears how he or she will be received.

Typically, the best internal person to conduct these reviews would be someone in human resources that the team member does not report directly to and does not interact with on a regular basis. If no such person exists in your firm, hire someone outside the firm to conduct these meetings. The expense is well worth it.

You will get the most valuable feedback from team members who do not believe there will be any negative consequences arising from their disclosures. If it is possible, have the feedback presented anonymously. Of course, if you have an internal team member conduct the review, the person conducting the review will know who the team member is. However, the person conducting the review does not need to assign a name to the feedback when it is passed along to the direct supervisor.

These reviews will only be useful if you implement some of the suggestions made by your team members. If they learn through the years that the firm takes action based on their feedback and there are no penalties for honesty, they will invest their time and effort into providing thoughtful comments. However, if you consistently ignore their feedback, they will learn that the exercise is a waste of time and put as little effort as possible into it.

There should always be an open door for team members to report concerns or provide suggestions at any time, not just when the review is being conducted. However, there should be a consistent routine as to when a formal review will occur so that the team member can take time to prepare his or her comments.

Termination of Team Member

The first question you have to answer is, "What is a firing offense?" There are certain things, such as assault, stealing, or harassment, that do not require any discussion. Those team members must be terminated immediately.

If a team member does not meet one of these "no brainer" criteria, the termination is a process. When the team member starts to underperform or violate a policy, notice of the issue must be provided to the team member and the team member should have an opportunity to address the issue. We encourage you to follow these steps regardless of whether your state requires you to do so or not. The termination process should give the team member a reasonable chance to retain his or her job. Even if you eventually have to terminate the team member, the separation is likely to go far more smoothly if the team member feels he or she was treated fairly. An equally important reason to give the team member a fair chance is to show the team members who are not leaving that you are not being arbitrary or capricious and that they have job security.

Pro Tip: When you are terminating a team member, there are certain precautions that need to be taken:

1. Safety: Evaluate whether there is a potential risk to your team members, and if so, be proactive.
2. Firm security: Make sure that the team member does not have access to sensitive firm information or the ability to harm firm systems.
3. Plan: Have a specific plan of action that includes when you will notify the team member, when that team member's benefits will end, when that team member must leave the premises, what that team member may take with him or her, and the logistics of the team member returning any firm property and keys or other means of access to the office and/or computer systems.

Although you never want to fire someone, it would be easier if a team member's behavior made the decision simple and straightforward. Unfortunately, that is rarely the case. It is not unusual to be faced with difficult scenarios such as when a team member is well liked but cannot handle the job responsibilities or the team member is great at handling the job responsibilities but is universally disliked. In both of these scenarios, your firm will be operating at less-than-optimal efficiency if you let this team member remain employed. These are hard decisions, but you cannot shy away from them.

No one wants high or premature turnover, but retaining a team member who does not fit only exacerbates the costs. What are you telling your other team members when you keep a team member who cannot do his or her share? Now others start to see that they do not have to do their share to stick around, or they become bitter that they have to pick up the slack for the poorly performing team member.

Most employees can understand and forgive a poor hiring decision, as no interview process is perfect, but what they cannot understand or forgive is you keeping a team member after there is proof that the team member does not fit in or cannot carry his or her weight. Retaining the team member will make your good team members question your judgment and leadership skills.

We do not subscribe to the Jack Welch theory that the bottom 10 percent should be replaced every year. However, we do believe that you need to evaluate your team members regularly to ensure that they are meeting the goals you set for them. If they are not meeting the goals and they cannot correct their behavior to reach those goals within a reasonable time period, then you need to terminate them.

Human Resources Section of Your Business Plan

We anticipate that your answers to the questions below will serve as an outline for the human resources section of your business plan. These answers will form the foundation for how you will manage your human resources.

1. Who will establish the human resources plan?
   a. How will the human resources plan be communicated to team members?
   b. What will your organizational chart look like?
2. What will your firm culture be?
   a. How will you develop this culture?
   b. Who will be responsible for developing this culture?
3. What is the job description for each team member?
4. What will your recruiting process look like?
   a. Who will be part of the recruiting process?
   b. Where will you find potential recruits?
   c. How will you advertise your available positions?
   d. Will you have different processes for different positions?
5. What is your hiring process?
   a. Who will make the hiring decision?
   b. How will the hiring decision be conveyed to recruit?

6. What benefits will you provide to your team members?
   a. Compensation structure
   b. Vacation/personal/sick time
   c. Other benefits
7. How will you manage or enforce your systems?
   a. What will your office manual say?
   b. Who will draft your office manual?
8. Reviews
   a. Who will conduct reviews?
   b. What are you hoping to accomplish with your reviews?
9. Termination of a team member.
   a. What will be considered a firing offense?
      i. *Absolutes (e.g., crimes, harassment, unethical actions, etc.)*
      ii. *Underperformance*
   b. Who will make the decision whether a firing offense has occurred?

See the Appendix of this book for a sample Office Manual, Self-Evaluation Review Form, and Employee Review Form that you can customize for your firm's needs.

6

Training: Making Your Team Efficient and Productive

Now that you have selected your team, it is time to make them efficient and productive. It is not enough to simply hire people, compensate them well enough to retain them, and then hope for the best. Even though you may have just paid a significant sum to recruit a new team member, that should be the beginning of your investment in the team member, not the end.

From our perspective, the most efficient and productive office is one that works together as a team. Everyone plays an important role on the team, and as the old saying goes, your team is only as strong as its weakest member. Another old but applicable adage is that you want everyone on your boat rowing in the same direction.

An efficient and productive team starts with strong leadership. The leaders must be able to identify the roles that need to be filled, choose the best team member to fill each role, and be able to communicate what those roles entail to each team member. After identifying each role, the leaders need to put the team members in position to excel.

Training Philosophy

There is no question that there are still many firms that subscribe to the sink or swim philosophy. We are not fans of this approach. People who learn to swim on their own are far more likely to learn strokes that work well for them individually rather than ones that are team oriented. Team members who learn on their own may become proficient at their "job," but if they do not fit smoothly into your team concept, the team will not be as efficient or productive as it could be. Moreover, some team members will sink, and they will take your firm's clients and reputation down with them.

We recommend investing the time, money, and energy necessary to train your team members not only to perform the tasks specific to their job but also to integrate them into your entire team. We recognize that it may feel counterintuitive to spend these resources on team members you just hired because you determined them to be qualified to fulfill the responsibilities in your job description, but if done correctly, this investment in your team will more than pay for itself.

We cannot overemphasize the importance of each team member understanding your firm's goals and the systems and procedures you have developed to achieve them. Team members are far more productive, especially in terms of attitude and morale, when they are working toward a known goal and when they can understand why and how their role will help achieve the goal.

Most lawyers can accept that new team members need to be taught how the firm does things, but many struggle with the concept of dedicating time to teaching a team member how to do his or her job. Even if the team member can perform the job's tasks, he or she can always improve with additional training. This alone would make training worthwhile, but there are other benefits that are even more valuable.

By training your team members, you can ensure that they will do their tasks in the manner that you want them done. When all team members are performing their tasks in the same way, the overall efficiency of the firm will improve. Each team member will fit more cohesively within the team structure, and the training will reinforce the importance of teamwork.

Perhaps the most important benefit of training your employees is that they feel valued when you invest in them. As with most things in life, you get out of something what you put into it. When you invest in your team members, you are likely to receive greater returns in the form of better performance.

Training can be done in-house, off-site, and online. We recommend a combination approach that works within your budget. If you can afford it, paying for off-site training in a nice location shows the team members that you value them and the importance of training.

The team members are likely to show their investment in the firm through greater loyalty. The more loyal your team members are, the less turnover your firm is likely to have. Although you invested more in each team member, you avoid the costs of repeated recruitment and training and the disruption caused by any gaps between the time one team member leaves and another arrives.

Scope of Training

The more challenging question is what the scope of the training should be. Should your training focus on the team member's current responsibilities, or should it be designed to help the team member take on more responsibilities? The answer to this question will depend partly on the team member's position and partly on the team member's individual abilities.

Onboarding Training

At a minimum, all new team members should receive training on your firm's policies and procedures. You cannot assume that a team member will show up and be able to master your firm's policies and procedures from the outset. The new team member needs time to digest these and to learn how you want them implemented.

Look at it from this perspective: even though every state sets forth rules of procedure that apply throughout the state, each local jurisdiction develops its own interpretations of those rules that become the "local procedures." Your new team member needs to learn your firm's "local procedures." This is your opportunity to instill your firm culture in a new team member from the outset.

It is worthwhile to dedicate significant time to allow the new team member to become familiar with these firm procedures. Not only will the team member have the time necessary to learn firm procedures, but by setting aside specific time you are also making it clear to the team member how important these procedures are.

You should document these procedures and store them in such a way that the team member can easily retrieve the necessary information. For example, if there is a particular way you prepare a certified mail packet, there could be posted steps in the mail room or in an administrative file. You could also elect to do educational videos on key topics. The key is that your process is communicated clearly to your team members and that they can articulate their comments and questions back to you.

While new team members may understand what your firm does in very broad terms, most new team members will not understand your firm's specific goals and the systems you have implemented to achieve those goals. We strongly recommend that you take the time as part of the onboarding process to lay out the firm's goals and systems in addition to explaining the procedures the new team member will have to perform. Team members who can see how their tasks fit into the "big picture" are much more likely to view themselves as important and/or valuable, and they are likely to take their job more seriously as a result.

Training to Improve in Current Positions

Each firm probably has certain positions that are unlikely to lead to advancement unless the team member in the position demonstrates potential. For example, receptionist or filing clerk positions are probably not stepping stones to higher-level positions. The training for those team members should focus primarily on their current responsibilities. However, there may be individuals in higher levels of your firm who you believe have reached the peak of their potential. Again, their training should focus on improvement in their current roles.

The trainings that focus on improvement in current roles should include a review component. As much as we would like for our team members to be trained once and to retain those lessons indefinitely, that is rarely the case. Therefore, you should periodically evaluate which procedures, tasks, and so on need to be reviewed in one of your periodic trainings.

Pro Tip: Solo practitioners need to go outside of their comfort zone when scheduling training. You cannot limit your training topics to the legal topics you enjoy. Because you are responsible for running a business and you will be doing most of it on your own, your training must include management, business, technology, and other topics you might prefer to avoid.

Training for Advancement

Of course, there are exceptions to the general statement that certain positions are unlikely to lead to advancement. While you may not have designed the receptionist or file clerk position to be one that leads to advancement, you may discover a talented team member in one of these positions. When you hire a young and/or inexperienced team member for one of these positions, you may discover that the person has far more potential and ambition than you expected. If you find a team member who shows potential, regardless of his or her current job position, you should consider expanding the training beyond his or her current responsibilities.

There are other positions in your firm that should be designed to encourage advancement. The team members in these positions should receive training not only for their current roles but also to prepare them for the roles you want them to grow into. Depending on your firm, there could be a wide variety of positions that may fit into this category. The most common example of a team member that firms anticipate will advance is an associate progressing to become a partner. Firms that focus solely on attorney advancement miss out on huge opportunities when they overlook potential advancements for paralegals, billing assistants, legal assistants, and others.

You should invest in those positions likely to lead to advancement and team members in whom you see a great deal of potential. Generally speaking, promoting team members from within will pay dividends. Promoting internal candidates allows you to build your firm with team members who already know your culture and systems, and they already have some level of loyalty. It also shows your other team members that there are opportunities for advancement when they perform efficiently within the team model your leaders established.

Training Topics

We have already mentioned the obvious training topics: your firm's procedures and legal training. Those topics are very important, and your firm should conduct regular training on these topics. Rather than going into more detail on those topics here, we want focus on topics that are not considered as often.

Most team members, particularly attorneys at a law firm, will be asked to perform tasks for which they did not receive formal training. For example, partners will be asked to manage associates, delegate work, deal with human resource issues, and make business decisions. Associates will be expected to delegate work, and eventually they will be expected to make firm management decisions when they become partners.

We do not recommend allowing your team members to learn these skills through either osmosis or "sink or swim" any more than we recommend letting a brand-new attorney take your client into court without any training or guidance. Just because partners have observed how assignments are delegated or how human resource issues have been handled does not mean that they are well equipped to handle those tasks on their own.

You should identify the tasks that are outside of your team members' formal training and look to provide training for those tasks. In short, training should be used to strengthen your team members' abilities, whether for the role you are currently asking them to fulfill or for the role you anticipate they will fulfill in the future.

Legal Services Training

Your firm should establish a strategy for legal services training. All jurisdictions require attorneys to complete a certain number of continuing legal education (CLE) courses. Of course, all the attorneys in your firm should at least meet the minimum requirements.

Although paralegals and legal assistants are not typically required to attend any courses, we recommend that you encourage or even require that they attend certain courses. When your team members understand more about the legal product your firm is providing, they will become more efficient.

In addition to taking courses, we strongly recommend that you create opportunities for team members to teach one another. If one team member attends a course, he or she should summarize the highlights of the course for the remainder of your team. If one team member has become proficient in a subject or demonstrated an interest in one, encourage the team member to give a presentation to your firm. (See Chapter 11 regarding legal services.)

Technology Training

You should arrange to train your team members on technology frequently. Technology changes rapidly, the changes are often significant, and they impact everyone. Whenever you obtain software updates, you should arrange for your team to be trained in the new technology. An upgrade will not be very productive if your team does not know how to take advantage of it.

Your team members should attend trainings offered by vendors and other providers to look for technology that can improve the services you provide. Technology is one of the few ways a law firm can take a huge leap forward in efficiency and effectiveness as long as your team knows how to use it.

Pro Tip: Train everyone in your firm. It makes each team member feel important and valued.

One year my firm offered to send our administrative assistant to a training seminar of her choice as one of her administrative week gifts. Although this team member had been in the same role for approximately ten years and she had no desire to "advance," she was overjoyed with the gift and registered for a course within days. In previous years, we had given her flowers, restaurant gift cards, and other traditional gifts. She told us that the training gift was her favorite.

One critical aspect of technology training is security. Your firm will be handling incredibly private and sensitive materials, and everyone on your team needs to know how to protect that information. This training must cover the following: (1) how your team members will protect confidential information when transmitting it both within and outside the firm, (2) how team members can avoid phishing or other scams, (3) how your team members can safely access firm information remotely, and (4) how to protect mobile devices. The most powerful step all team members can take is to use two-factor authentication everywhere it is available.

It is not realistic to think that your firm's confidential information can be stored in a vault that is locked every night when the managing partner goes home. The confidential information leaves your office every time a team member logs in remotely and/or takes his or her mobile device out of the office. The last thing you (or your clients) want to read about is how your firm exposed all of its privileged information when a team member left his or her smartphone, laptop, or other mobile device on public transportation without even making the device password protected. Annual cybersecurity training is highly recommended.

Who Will Receive Training?

Who should you spend resources on to train? That's an easy one—all of your team members. Every employee is a valuable member of your team. If you do not believe the team member or that team member's role is valuable or worthy of training, the position should be eliminated.

Consider this from a sports perspective: even the world's best teams train. The training is designed not only to improve each individual's skills but also to ensure that everyone knows his or her role and to improve everyone's teamwork. Your law firm is no different than a professional sports team. If they can benefit from ongoing training, so can your firm. Every team member in your firm can improve his or her individual skill set, and every team member needs to practice to know his or her role and to work efficiently with others.

Who Will Do the Training?

The answer to this question will likely depend on what you want your team member to learn. When firm procedures are being taught to new team members, an office manager, supervisor, or team member who has the same role as the new team member should be able to conduct the training. Often, the best trainer is the colleague who has to perform the same tasks as the new team member and is in a position to explain not only the procedures but also how they will apply on a day-to-day basis.

When you want your team members to learn new skills, you have to gauge whether you have a team member who is knowledgeable enough regarding the new skill to teach it to other team members. If there is a team member who knows the material well enough, an equally important question is whether that team member is an effective teacher.

If you do not have a team member who is both knowledgeable enough about the topic and an effective teacher, it is worth it to pay a third party to train your team. There are many trainers who will come to your office to conduct the training for no cost.

This is particularly true when you are looking for training in which your vendors have expertise. For example, your malpractice carrier will probably come to your office to give your attorneys training on ethical issues to help prevent potential issues. Companies that provide programs to help with electronic evidence will likely be happy to come to your office to conduct a training/sales pitch. Just because something is designed to be a sales pitch does not mean that you cannot learn from it.

Pro Tip: Build the training manuals piece by piece. Each time you do a new task, write down how you did it. When you learn a shortcut, update the instructions. Before you know it, you will have a manual that covers virtually everything that gets done in your office.

At the outset, we anticipate that you will be doing most, if not all, of the training yourself. This is particularly true if you wore all the hats in the office when you first opened the firm. You will be in the best position to pass down the procedures you learned through your own experiences.

Although it may be possible to arrange for someone from your own firm to present courses that will qualify for CLE credit, most firms will need to send their attorneys and paralegals to outside providers. Furthermore, it is important to attend trainings done by third parties to ensure that team members hear viewpoints from sources outside the firm.

Whenever a team member attends a course presented outside the office, the team member should be required to share what he or she learned with the rest of the firm. This does not need to be a formal process. At a minimum, the team member can draft a memorandum, give a short presentation that outlines the highlights of what the team member learned at the course, or even send an e-mail with bullet points. Since the firm likely paid for the training, the entire firm should benefit even if only one team member attended the training.

What Training Guides Will Your Firm Have?

The short answer is that your firm should have training guides for everything you want your team members to know. These guides should be available for any team member to review at his or her convenience. The training guides are there not only to help new team members learn but also for experienced team members to review, particularly when they are faced with a task that does not arise often.

Regardless of whether you plan to provide training orally or through a demonstration, there should be a written outline of the training. Some team members will absorb training orally or through a demonstration, and others will absorb the information better by reading it.

Taking the time to prepare training guides will provide two additional benefits. First, having a guide will save you from reinventing the training process when your trainer leaves the firm. Second, you can ensure that the trainings are done in accordance with your expectations because you can review and monitor the trainings that are being provided to your team.

When it comes to legal training guides, such as CLE outlines, your firm should maintain a library of training materials from courses your team members have prepared or attended. Your team members should be encouraged to view CLEs as more than just an obligation to fulfill the continuing legal education requirements of the state bar. CLEs and other legal presentations are truly an opportunity to learn how the individual team member and firm (if the information is shared) can improve the legal services provided.

Certainly, your legal training guides should not be limited to notes and materials your team members bring back from CLEs. Your firm should purchase treatises, access to online research libraries, and whatever other formal resources your team members will need to provide their legal services. At this point, your firm's library should be primarily, if not entirely, electronic.

How Much Time and Money Will You Allocate for Training?

We recognize that you have limited time and money. You cannot spend all your time in training because you will never get anything accomplished, and you cannot attend every training that would be beneficial because you have limited money.

However, if you want to avoid miscommunications and ensure that the work product is done to your standards, we encourage you to invest in training. This is a responsibility you cannot abdicate. Too often, we see attorneys complaining that their secretary cannot prepare a letter properly, laying all the blame on the secretary. We see this as the attorney's failure to properly train his or her secretary.

Because it is easy to overlook training when you have case deadlines, trials, and other business decisions to handle, we strongly recommend that you budget how much time and money you will invest in training. Once it has been budgeted, it will be much easier to follow through.

We also recommend that trainings be done on a consistent schedule. Your team members should learn to expect the trainings and appreciate their importance. For those of you who think that training should be a one-time or infrequent task, please consider how often professional athletes receive training. They certainly do not stop receiving training once they become part of a professional team. In fact, the highest levels receive more and better coaching/training than amateurs. Good training will lead to better team members, which will lead to a more productive (and profitable) firm. (See Chapter 14 on finances.)

Training Section of Your Business Plan

We anticipate that your answers to the questions below will serve as an outline for the training section of your business plan. These answers will form the foundation for how your firm will train its team members.

1. What will your training philosophy be?
   a. New hires with experience
   b. New hires without experience
   c. Established team members
2. What are you hoping to accomplish by training your team member?
   a. Proficiency in current position
   b. Ability to advance in career
3. Who will receive training?

4. Who will do the training?
   a. Internal training
   b. External training
5. What training guides will you have?
   a. Firm policies or procedures
   b. Position performance
6. How much time and money will you allocate for training?
   a. Frequency
   b. Dollar amounts

7

Managing Your Time: Vacation, Money-Making, and Preparation/Clean-up Time

Managing Your Time

Attorneys need to recognize that there is nothing more precious than their time. This is true for all attorneys, but even more so for attorneys who bill by the hour.

Pro Tip: Scheduling is much harder and more time-consuming than it appears; however, a properly managed calendar will enable you to work efficiently and will save you time in the long run. As silly as it sounds, you need to plan to make a plan.

Nevertheless, we consistently see attorneys focus on their time management *last* when it should be *first*, regardless of whether you are setting up or managing your firm. Your goal should be to coordinate your schedule to allow you to be efficient and productive in performing your work and simultaneously allot reasonable time for your personal life.

We have found that the best way to avoid getting distracted by e-mails and phone calls, sidetracked by needy or overbearing clients, or interrupted by your team members is to have a game plan for the limited time you have. It is not enough to think about how you want to allocate your time—you need to map out how your time will be allocated.

Allocation of Time

As you put together your schedule, the first step is to determine how you want to allocate your time. We suggest that you divide your time into at least the following three general categories: (1) vacation time, (2) money-making time, and (3) preparation/clean-up time.

Any time when you are not working is considered vacation time. This may include travel but not necessarily. Vacation time can also include lunches, evenings, and weekends.

Money-making time is either when you conduct the work that generates future business or when you perform the work that your clients have hired you to do. In short, this category is exactly what its title indicates. It is the time when you will earn your living.

The final general category of preparation/clean-up time is when you handle those miscellaneous and administrative tasks that must be done. You may not be able to bill this time, but these tasks must be completed to put you in position to maximize your money-making time.

Vacation Time

It may seem counterintuitive to schedule your vacation time first, but we recommend that you take this step. We have found that attorneys who do not plot out their vacations tend to push them off. If the vacation time is not put on your calendar, something always seems to come up, and before long there is no time left for a vacation.

Give some thought to how much time you want for yourself. Remember that there should be a reward (not always more money) for your hard work, and you need to take time for yourself to recharge your battery to make yourself the most productive attorney you can be.

No one who stays awake for 48 straight hours can expect to be able to perform at his or her peak. Likewise, you should not expect to work 48 straight days and be able to perform at your peak levels.

Taking Days Off

When you are planning to take a day or multiple days off, we recommend planning your vacation time for at least the next six months. Mark all of the time when your goal is to *not* work at all. This means that you do not touch your phone for business matters, look at e-mails, or even think about work.

While many feel that this is counterintuitive and that "ignoring work" will lead to sure failure if you are not working, we have found the opposite is true. You need that time to recharge, and you will be far more productive when you are fully rested physically and mentally.

Yes, this really means that you do not check your e-mails (take your business e-mail account off your phone if you can't help yourself from looking every time you see one more unread e-mail), and do not check in with the office to see what is waiting for you.

Preparation for Days Off

Regardless of the size of your firm, you need established systems and procedures your team can implement in your absence. You have to trust not only these systems and procedures but also your team. Once you establish this trust, you will be comfortable leaving the office and knowing that everything will not crumble. The lights will still turn on when you return.

You will need to prepare your clients and team members for your vacation time. You cannot simply go dark on everyone. One of the reasons we recommend planning your days off so far in advance is to enable you to provide ample notice of your plans to your clients and team members.

Your clients will be much more understanding and respectful of your personal time when they know about it in advance. The advance notice will give your clients confidence that you will make appropriate arrangements to ensure that their case will be in good hands in your absence. In addition, the notice will enable your clients to plan around your schedule.

Your team members will also need to be prepared for your vacation time. They need to know what has to be done on each case while you are gone and also what the protocols are in the event of an emergency or unexpected development.

Time Off during the Workday

We encourage you to consider scheduling vacation time during "standard" working hours. Very few of us can maintain our stamina for eight or nine straight hours without a break. Vacation time during working hours does not need to be an extended period. It can be your lunch break or even just a few minutes to step outside for some air.

Time Off during the Workweek

While it may seem to be obvious that you will not work all night every night, we find it worthwhile to identify when you want to go home each day. There will be very few days when you have completed absolutely everything you want to do by the end of the workday. If you do not make a conscious decision to stop working, you could be at your desk all night.

Your schedule should identify what time you plan to arrive and leave every day. More importantly, since so much work is done remotely these days, your schedule should identify when you will turn off all work activities and what time you will start again.

Planning Your Vacation Time

Now that you understand the rationale behind allocating vacation time, get your calendar out and visualize how you want your whole year to look at least with regard to your days off.

When we first started practicing law, a local attorney took a month off each summer. As his career progressed and his practice boomed, he increased his vacation time each year until he reached the point at which he got on his sailboat around Memorial Day and returned around Labor Day. While taking a couple of months off is a goal, we have not managed that yet, but we have each taken two to three weeks off at a time.

So, let's get to the fun part. Think about how much vacation time you ideally would like to have. What do you want your workweek to look like? Do you want to take Fridays off? Weekends only? Wednesday afternoons? This is your chance to shape your schedule before someone else (like your client) starts doing it for you.

Remember that you do not need to plan an extravagant trip to call it vacation time. Maybe you are going to exercise, read a book, take a walk, spend time with your family—you name it! The only requirement is that you do not work.

Pro Tip: Balance your time between performing legal services and working to generate new legal work. Set aside time regularly to generate new work to ensure that you have a constant flow of work to perform.

Mark those days and times clearly on your calendar as vacation time. Have fun with it. Even though you may think there is no way you can take that much time away from the business, let your hair down and go for it. This part should be enjoyable to you and hopefully eye-opening.

In our experience, you will take that vacation time if you block it off on your calendar. However, if you do not plan for the vacation time, you are not likely to take that time as vacation time and you will be relying on sheer luck to increase your vacation time from year to year. Without a clear allocation for this time, everyone (clients, team members, and others) will pull you in various different directions and demand that you allocate that time to their needs.

From our perspective, vacation time is critical for the long haul to keep you ready mentally and physically for the money-making time. The quality of your work will increase when you take time to recharge. When your work quality increases, your profit margins increase. When your profit margins increase, you can earn the same amount without working as many hours, and then maybe you too can set sail on Memorial Day.

Money-Making Time

Now that you have set aside time for yourself, it is time to designate when you plan to focus on your highest money-making activities. In short, these are times when you are either marketing your services or performing the work you have been hired to do.

Examples of tasks you may perform during money-making time are client presentations, client proposals, delivering on a proposal, marketing to key people or organizations, networking, depositions, settlement conferences, drafting agreements, and trials. The nature of your firm and practice areas will dictate what tasks you will perform during money-making time.

Amount of Money-Making Time

How much money-making time you have will depend primarily on your financial goals, but it may also depend on what phase your firm is in—for example, start-up, mature, or winding down. No matter what your financial goals are or what stage you are in, you must dedicate time to doing the work that generates revenue and profits.

Within your money-making time, you will have to balance how much will be allocated to generating new work and how much will be allocated to performing the work you promised your clients you will do. In a perfect world, you will find a consistent balance for these two tasks.

In reality, it is very hard for most attorneys to balance the time they spend on these tasks. As your case load increases, and particularly if you have a heavy trial schedule, it becomes harder on both a practical and a mental level to find time to generate more work.

First, your case work takes more time, and there simply is not time for other tasks. Second, it is very hard to get motivated to seek more work when you are overwhelmed with the work you already have.

If you do not find a way to balance the time you spend generating work and doing work, you will find yourself in a boom and bust cycle. In the boom cycle, you will have as much or more work than you can handle. When the boom period passes, you will have nothing to do because you did not spend any time finding new work. In the bust period, you will spend all your time generating new work. In all likelihood, since the new work will start at roughly the same time, the deadlines and intense periods of work for the new cases will overlap, leading to another boom period.

Pro Tip: Putting off a task is almost the same as not doing it. At the extreme end of the spectrum, we have heard stories about attorneys who put off filing tax returns and eventually just stopped filing them, leading to the implosion of their firm. Most procrastination will not lead to such catastrophic results, but all procrastination will be a drag on your firm's efficiency.

We urge you to map out the time you will spend generating work and the time you will spend doing the work. By allocating time to generate work, you are far more likely to actually follow through. Furthermore, if you have scheduled how much time you have to do the work, you will limit the work you agree to handle to what you can accomplish within the scheduled time.

Focus on Money-Making Tasks

It is very easy to get sidetracked by seemingly simple tasks, and without even knowing it, the whole day has passed by and you have not done the project that means the most to you and your client. When you schedule money-making time, you need to ensure that you have sufficiently large blocks of time to accomplish the money-making tasks.

Take a moment to think about how often you are interrupted by an e-mail or text throughout the day and what happens when you receive that message. You stop working on your project, and you answer that e-mail thinking that it will take only a minute or two to respond.

While the e-mail may only take a few minutes to answer, it will take you a few more minutes to get your mind back on your project and on task. Now multiply that by three times per hour—we all get at least that many e-mails per hour, especially when you include junk or spam e-mails.

If you allow yourself to read and/or answer each of those e-mails, you will lose 25 percent of each hour. Even if the time was not completely wasted, it was not spent on your money-making tasks.

We encourage you to minimize your e-mail program and put your phone on "do not disturb" until you finish the money-making project. Turn off the audible alerts and the pop-up notifications that let you know that a message is there waiting for you. This will enable you to focus for blocks of time.

If you have systems and procedures in place that enable you to take days off for vacation time, your clients and team members can certainly survive a few hours or even days while you work on the project. Everyone has had a sick day when he or she did not respond to clients or the office, and everyone survived. The same principle applies here.

Avoid Procrastination

Attorneys are human, and we certainly are not immune to procrastination. While procrastinating is never productive, it must be avoided whenever possible when it comes to money-making tasks.

We recognize that money-making tasks can be challenging and exhausting, and as a result, there is a greater tendency to put them off until a hard deadline is approaching. If these tasks were easy, you would not be getting paid the big bucks for doing them.

These are tasks that must be completed, and if they are not done in the time you set aside, you will have to invade time you had allocated for something else. This will have a trickle-down impact on all your strategic plans.

Scheduling time to complete these tasks is the first step. When scheduling time, make sure to schedule sufficient time to finish the task. Also, if the task is going to be mentally challenging, pick a time when you will have the most energy or stamina.

Attorneys trick themselves into thinking they are not procrastinating because they are doing work that needs to be done, but they are putting off their money-making tasks. Do not fall into the trap of working on less important tasks during the time set aside for your money-making tasks.

Results

Your clients and team members will be thrilled when they see the results you generate when you are able to focus on their project. One way to think of your money-making time is to think of it as your "game day."

Just like professional athletes do not have games every day, you will not have money-making time every day either. You cannot sustain that level of focus for five, much less seven, days a week. Review your calendar and mark the time when you will be ready for your "game day" and focused on what makes you the most money.

Preparation/Clean-up Time

Finally, it is time to schedule preparation/clean-up times on your calendar. These are times dedicated to getting organized, returning client calls and correspondence, coordinating with your team members, and preparing for your money-making time. Just like athletes have to prepare for their games and the important play that determines the outcome, attorneys need to prepare for their money-making activities and the one moment that can change the outcome.

Examples of preparation/clean-up time tasks include taking care of (and/or delegating) administrative items, responding to e-mails/phone calls, getting ready for client meetings, preparing for trials, and researching to prepare you for your highest money-making activities. These tasks must be done in order to put you in position to perform at your best during your money-making time.

Scheduling Preparation/Clean-up Time

Most attorneys do not schedule preparation/clean-up time. Instead, they fit these tasks in whenever they have time. While some preparation/clean-up time tasks occur repeatedly on a relatively consistent time line, many of them arise at haphazard times. In addition, preparation/clean-up time tasks often can be completed in a relatively short period of time Therefore, it feels easier to do them between other tasks as opposed to blocking off time for them. Often, this causes the attorney to invade vacation and/or money-making time. If you block off time for preparation/clean-up tasks, you will not feel compelled to interrupt your vacation or money-making time because you will know that there is sufficient time set aside to complete the preparation/clean-up time tasks.

We encourage you to set aside at least a little time for preparation/clean-up time several days a week. Preparation/clean-up time tasks arise frequently, and at a minimum, you need to ensure that you have time to communicate with your clients in a timely fashion. These small blocks of time will allow you to keep up with the maintenance items that need to be done.

There will be additional preparation/clean-up time tasks that will occur less frequently but may be more time-consuming. You should set aside sufficient time to address these on a weekly or monthly basis.

Preparation/clean-up time will differ for different types of attorneys. Attorneys who deal in time-sensitive matters or matters in which clients demand extensive access may need to allocate small blocks of time on each day, whereas attorneys who work on larger, long-term projects may be able to consolidate their preparation/clean-up time tasks (other than client communication) on a day or two each week. You need to balance the benefits of having uninterrupted time to complete money-making tasks versus your clients' and/or team members' need to communicate with you.

Delegation

An important part of managing your calendar, and in particular your preparation/clean-up time, is determining whether you or someone else on your team should be performing the preparation/clean-up time task. Many of these tasks can and should be delegated.

One of the most challenging professional responsibilities is learning to delegate effectively. Attorneys often believe that they are not only the best person to perform a task but also the only person who can perform the task.

While the attorney may be the best person to do it, he or she is rarely the only one who can perform the task. The most efficient attorneys delegate tasks to their team members. As your practice develops, the goal should be to delegate as many of the preparation/clean-up time tasks as possible to other team members so that you can focus on your vacation and money-making time.

You will never be able to eliminate all your preparation/clean-up time tasks. Moreover, when you start delegating these tasks, you will have to add time to manage and supervise their execution. Delegating work to another team member rarely means that your involvement ends, but it should mean that the time you spend on the task is greatly reduced.

Making Your Calendar Practical

Now you have your perfect calendar—if only we could stop there. Save that calendar; it is your gold standard and your ultimate goal.

Understand that you may have to revise the calendar to ensure that it is practical given your practice's current stage. This is not an exact science, and your calendar strategy will be a never-ending work in progress. You will routinely adjust your days and weeks depending on the status of your practice, work load, and team members.

The goal of time management is to allow you to work efficiently and at your highest level of productivity. Setting aside time for specific tasks is critical to accomplishing this.

The most successful attorneys are the ones who are able to maintain consistent schedules. Do not schedule a recurring team meeting for a different time each week. Find the time that works best for everyone, and stick with it.

Sample weekly calendar without court appearances:

Monday morning: Plan work projects for the week

Monday afternoon: Address any pressing and/or unexpected case issues that arose over weekend

Monday evening: exercise

Tuesday morning: Meet with team members you work with regularly to review and assign work

Tuesday lunch: Networking lunch

Tuesday afternoon: Work on one aspect of your business

Wednesday: Client meetings

Wednesday evening: exercise

Thursday: Perform work identified in team and/or client meetings

Friday morning: Client meetings

Friday afternoon: Partner meeting

Saturday: exercise and free time

Sunday: free time

Saving Time

While we cannot add hours to the week, there are ways to accomplish more within those hours.

Use Technology

Leveraging the right technology and platforms can significantly increase your capacity. Invest the time and money into investigating and purchasing the right technology for your firm.

Many tasks that are repetitive can be handled by technology. Even if a task takes only a moment to complete, you can create huge time savings over time by eliminating that task.

The mobile aspects of technology allow us to create time where none previously existed. You can make your commuting time productive with voice-activated software for drivers and mobile devices for rail or bus riders.

Technology should be integrated into all areas of your firm. While new technology may take some "start-up" time, the long-term time savings will make this investment worthwhile.

Avoid Distractions

Address those common "distractors" that you know will arise. We all encounter the following scenarios: "A client must talk to me right now." "I have to answer this e-mail right now." "My assistant needs to talk to me right away." "A prospective client is calling and is interested in my services." "Opposing counsel wants to talk now." We are sure that you thought of several more as·you were reading this chapter.

Make a list of the common distractions you face and develop a strategy for dealing with each of them. Perhaps, instead of answering the phone every time a client calls, you give your assistant specific times later in the day and/or week when you will return the client's call.

If your assistant has a habit of coming into your office every 30 minutes to chat or even to discuss work-related issues, instead of having your office door open all day, you let your assistant know that you will check in at the beginning of the day and at certain times during the day and that questions will need to be saved until those times. Having established procedures in place to deal with the common distractors will reduce the interruptions to only the true emergencies.

Commit to a Schedule

As you read this chapter, you probably thought, "There is no way my practice will allow me to adhere to such a defined schedule." We are confident that this schedule will work for any practice. Give it a try!

Patterns

Once you take time to review your practice and the tasks you handle regularly, we anticipate that you will start to see more patterns in them than you think exist. Attorneys are creatures of habit, and when you start to analyze your workweeks, you will probably see that you already have a loose structure in place.

The key is to solidify that structure. As you solidify the structure, you need to be certain that you set aside time for your most valuable work and for the work that you try to avoid. All of it needs to get done.

Again, we cannot emphasize this enough: it is far more likely to actually happen if you write it down. Just thinking it is not enough. Most of us are much less likely to follow a mental plan than a written plan. Remember how valuable your time is, and do your best to maximize it.

Adjustments

Adjust your calendar as necessary, but make sure to identify the adjustments you make and why. Write down exactly what cases made you adjust your schedule, and what phone calls, e-mails, or team members distracted you. Was this essential to deal with at that specific moment? Why?

Use your lawyer skills to determine where your calendaring system broke down. A well-oiled machine is efficient and has a consistent flow. Why is your flow being disrupted?

The majority of attorneys we know spend little or no time reviewing how they got sidetracked, and as a result, they do not know how to use their time efficiently the next time the issue arises.

Time Management Goals

Of course, you cannot make every day vacation time. You will have to put in the work, and if you are starting up your firm, you will be working long hours until you get past the start-up phase.

Over time, assuming this is your goal (it is *our* goal), you will be able to work 40 hours or less per week while running a profitable practice. Moreover, you can take long vacations where you are actually enjoying the vacation and not feel as if you are just working in a different location.

Being present *where you are* is a common theme throughout this book and will serve your personal and business lives well. We have colleagues who spend half the time they are on vacation on their phone or e-mail. We see their stress actually increase on their "vacations."

It is laughable but true, and you may see this with your colleagues or even in your own lives. Does that sound like a vacation to you? What type of quality time is that with your family? Your body and mind need to disconnect so that you can be focused and on your game when it will make the most money or impact for you. You can implement this approach if you plan it right.

Managing Your Time Section of Your Business Plan

We anticipate that your answers to the questions below will serve as an outline for the managing your time section of your business plan. These answers will form the foundation for how you will manage your time efficiently.

1. What do you want your work/life balance to be?
2. How will you categorize your time?
    a. Vacation time: how much free time do you want?
    b. Money-making time: how much time can you allocate to this?
    c. Preparation/clean-up time: how much time do you need?

3. What does your ideal week look like?
   a. When will you handle your management responsibilities?
   b. When will you work on your business strategy?
   c. When will you market your firm?
   d. When will you actually practice law?
   e. When will you take time for yourself?
4. Break your ideal year into quarters.
   a. How much vacation or free time will you have each quarter?
   b. How much work do you want to accomplish each quarter?
   c. What will your ideal year look like today (when you open your firm), three years from now, and ten years from now?
5. What calendar system will your firm use?
6. How will you delegate tasks?
   a. How will you focus on the most valuable tasks?
   b. Will you continue to handle tasks you like even if they are not the most valuable?

8

Ideal Client: Building a Profile of Your Ideal Client

Every attorney should strive to represent his or her ideal client in every case. We urge you to look much deeper than whether the potential client wants to hire you and can pay your bill.

Many of the frustrations and setbacks lawyers deal with stem from working with the wrong clients. Every time you work with a client that is a poor fit, you run the risk that you will not have the time or opportunity to work with your ideal client.

Pro Tip: Make a real effort to list the characteristics of the clients you want to represent. Very few of your clients will check every box on your list, but having the checklist will guide you to clients who are much closer to your ideal.

We realize that many attorneys do not want to turn away paying clients because they fear that they will lose income. However, we encourage you to turn away the potential clients with red flags so that you can focus on working with the clients you enjoy representing.

Although it would be fantastic if every client was an ideal client, we realize that we operate our firms in the real world. It is not realistic to expect every client to be perfect, but the more often you look for your ideal client, the more often you will find yourself working with a very good, if not ideal, client.

Define Your Ideal Client

The first step toward working with your ideal client is to identify the characteristics that this mystical person or entity has. We encourage you to list all the characteristics that matter to you and then to prioritize them.

As we describe some of the potential characteristics, we realize that there are stereotypes. Everyone does not fall into these stereotypes, and you can and should make case-by-case decisions as you meet potential clients. Next, we have outlined a few characteristics that we believe can tell you a great deal about a potential client and our experiences with clients who have these characteristics.

Legal Services

The first criteria is that the client needs the legal services you provide. Most attorneys prefer to handle specific aspects or subparts of the scope of legal services they provide. The ideal client will want you to perform the legal work you truly enjoy handling.

Within your specialty, you should differentiate between clients whose issues are simple or straightforward and simple cases versus those whose cases are complex. Although the case falls within your specialty, the complexity of the case will make a huge difference in what it feels like when you are representing the client.

Finances

This will sound obvious to most of you, but most attorneys want to be paid for their services. We would argue that not every dollar paid is equal. The most desirable situation is when your client pays your entire bill in a timely manner.

The next level down is the client who seeks a discount or attempts to negotiate the bill but ultimately pays most, if not all, of the bill. This case is likely to be profitable, but some of the profits are lost in the time you and/or your team members spend dealing with the client and the bill.

Then there are clients who eventually pay but not without forcing you to spend time collecting the fees and/or negotiating the amount. Not only have you spent time working to collect a fee that you earned but also the longer it takes to collect the fee, the less valuable it is to you.

In a perfect world, we would only have clients who paid for our services when payment is due without raising any questions or complaints. However, we recognize that is not reality. Nevertheless, there is a difference between clients who question and negotiate each bill and clients you have to track down for partial payments.

A potential client's ability to pay fees is not important for every attorney. There are many attorneys who prefer to handle pro bono cases or have different objectives.

We spoke with an attorney who had a disabled child. This attorney's definition of success was helping as many parents of disabled children navigate the public school systems as possible. The attorney had little interest in earning a lot of money, and she planned to charge her clients on a sliding scale.

Organized or Disorganized

Some attorneys strongly prefer to work with organized clients, whereas other attorneys are not bothered by disorganized clients. Organized clients tend to make it easier for you to put together your case, but they may insist that you be as or more organized than they are.

Dealing with disorganized clients can be frustrating. Certainly, there are some attorneys who cringe when the client walks into their office with documents stuffed into a box in no particular order. Other attorneys are not bothered in the least by this and look at that box and think, "More billable hours."

Personality

We find that many attorneys overlook the importance of a potential client's personality when deciding whether to take a case. Even when the legal issues in a case are exactly what you like to do and the client is more than willing to pay your fees, a case can be extremely unpleasant if you do not enjoy interacting with your client.

You need to honestly assess what type of personality you have and what type of personality you want to work with. In your early years, this assessment may extend to what type of personality you can manage to work with effectively even if not desirable.

As you are aware, people come in all shapes and sizes. Most people who are involved in a legal matter are under more stress than they otherwise would be, and as a result, their personality characteristics are often exacerbated. We cannot try to describe every possible personality you may encounter, but here we provide a few general categories that we encounter frequently:

- The client who needs his or her hand to be held. This client will need things to be explained repeatedly. This client will require extra time and attention to get through even the most basic steps of representation.
- The client who knows more than you do. Often, this client wants a lawyer to act as his or her mouthpiece. These clients may have more knowledge than you do about their business or experiences, particularly if they work in a highly specialized or technical field, but they do not know more about the legal aspects of their matter. Other times, these clients feel that their experiences make them better strategists or negotiators than you. To work effectively with these clients, you will need to be able to redirect the client in the direction you feel is best without directly challenging their ego.
- The client who wants you to make all the decisions. This client either does not want to participate in the process or has self-esteem issues and he or she wants you to decide everything. For an attorney, this can be exhilarating or very stressful. There are attorneys who are happy to make all the decisions, as from the attorneys' perspective, this allows them to put the case on the path that they feel is best without any disruptions. There are other attorneys who do not want 100 percent of the responsibility for the case. These attorneys want the client to participate in the decision-making process so that both the attorney and the client share responsibility for the outcome.
- The client who wants to make all the decisions. This client recognizes that he or she needs a licensed attorney, but the client intends for that attorney to be his or her puppet. This client often is motivated by more than just the desire to obtain a good outcome. This client may let his or her emotions drive the decision making or may be as concerned with how the litigation steps impact the other side throughout the process. As long as the attorney follows the client's directions, they will have a good working relationship.

Education

A client's education level can provide some key indicators. Clients with high education levels are likely to earn more money, and they probably will be better equipped to participate actively in decision making throughout the case.

Highly educated and actively engaged clients often can grasp the logic and rationale behind the options you provide and the basis for your recommended approach. However, these clients are more likely to think that they can perform the analysis better than you, and if their analysis comes to a different conclusion than yours, they are less likely to follow your advice.

We have also observed that clients with higher levels of education are more likely to accept coaching from you. These clients are used to being "taught" by professors, tutors, and so on. As a result, they expect you to educate them about the legal process (just like every other subject they have studied), and they expect that you will provide some amount of guidance.

The type of education someone received can also be very telling. For example, someone who has an advanced accounting or engineering degree will probably be highly organized and will come to your office with spreadsheets and supporting documents that are already in folders. Alternatively, an art major might be more likely to show up in your office with a box filled with random documents, unopened letters, and whatever else fell into the box—he or she will look to you to make sense of it.

Professional/Employment Background

We have found that a client's professional or employment background can provide a great deal of insight into how the client will approach his or her relationship with you. The characteristics that make people good at their jobs usually carry over into their personal lives and the ways they interact with others.

For example, people who need to be precise in their professions, such as engineers, auditors, and certain types of doctors, tend to want their attorney to be precise. These clients will not be happy when their attorneys glosses over something or tells them to consider something a wash and to move on.

Successful business owners and successful professionals frequently approach their legal matters from completely different perspectives. Business owners have to make adjustments to competition, interact with clients, and find practical and realistic solutions. As a result, business owners often look for practical solutions that balance value and cost.

Successful professionals who do not have any ownership responsibilities are often responsible only for performing specific tasks within their specialty that have been assigned to them. These clients are more likely to focus on what they believe to be the "right" solution rather than the practical one.

Attorney Shoppers

The client who visits three or four attorneys before retaining one is the client who is doing his or her due diligence. This is a client who will be thorough and expect you to present him or her with multiple options and explanations regarding the pros and cons of each option before moving forward with a selection.

The client who has been represented by several attorneys in the same matter before coming to see you is a bright flashing red flag. You have to ask yourself, what is it that I am going to be able to differently than those other attorneys? Why is this client going to be happy with me when the client was not happy with anyone else?

Price Shoppers

It is one thing for a client to interview multiple attorneys before retaining one, and certainly, the client will and should get detailed information about your billing rates and fees. This approach makes absolute sense, especially when the legal fees are going to be substantial.

It is something else completely when a potential client asks you to reduce your rates before you have been retained. This potential client is looking for the best possible deal, and even if he or she likes your legal work, he or she is likely to try to get a discount at some point in the process.

Age

Age may matter to you for several different reasons. On a personal level, you may have preferences as to whether you work with clients who are younger, older, or in your age range.

Your client's age may impact how he or she approaches his or her legal matter, but it almost certainly will impact how he or she wants to communicate with you. For example, older clients are more likely to want to meet in person, whereas younger clients will want to communicate by e-mail or text.

It may make good business sense to work with clients who are in your age range, particularly if these clients are likely to have ongoing or recurring legal needs. Once you begin working with these clients, you can continue working with them throughout your career.

Attorneys with certain practices may seek clients within a certain age range. For example, trusts and estates attorneys may prefer to work with clients who are older.

Emotional Considerations

Looking at the emotional profile of your client will also lead you to the right client. Clients who work with you because they know that they need help and they are ready to accept your help will interact very differently with you than those clients who feel compelled to hire an attorney but do not really think they need one.

Some clients will approach legal matters with a sense of fear. These clients will need more reassurances and comfort.

Rather than fear, some clients will approach legal matters with a sense of opportunity and the belief that your legal assistance will help them achieve a goal. Helping a client reach a goal can be very rewarding, especially when you view the goal in a positive light.

You are likely to encounter clients who want to use the legal system to punish or take advantage of someone. There is no question that there are many attorneys who have no qualms with this client goal so long as they pursue the goal within the ethical and professional guidelines and the client is willing to pay the bill. However, these clients are not for everyone.

Communication

From our perspective, one of the most important considerations is the level of communication the client will want or demand. The level of communication can mean the frequency, method, amount of information, or tone/attitude during your interactions.

Certain clients will bombard you and your team with e-mails and calls and demand immediate responses. You have to determine if you and/or your team are equipped to deal with this type of client.

On the other end of the spectrum, you will have clients who are very reluctant or even refuse to communicate with you even though it is detrimental to their case. You will have to expend a great deal of time and effort dragging the information you need out of your own client.

Clients often have a preferred method of communication, such as in person, telephone, electronically, via videoconferencing, and so on. Similarly, most attorneys have a preferred method of communication. These preferences need to be in alignment for your representation to be effective.

Another aspect of communication is whether you need your client to convey information to you in writing, orally, or visually. You will want to know if your client can provide information to you in the way you digest and process information efficiently.

Inquisitive Nature

Do you want clients who really want to know what is happening every step of their case and why? Depending on your perspective, these clients can be considered partners in the legal matter or they can be considered demanding. They actively participate in all aspects of the case, and they routinely ask questions.

Alternatively, there are clients who have no interest in the means; they only want results. These clients may not seem interested in the case, and the attorney may feel as if he or she is unilaterally making decisions. As the attorney, you may feel isolated and responsible for the outcome of this client's legal matter, or you may feel free to run with your preferred approach.

Expectations

What are the client's expectations? Ideally, you and your client will have similar expectations about every aspect of the legal matter, but there are two particular expectations that must be similar.

First, you and your client have to be on the same page in terms of access. If you never work nights or weekends but your client expects you to be available 24/7, there will be problems. We cannot emphasize how important it is to be clear with your clients regarding your hours of operation and accessibility.

We know an attorney who told his clients that he would provide them with his cell phone and that they could call him whenever they wanted with one condition: his hourly rate doubled for the time spent on a phone call when the client called his cell phone. Remember, you get to set the ground rules.

Second, your client's expected outcome must fall within a range that you think is reasonable. If the client expects you to provide a result that you cannot achieve, you and your client will have major problems when you do not deliver what the client expects.

Be very, very cautious about taking the approach that you will be able to change the client's expectations as the case progresses and you have had an opportunity to educate the client about the case. Rather than changing his or her expectation about the outcome, this client is more likely to feel as if you pulled a bait and switch. He or she will think that you promised the world to get him or her to retain you and now that he or she has incurred significant fees with you, you are telling him or her that you cannot deliver what the client thought he or she was buying.

Geographic Considerations

Years ago, most clients probably lived or worked in close proximity to their attorney's office. With the advances in modern technology and ease of travel, clients no longer need to be located near their attorney.

Many attorneys interact exclusively with their clients online, by telephone, or through videoconferences (see Chapter 15 regarding technology). These attorneys probably do not care where their clients are located, provided that their legal matter is located in a jurisdiction where the attorney is licensed.

For those attorneys who prefer to meet with clients in person or those who have to meet in person to provide effective representation, the client's location matters a great deal. These clients will need to be able to reach your office relatively easily unless you are willing to travel to them.

The geographic consideration is not limited to how close your client's home or office is to your office. You must also consider how far you are willing to go to litigate a case. Given the ease of travel, modern attorneys are far more willing to travel to distant jurisdictions to litigate cases.

Relationships

Many attorneys generate referrals through their personal relationships. It is one thing for an attorney to represent a client who is referred by someone with whom he or she has a personal relationship. It is another thing altogether for the attorney to represent the individual with whom he or she has the personal relationship.

We encourage you to carefully consider the pros and cons of representing a family member, close friend, neighbor, and so on. These clients may blur the line between professional and personal, and they may expect you to treat them differently than other clients.

Other Demographic Characteristics

In talking with other attorneys, we have heard attorneys talk about the following characteristics as well: gender, marital status, net worth, income, family status, home value, debts, cars, disabilities, and mental health, among others. The characteristics listed and discussed in this chapter are not intended to be an exhaustive list.

While we have covered characteristics that we believe are most likely to provide the best indicators about a client, we are certain that there are other characteristics that you feel would provide more valuable information about your clients. Take the time to determine what those characteristics are so that you can build a detailed description of your ideal client.

Where Do You Find Your Ideal Client?

One reason to take the time to identify your ideal client is that it will allow you to create a much more effective marketing plan. Your marketing efforts can specifically target places where individuals or businesses with the characteristics that you identify as ideal are most likely to look.

Define the Clients You Do Not Want to Represent

We encourage you to focus most of your efforts on identifying the characteristics that you want your clients to have, but you should not ignore the other end of the spectrum. You should spend some time listing the characteristics that you want to avoid.

Be honest with yourself, and list the behaviors that you do not want to deal with even if the client is paying every penny of your fees. By the time you factor in your heartburn over dealing with these clients, it will not feel as if the fees were worth it.

Time after time, we hear stories about attorneys who knew in the initial meeting that they did not want to work with the potential client. Instead of declining to represent the client, the attorney quoted a huge retainer fee, thinking that the client would not be able to or would not want to pay the fee. The client pays it every time, and now, you are stuck representing a client that you do not want. The better practice is to decline to represent that client and trust that a better client will come along.

Categorizing Potential Clients

Having a definition of your ideal client and knowing which potential clients you want to avoid is useless if you do not have a system to vet your potential clients. You need to develop a system that will let you categorize potential clients quickly.

As your practice grows, you should maintain a list that identifies the characteristics of clients that you either really enjoyed working with or would prefer to never see again. Over time, we anticipate that you will see certain characteristics repeat themselves for clients at both ends of the spectrum.

Once you know which characteristics are most likely to lead you to an ideal client, it will be much easier to identify them. In addition, it will also be much easier to weed out the clients that you do not want to represent.

How to Use the Ideal Client Definition

The primary purpose of defining your ideal client is to focus your efforts on working with clients who check off as many boxes as possible in your definition. A significant additional benefit is that having a definition of an ideal client will enable you to target your marketing to those individuals or businesses that are most likely to be ideal clients.

Today there are many ways to market to very specific audiences. Internet ads can be designed to appeal to users with certain characteristics.

Furthermore, you can place your advertisements or marketing efforts in places where your ideal potential clients will be looking. For example, attorneys whose ideal clients are highly educated may look to place an ad in college alumni magazines, or attorneys whose ideal clients are located within a particular neighborhood may send promotional materials to a particular zip code.

By using your ideal client characteristics to focus your marketing efforts, your marketing will be far more efficient. Your marketing strategies will stop feeling scattered and instead will target the audiences you want to reach.

Advantages of Representing Ideal Clients

When you are representing your ideal client, it will feel great. You and your client will work well together, and you can focus all your efforts on the actual legal work—legal work that you enjoy doing. You will not have to expend extra time or energy dealing with tangential issues.

Pro Tip: Do not ever underestimate the emotional strain on you and your team when you represent an undesirable client.

Many attorneys tell us that they do not feel as if they are working as hard when they represent their ideal clients. This is true because these clients do not compel you to spend time and energy on issues that are not going to advance their case. In addition, you will be happier, and work progresses more smoothly when you are interacting with someone you enjoy being around and you are doing work you enjoy.

From a marketing perspective, every time you work with an ideal client, you are likely to attract more ideal clients in the future. The best possible referral is an existing client. Since existing clients are likely spending time with people who have the same behaviors or values, they can share your contact information with a larger pool of ideal clients.

Consequences of Representing Undesirable Clients

An undesirable client is one that does not have any of the characteristics of an ideal client. Agreeing to represent a client you do not want to work with is not a harmless error. Many attorneys have told us that it is no big deal to take on a bad client once in a while. We disagree.

The most common refrain we hear is that the attorney needed more work and feared that he or she would not have enough revenue without the new case. Resist the urge to take on this client because you feel as if you need more clients or more work. Trust us when we say that the bad clients are not worth it. They cause immeasurable damage.

Regardless of whether the client pays his or her bill every time, when the case is over, you will feel as if you were not paid nearly enough. Clients that you do not want to represent are emotionally draining—not only for you but also for your team members.

Attorneys and team members often feel more exhausted after meeting with this type of client or working on that case. When one client tires you and your team out, your other clients may suffer.

One hidden cost of agreeing to represent a bad client is that it takes away the opportunity to work on a better case. You have limited resources, particularly your time. Once you devote that time to an undesirable client, that time is no longer available for an ideal client. You will be far better off in the long run rejecting the undesirable client and waiting for an ideal client to come along.

The real dangers of representing a bad client rear their ugly head when you do not provide top-notch representation. Every attorney says that he or she provides competent and zealous representation to all his or her clients, but that does not mean that every attorney provides the same level to every client.

Every attorney has a case that gets pushed to the bottom of the pile and whose tasks get pushed to the end of the to-do list. These clients do not get a prompt return phone call or e-mail. Not only does this behavior increase the risk of a mistake in the case, but also it is likely to cause the client to be unhappy with you.

Nothing good will come from an unhappy client. In our experience, dissatisfied clients react in one of the following four ways:

1. Suffer in silence: This client is unhappy but does not say anything to anyone. The client never returns to you for assistance and certainly does not recommend you to anyone else who needs legal work done. This is your best-case outcome.
2. Tell the world: This client tells his or her circle of friends and/or colleagues what a crummy job you did. Not only does this client never return to you and never refers anyone to you, but also this client damages your reputation. This client posts negative reviews online. Negative feedback travels much further and is more memorable than positive feedback.
3. Complainer: This client complains to you about the level of service he or she is receiving. In addition to providing ordinary legal services, you have to take extra time to address the client's complaints. Since you probably cannot charge the client for the time you spend assuring them that you have his or her case under control, ultimately you will be paid less for this case than an ordinary case.
4. Bar or malpractice complaints: This client becomes so frustrated with your communication (or lack thereof) with him or her that a bar complaint is filed, or the client is so unhappy with the result that a malpractice claim is filed. In this scenario, you get the added burden of paying an attorney to represent you as you navigate the disciplinary and/or malpractice field. Instead of making a profit on the case, you are now losing money and valuable time cleaning it up.

Advantages of Representing an Undesirable Client

There must be advantages of representing an undesirable client. Otherwise, why do so many attorneys represent them? The two most common reasons we hear from attorneys when asked this question are money and experience.

Inevitably, when an attorney is having a slow month or has just finished up several big cases, an undesirable client will walk through the door. There is no guarantee that an ideal client will walk in the next day, and the attorney who is starting to feel desperate for more business agrees to take the case. However, as mentioned previously in this chapter, this case may cost as much or more than what the attorney is paid.

New attorneys frequently take less-than-ideal cases to get experience. New attorneys may not have the option of working with the better clients until they have gathered some experience, and taking on a lousy client may be the fastest way to get that experience. There is no question that the experience can provide valuable lessons for future cases, but you need to be aware of what you are paying for that lesson.

There may be scenarios in which representing a lousy client offers some benefits. However, we would argue that the risks outweigh the potential benefits.

Ideal Client Section of Your Business Plan

We anticipate that your answers to the questions below will serve as an outline for the ideal client section of your business plan. These answers will form the foundation for how you will identify and attract ideal clients.

1. What are the characteristics of your ideal client?
   a. Age
   b. Money
   c. Personality
   d. Education
   e. Geography
   f. Compatibility with your process
   g. Revenue on case
   h. Complexity of case
   i. Risk of the case
   j. Residuals/potential referrals from the case
   k. Payment of fees
2. Where will you find your ideal clients?
3. How will you reach your ideal clients?
4. What are the pros and cons of taking less-than-ideal clients or cases?
   a. Reputation
   b. Opportunity cost of missing better cases
   c. Potential malpractice or unhappy client
   d. Experience
   e. Cash flow
   f. Do you have the resources for the case?

9

Marketing: Getting Clients

The days of earning your law degree, hanging out your shingle, and sitting behind your desk waiting for your clients to walk through your door are over. Lawyers who think that they can sit back and have clients magically show up do not run successful or profitable law firms.

Pro Tip: These are our mission statements:

Cooper Ginsberg Gray strives to provide high-quality family law legal representation efficiently and at a reasonable price.

Insight Law's mission is to create plans that work for people who care.

Marketing is no longer optional. It is an absolute requirement. The competition among lawyers for clients is fiercer today than ever before. In addition to competition between attorneys, today's lawyers face competition from Internet legal services and non-attorney providers, such as mediators and financial planners, who did not exist previously.

Mission Statement

The first step in any marketing campaign is to develop your message. What is it that you want to tell your potential clients? What do you want to tell your team members?

We believe that every firm should have a mission statement. This statement needs to summarize the firm's goal in one or two sentences. There is no reason you cannot articulate your firm's overarching goal in one or two sentences.

The concept behind the mission statement should not be far from the 30-second elevator pitch. We have all heard the axiom that you must be able to describe what you do in 30 seconds or less. Think of the mission statement as a written version of this.

As we have emphasized throughout this book, WRITE IT DOWN! People are much more likely to follow through on things that are written down. When it is written down, the mission statement will not be altered each time it is passed verbally from one team member to the next, whether through word changes, body language, or the delivery tone and attitude.

Message

Not every message must include your mission statement, but every message must be designed to bring you one step closer to accomplishing your mission. You should design different messages for each audience or type of client you plan to target.

Your team members must be familiar with and believe in your messages. Ultimately, they are the ones who will have to "sell" the message to a potential client in an initial interview. If your team members do not know or believe in the message, they will not convey the message effectively.

We encourage you to collaborate with your team members to develop a message not only that they believe in but also that they believe they had a part in creating. Those messages will be delivered more passionately and effectively to your potential clients.

The best messages will tell potential clients what you do and why you are the right person to do it.

Billing Rates

This is not a typo. Your billing rates constitute an important part of your marketing strategy. Your rates send a strong message to your potential clients, and different rates will attract different types of clients.

Attorneys who charge very high rates may be exceptional lawyers, but they may also be looking to attract those clients who believe in the axiom "you get what you pay for." On the other end of the spectrum, bargain hunters or clients who believe that their legal matters are very simple may seek attorneys who charge low rates.

Pro Tip: Remember, you are providing a product. Some of your potential consumers will choose a provider based on price; others will make judgments about the value of your product based on what you think it is worth.

The billing rates will play a role in which law firms you are competing against and how you are viewed by your competition.

Competition

We encourage you to develop at least the first draft of your mission statement and the message you want to deliver to your potential clients independent of your competition. The message that comes from you will be far more powerful and effective than one that comes across as a defense against your competition.

Pro Tip: Get to know your competitors. You will be surprised by how many referrals come from your competitors. Keep in mind that your competitors will come into contact with individuals who are looking for the services you provide and may decide that they would prefer to receive the services from you.

That said, every business must determine who its competitors are. Your firm's marketing plan should explain how you are different from and/or better than your competitors.

The competition for legal services has become far more intense and varied in recent years. The lawyer located in the firm next door is no longer the only competition. Certainly, other lawyers are competitors, but even this category can be divided into many subparts.

Other Lawyers

When looking at competition from other lawyers, technology has expanded the number of potential competitors exponentially. Thanks to technology, attorneys do not have to be located in geographic proximity to their clients. In addition, technology makes it much easier to reach and recruit clients who are located great distances from the attorney.

At first glance, you might think it does not matter what size firm your competitor is in. We disagree. Your marketing strategy should be altered to showcase the strengths that differentiate you from a solo practitioner, small firm, department of a large firm, or an attorney who dabbles in your practice area.

Internet

Legal services are available through the Internet more and more every day. Billion dollar companies like Legal Zoom enable your potential clients to put together legal documents at a fraction of what most attorneys charge.

Other Professionals

Services that once were the sole domain of attorneys are now offered by other professionals. Consider the examples below of how a family law client can obtain legal services from nonlawyers.

Washington state has authorized nonlawyers to help litigants navigate the legal system and to appear in court with clients. We can envision a scenario in which more states approve procedures that allow nonlawyers to hold a client's hand through the litigation process.

Many family law cases are resolved through mediation. Many states now require family law litigants to participate in mediation before they can argue their case in court. The mediator may be a lawyer, but this is not a requirement.

In any event, the mediator often provides two critical services in lieu of an advocate attorney. The mediator helps the parties negotiate a settlement and then drafts the settlement agreement. Not only does the mediator handle two important and profitable aspects of the representation, but also the mediator handles two potential clients at a time.

Pro Tip: The themes and concepts of your message should not change from audience to audience, but your delivery and packaging of the message should be tailored to the target audience.

Many family law attorneys talk about how a significant aspect of their time is devoted to social work or "legal therapy." No more. As the stigma of seeking mental health treatment recedes and the number of mental health providers multiplies, clients no longer need attorneys to be their emotional sounding board. The client can obtain this service from someone who is better trained than they are to deal with it as well as someone who typically charges much less.

From time to time, financial planners, accountants, and other lawyers handle portions of family law cases. These professionals may not get involved in family law cases as routinely as mediators or mental health professionals, but every time it results in less work for the family law attorney.

Who Is Your Audience?

Of course, you have to convince the potential client to schedule that initial meeting before your team member even has a chance to persuade the potential client to hire your firm. So where will you have the best chance to find potential clients?

While there may be countless potential audiences, there are three categories that we urge you to consider: (1) your current and former clients, (2) referral sources, and (3) the general public. You do not have to market to each of these categories, but each should be considered. Depending on your practice, you may find it necessary to divide these categories into smaller groups.

Current and Former Clients

The easiest audience to reach and, one hopes, the most likely audience members to hire you are your current and former clients. These clients have already chosen you once, and if you have treated them well and stayed in touch with them, they will be inclined to choose you again.

From a client's perspective, the clients would be thrilled to hire a lawyer that they know will accomplish their goals without having to go through the exercise of finding a lawyer. If you have done your job, the first and only place they will look for representation is you.

From our perspective, your marketing should begin with your first interaction with a potential client and continue indefinitely. Every contact you have with a client is a marketing opportunity. Clients measure each interaction on at least two levels: (1) how you are treating them, and (2) how effective the law firm is at accomplishing their goals.

You have complete control over how your clients are treated, and therefore, there is no excuse for clients to develop an impression of your firm that differs from how you intend for them to view you. Take advantage of this opportunity.

Above all else, your clients want to be respected and treated with dignity. Clients are not always able to gauge the quality of the legal services they receive, but they can always gauge whether they were treated well.

Clients who wait for long periods in the lobby, do not get return calls, and do not understand what is happening in their case are not likely to remember your firm fondly. However, clients who feel as if they are a top priority and who feel as if you are doing your best to address their needs will give positive reviews of your firm to friends, colleagues, and online.

From most clients' perspectives, we have found that the clients' satisfaction level with their attorney depends much more on how they are treated rather than the outcome of their litigated case. It is well worth your time and effort to ensure that your clients are well-educated about every aspect of their case. They should know that going to trial entails risks. We have found that these clients are willing to accept defeat at the hands of a judge or jury, but they are not willing to accept being left in the dark by their attorney and/or being patronized.

Pro Tip: Do not underestimate the potential value or ignore the potential opportunity that your bills provide. This is your chance to show your clients what you have done for them and how valuable that service is to them.

The most consistent communication you have with your client is your monthly invoice. Most attorneys ignore the opportunity this regular communication presents. Use your invoices to explain to your clients what is happening in their case, why it is happening, and that they are getting a good return on their investment in your services.

Of course, all clients want you to accomplish the legal goal they hired you to address. In a best-case scenario, you would fulfill their wishes every time. This is not possible in litigation practices in which a judge or jury controls the results. For this reason, it is even more important in those practice areas to ensure that you are attending to the way that the client feels about the services you are providing.

When marketing to your existing clients, the services you provide are your marketing messages. You do not need to prepare glossy promotional packages or give glitzy presentation to your clients. Your services should speak for themselves.

One glaring omission we see attorneys routinely make when interacting with their clients is the failure to tell their clients that they would appreciate a referral, much less ask their clients to refer them to anyone who may need their services. The simple act of letting clients know that you are interested in cases like the one the client had and that you would appreciate your clients letting their network know will result in a significant increase in referrals from clients.

Another significant omission is an attorney's failure to stay in touch with former clients. Most marketing plans are designed to put you in touch with potential clients or people who can refer you to potential clients. Your former clients fit perfectly in these categories, you are already in touch with them, and you have all their contact information.

Time after time, we see attorneys send a closing letter, toss the client's contact information into storage, and move on. The client's contact information is the single most valuable piece of marketing information you have. Use it. Your client has already needed legal services once and therefore is more likely to need or want more legal services.

Potential clients who need legal services are far more likely to choose a law firm when a friend, family member, or colleague has referred them with a personal reference. Your former clients can only make this personal referral if they remember who you are.

Referral Sources

Regardless of your practice area, you can identify individuals or entities that will interact with your ideal clients more often than others. Not only do these individuals and entities interact with your potential clients; they are also typically in a position of trust and/or influence.

The most common referral source for attorneys is other attorneys. In many cases, someone looking for an attorney only knows one attorney. Regardless of that attorney's practice area, the potential client contacts that attorney to be pointed in the right direction.

The potential client will likely trust the recommendation the attorney makes because the potential client often does not have a better way to evaluate which attorney is best qualified to help.

Think about your potential clients' spheres of influence. For example, potential family law clients are likely to interact with marriage counselors, therapists, mediators, financial advisors, accountants, and so on. Everyone seeking legal help will have spheres of influence. You need to determine which ones apply to your ideal clients.

Your goal is to provide your referral sources with the confidence to recommend you. The hardest referral to obtain should be your first one. You need to convince the referral source that you are qualified to accomplish whatever the potential client needs. Once the referral source knows that you can provide the services you say you can, he or she will be even more confident sending clients to you.

The perfect scenario is when the client who came from a referral source reports back to the referral source regarding his or her positive experience with you. Without violating any client confidences, you should work to ensure that the referral source knows that you did a good job for the client.

Potential clients are much more likely to retain you when they reach you through a referral. The fact that a third party, especially someone in a position of trust or influence, has recommended you will make the potential client far more likely to become a current client.

We recommend spending a great deal of time and effort recruiting referral sources that are likely to interact with your ideal clients. While not as efficient or inexpensive as marketing to your existing and former clients, this is the next best approach.

General Public

Attorneys should not ignore the general public since there are many potential clients who have not needed legal services previously and may not have a social or professional network that puts them in contact with your referral sources. That said, pursuing clients through the general public is the least effective approach.

When you are targeting the general public, the goal is to place your message in a place where the most people will see it with the hope that some segment of that group will need your services. Any marketing strategy aimed at the general public will reach some potential clients, but the percentage of the general public who need your services is probably very low. When measuring this approach in terms of return on investment, this is typically the most expensive approach.

Pro Tip: Find out what the mindset of your potential client is, and adjust your message to address the factors that your potential clients will consider when deciding whether to hire an attorney and whether to hire you.

Marketing to Different Types of Client

Clients typically either need legal services or want legal services. There is a big difference in the mentality of a client who needs versus one who wants legal services, and therefore, the marketing strategy for these potential clients is very different.

On the one hand, clients who need legal services are definitely going to hire an attorney. The only question is which attorney they will hire. These clients are comparing attorneys based on skill, cost, and so on, and your marketing strategy should be designed to differentiate you from your competition. Clients who have been charged with a crime, whose spouse has filed for divorce, or whose business partner has sued them need an attorney.

On the other hand, a client who wants an estate plan or to revise the office employment manual does not need legal services. Instead, that client wants legal services. Very few people looking for estate planning documents think that they are on the verge of dying. Therefore, while they know that they should have an estate plan drafted by an attorney, they do not think they must have one immediately. This potential client needs to be convinced not only that they should pay for legal services now but also that you are the right attorney for the job.

Delivery of Your Message

Once you have figured out what your message is and who you want to receive the message, the next step is to determine how you will deliver the message to your audience. You should expect to deliver your message differently to each audience.

Pro Tip: Social media is becoming more important every day. Learn how to create accounts on various social media platforms, such as LinkedIn, Instagram, and Facebook, and to build communities on each. Each platform has its own style and rhythm (formal versus informal, post daily versus weekly, pictures versus text, etc.). Take the time to find out what will work on each platform, and adjust your content to appeal to each audience.

Clients and Former Clients

As we have stated previously, every interaction with your clients should be treated as an opportunity to demonstrate that the client made a good choice. Many consumers need reassurance that they made a good choice, particularly when the cost is significant.

In addition to ordinary attorney-client interaction, we encourage you to serve as a general legal resource for your clients. When a client calls you to ask if you can handle a legal issue that is outside the scope of what your firm handles, do not simply reply that you cannot help him or her and hang up. Take the time to find an attorney who can help your client. Providing assistance like this will leave your client with a positive impression.

Also, we encourage you to host events for your clients. These can range from seminars that educate your clients about common issues you anticipate they will encounter to events that are purely social functions.

There are countless ways to market to your clients and former clients. The following are a few that we believe can be effective if done properly, but this is no way an exhaustive list: blogs, newsletters, holiday and/or birthday cards, end-of-case gifts, social media, videos, announcements, and promotional items with your firm name/logo.

Referral Sources

The single best way to get referrals is to give referrals. When there is an opportunity to refer a client, colleague, or friend, send him or her to a potential referral source you trust. After receiving referrals from you, this referral source is far more likely to think of you when he or she is looking for an attorney for his or her own contact.

Referral sources, particularly ones in a professional field, want to have confidence that you know what you are doing. When you are trying to impress other lawyers, the best way to do this may be to write an article or present a seminar in your field.

Another effective way to give other lawyers confidence in your abilities is to participate in law-related committees with them. While you are not likely to have an opportunity to demonstrate your skill in your practice area, you will have numerous opportunities to show the other lawyers on the committee that you can be relied upon. By being punctual, finishing the tasks assigned to you in a timely manner, and working cooperatively with the committee, you will demonstrate your work ethic.

For those professionals who are not attorneys, you may be able to present a seminar as to how your legal field impacts their profession. In a best-case scenario, you can work hand in hand with them to help mutual clients.

We encourage you to participate on nonprofit boards and other groups where you will be able to show that you can act professionally and responsibly. Similar to the law-related committees, you will not have the opportunity to demonstrate your legal skill, but you will be able to showcase other skills that will give the professionals the confidence that their referrals will be in good hands with you.

Pro Tip: Pay careful attention to the financial aspect of your marketing efforts. Each effort has a monetary and nonmonetary (how much time you spend on the marketing effort instead of another task) cost. You must track how many new clients you obtain through each individual marketing effort and the average revenue/profit generated by each client. Knowing the total revenue/profit generated by each marketing effort will tell you whether the marketing effort should be continued, expanded, or terminated. (See Chapter 14 regarding budgeting.)

We have found that you can find referral sources in any group. As an example, we have found valuable referral sources in a weekly pick-up basketball game and when coaching high school lacrosse. Get to know the people in your social circles and let them know what you do for a living. Not everyone will turn into a referral source, but if no one knows what you do, you will never cultivate any referral sources.

General Public

Some attorneys still rely on print advertising to reach the general public. One advantage of print advertising in today's market is that you can usually reach a very specific audience. Many magazines are geared toward one audience, such as university alumni, local geographic areas, zip codes, and so on, and therefore, your advertisement will go to that select audience.

Certain practice areas still rely on direct mailers. Direct mailers are likely to generate only a small rate of return, but if done properly, they can still be profitable. There is a reason you receive dozens of letters from traffic attorneys offering their services when you receive a ticket.

Attorneys still use billboards, written or television advertisements, flyers, sponsorships, and direct mailings to promote themselves. All of these approaches have merit and should be considered.

You should not ignore the general public, particularly when you are a new attorney who does not have many clients or former clients or a strong referral network. However, we recommend that you focus your approach on the audiences that are most likely to be receptive to your message.

Pro Tip: Your website is often your potential client's first impression of you and your firm. Make it a positive one!

As technology continues to improve, it is becoming easier and easier to define and reach your target audience. As you learn which groups are more likely to have members who need your services, you can narrow your target audience to those groups. When you shrink the size of your target audience, your return on investment will increase.

Website

We have set the discussion of your website into a category of its own because it impacts all three audiences (clients/former clients, referral sources, and the general public). The fact that all three audiences will use your website, and that they are likely to be using it in different ways, will present web design challenges.

Your clients and former clients will likely use the website to reinforce their belief that they made the right decision to hire you. They will review the website periodically to see what articles you are publishing, where you are speaking, and what awards or recognitions you have received. All of these items will give them confidence that they made a good choice.

In addition, clients and former clients will review the website to familiarize themselves with team members they interact with. In particular, if they were not introduced to a team member who is now an active member of their legal team, the client will want to see what this person looks like and review his or her bio.

Referral sources will look at the website to refresh their memory as to what services you provide and to obtain contact information to pass along to the potential client. Once the contact information is passed along, the potential client is highly likely to review the website before contacting your office to schedule an appointment.

The general public will typically reach your website through a search. The individuals who reaches your website will have no advance knowledge or information about anyone at your firm, and they will be looking to see if your firm appears to be a good match for them.

Every attorney should have a website, but a substantial number of solo and small firms do not. Virtually all potential clients will expect you to have one, and it is a relatively easy way to provide valuable information about your firm. Unlike written promotional materials, websites are easy to update with current events and can be easily shared with your contacts.

Remember that many potential clients will be looking for a lawyer on their mobile phone, so your website must be mobile friendly in design.

Your website should be updated frequently to avoid becoming stale and to increase your standing in the mysterious search engine algorithms. You should consult with a website designer or search engine optimization expert to do whatever you can to move your website to the first or second page of the search results. Potential clients are not likely to look through multiple pages of search results to find you.

Gift ideas: Food or a gift certificate to a good local restaurant are always safe choices.

Promotional items that include your firm name are often seen as a marketing effort rather than a genuine thank you gift.

Social Media

Law firms are increasingly finding that a strong social media presence on a variety of platforms, such as Facebook, Instagram, and LinkedIn, is a good way to share information and news to a virtually limitless audience.

Many firms announce new employees, awards, accomplishments, published works, charitable work, and other notable events on social media. With the ability to "tag" and link to the pages of related professionals or organizations, the news can spread far beyond just the followers of your particular page.

As with all forms of marketing, you must be aware of your audience. People who join Facebook will consume information differently than those who join Instagram. Firms cannot hope to have an effective social media strategy by cutting and pasting one message into all their accounts.

Thank You Notes and Referral Gifts

Everyone who refers a potential client to you should receive a thank you note and possibly a gift as well. This rule applies to everyone who refers someone to you, whether that client retains your firm or not. Once the recommendation is made, it is your responsibility to convert the potential client to a client.

Referral sources cannot do more than recommend you. Take a moment to think about how valuable that recommendation is. A personal recommendation from a client, former client, or referral source is likely to lead to a high conversion rate. The bare minimum you can do is thank the referral source for making the recommendation that could lead to thousands of dollars in fees.

The thank you note and/or gift will let the referral source know you value and appreciate his or her effort. In addition, the thank you note and/or gift is the perfect opportunity to touch base with the referral source to keep you in the forefront of his or her thoughts in a positive way.

Ratings, Awards, and Recognitions

Many attorneys would say that magazine ratings, public awards, or recognitions are not good indicators of whether an attorney is a good attorney or not. That may be true, but for marketing purposes, it is beside the point.

Potential clients are looking for ways to differentiate one attorney from the next. Generally speaking, potential clients who do not interact with lawyers on a daily basis probably cannot distinguish one from another.

Another aspect of ratings is an attorney's Yelp or Avvo rating. Younger clients are as likely to rely on these ratings as they are on a personal referral. You must take the time to manage these ratings. You can invite clients to review you, and you have the ability to challenge unfavorable reviews.

When all things are equal, these potential clients will look to see which attorney has a good rating or has received awards.

Marketing Plan

From our perspective, there are no absolutes when it comes to marketing. We recognize that most lawyers did not study marketing, and no one went law school to become a marketing executive. The only approach that we strongly discourage is one in which you ignore marketing altogether.

As much as you want to be practicing law, the bottom line is that you cannot practice law without clients. In this day and age of heightened competition, you will not have any clients (or not enough clients to stay in business) if you refuse to market yourself.

Just like any other plan, your marketing plan should be well-defined. Too many attorneys approach marketing haphazardly. They agree to have lunch with referral sources when they bump into them at another event or agree to sponsor an event because a friend asked them to contribute. While these efforts have value, they may not provide the maximum value.

Your marketing plan should identify your message for each audience; who your target audiences are, and how your message will be delivered to each target audience. Your decisions to attend lunch with a referral source or sponsor an event, etc. should be based on whether the activity fits within your plan.

Pro Tip: Every team member has a circle of friends and a network of contacts. All team members, not just attorneys, should promote the firm to their connections. Make sure that every team member has talking points about your firm and is comfortable sharing them.

Be certain that your team is sharing all their marketing and networking efforts. This will allow you to ensure that efforts are not duplicated and that potential marketing opportunities are not being ignored.

Who Will Create and Execute the Marketing Plan?

You do not have to create the marketing plan or execute every aspect of it. You are welcome to hire someone to execute a marketing plan for you. However, you do have to participate in and help develop the overall message.

We strongly encourage you to consider every team member to be a marketer. Remember, when it comes to current and former clients, every firm interaction with a client is a marketing opportunity. Therefore, every team member needs to understand this responsibility and be trained to handle the interaction in a manner that leaves your client with the impression that you want the client to have.

Furthermore, every team member can be a valuable marketer not only with existing clients but also with potential clients. Your team members have their own friend groups, spheres of influences, and families, and ideally each team member will promote your firm within each of these groups.

All team members should be promoting the firm, and all marketing efforts should be designed to help the firm achieve its goals. However, we also encourage each partner or lawyer who aspires to become a partner to develop his or her own marketing plan within the parameters of the firm's marketing goals.

An attorney who develops his or her own marketing plan will reach his or her personal goals while simultaneously advancing the firm's goals. Attorneys who can attract clients on their own rather than depend on another attorney to funnel work to them are far more valuable to their firms, and therefore their careers will advance more quickly.

Quantifying Your Marketing Efforts

It is imperative that you measure your marketing efforts. You need to know what is working, what is not working, and how much each effort costs in terms of time and money. Without these measurements, you will not be able to make adjustments.

Marketing is not static. Strategies and approaches go out of style, and you need to be in the position to keep up with the current trends. For example, years ago many attorneys could not have imagined advertising anywhere other than the yellow pages and would not have considered advertising on television, much less online. Of course, as technology has moved forward, most attorneys have abandoned the yellow pages for all forms of online advertising.

On one hand, we urge you to track where your clients come from. At a minimum, every potential client who contacts your firm should be asked how he or she heard about your firm. This one piece of information can tell you a great deal about which marketing strategies are working. There is nothing more helpful than a good intake form.

The more information you gather about potential clients, the better. Every bit of information you have about your potential and current clients will help you identify where your clients come from, and that will enable you to tailor your marketing strategies to reach the people or entities who are most likely to become your clients.

On the other hand, you have to track how much time and money you spend on each marketing effort. In essence, each marketing strategy should have its own budget. Each budget should measure how much time and money you spend on each strategy.

The goal is to convince your ideal clients to retain your firm while incurring the lowest costs. We have discovered (the hard way) that some strategies that feel as if they are very effective are actually very costly compared to other strategies. It is very easy to fall into the trap that a particular method is effective, especially when that strategy comes with a good storyline or is the traditional way of doing things. We strongly encourage you to develop analytics that will give you an accurate measure of the strategies that work.

Marketing Section of Your Business Plan

We anticipate that your answers to the questions below will serve as an outline for the marketing section of your business plan. These answers will form the foundation for how your firm will reach your potential clients.

1. Draft a written marketing plan.
2. What is your firm's message?
   a. What is your overarching mission?
   b. What is your message to each constituency?
      i. Team members
      ii. Potential referral sources
      iii. General public
3. Who do you want to receive your message?
   a. Clients and former clients
   b. Referral sources
   c. Retail/general public
4. How will you get your message to your target audiences?
5. When are you marketing?

6. Who is doing the marketing?
   a. Will there be a leader of the marketing program?
   b. What is each team members' role in marketing?
7. Quantifying your marketing efforts
8. Economics of marketing
9. How you can use technology in marketing
   a. Quantifying and tracking your marketing efforts
   b. Delivering your message efficiently

See the Appendix of this book for a sample Intake Form for a Potential New Client and a Closing Letter that you can customize for your firm's needs.

10

Managing Clients: Keeping Clients

Successful attorneys actively manage their relationships with their clients. We have found that setting clear expectations up front creates the foundation for a good working relationship.

Everyone has heard the adage "location, location, and location" for real estate. When it comes to the attorney-client relationship, the adage is "communication, communication, and more communication."

We cannot emphasize strongly enough how important it is to set expectations and to communicate them to your clients. On the flip side, your clients should have reasonable expectations of you, and you should know what those expectations are.

Retainer Agreement

In most attorney-client relationships, you and your client will memorialize your expectations of one another for the first time in your retainer agreement. The most effective and efficient attorney-client relationships will require the attorney and the client to complete certain tasks.

All retainer agreements will state with a reasonable level of specificity what legal work you will perform. While you will perform the legal work, you will not be able to provide top-notch legal services without cooperation and information from your client. Your retainer agreement should make it clear what you will need from your client.

Every retainer should state exactly how and when the legal services will be paid for. Nothing sours an attorney-client relationship faster than a disagreement over money.

Finally, the retainer agreement should spell out how either the attorney or the client can terminate the relationship. The client needs to know that your representation will not continue unless a certain standard of behavior is met. However, the client needs to know that he or she does not have to continue working with you if you are not meeting his or her expectations.

Communication

The most common complaint clients make about lawyers is that they do not return calls or messages in a timely fashion. You and your client should have a clear understanding as to how and when you will communicate.

Your firm should have a policy as to how quickly you will return phone calls, e-mails, texts, and so on. This should be memorialized in your office manual (see Chapter 5). This policy should be shared with your client so he or she knows what to expect.

We have seen attorneys who make themselves available to their clients 24 hours a day and others who place strict limits on the times when they will take calls. We have not seen any appreciable difference in client satisfaction for either set of attorneys.

The clients who are unhappy with their attorneys are the ones who do not know when to expect a return call or message. When there is no set expectation, the client will fill in the gap with whatever he or she expects, which may be very different from what you think is reasonable. When you do not meet the client's unknown expectation, then the client becomes unhappy.

We have encountered lawyers who charge more per hour when clients call them on their cell phone, after-hours, or on weekends. This is permissible if this arrangement is clearly stated in your retainer agreement and explained to the client.

Pro Tip: Your out-of-office e-mail auto-reply message should include the following information: how long you will be out of the office, when you will return, a general estimate as to how long it will take to receive a response after you return to the office, and an alternate point of contact in the case of an emergency. Your voicemail message should contain the same information.

You should change your voicemail message every morning when you start work. The message should contain basic information. For example, if you are in meetings throughout the day, it should state that you will be available to return calls in the afternoon, so that callers have a general understanding as to when you are likely to receive their message and when their call will be returned.

The communication should always be professional. As communication moves from letters to texts, there is a tendency to use less formal language. While you do not need to speak in legalese, we do not recommend using emojis or slang to convey your message.

We strongly encourage you to speak to your clients in English rather than legalese. We find that many lawyers fall into the habit of using arcane legal terms or lengthy, convoluted sentences that most people, even those with advanced degrees, cannot understand. Even if everything that you say to your client is completely accurate and addresses all of the issues, it is worthless if your client cannot understand what you are saying. Make sure that you are speaking in a language that makes sense to your client.

Notices

E-mail and voicemail systems make it incredibly easy to set up auto-replies for when you will be out of the office and/or unavailable. Given how easy these tools are to use, there is no excuse for not using them.

Most attorneys are pretty good about changing these replies when they are going on vacation, but we encourage you to use them more frequently. If you are going to be in trial for several days and therefore unavailable to all of your other clients, we recommend letting everyone know. In short, whenever you know that you will not be able to respond as quickly as you ordinarily do, you should use the notices.

Keeping your outgoing voicemail message up-to-date is critical. You should not count on your receptionist to convey information about your return to all of your callers. In any event, your receptionist is not likely to be there in the middle of the night when your client calls to leave you a voicemail message. With an outgoing message letting the client know that you are unavailable, the client knows not to expect an immediate response.

If you know that you will be out of the office for several consecutive days, we encourage you to let your clients know in advance so they can plan around your availability. When you schedule a vacation several months in advance, you will have multiple chances to let your clients know about your plans.

In addition, your notice should let your clients know who can assist them in your absence. Although you and your clients can plan around your vacation schedule, inevitably, one of your clients will have an emergency. Make sure that client can be helped until you return.

Billing

It is worthwhile to take extra time to review and discuss your billing practices. While it will be spelled out in the retainer agreement, you and your client should make sure that you are on the same page. Whatever extra effort you put into clarifying and explaining your billing practices will pay huge dividends when your client makes timely payments.

The billing discussion needs to explain how much you are charging for your services. When you are billing by the hour, it is typically impossible to provide your client with a specific amount that he or she will pay for the entire case. Although you cannot provide a specific amount, you can provide guidance to your client as to what may increase or reduce the case costs.

If you are charging a flat fee, it is critical that the client understands exactly what is or is not covered by that flat fee. This is particularly important if there is related legal work that is not covered by the flat fee. Your clients will be incredibly frustrated to learn after their flat fee has been exhausted that there is more work that should be done, and that it will cost more.

Pro Tip: Do not dance around billing issues. Be up-front with your clients about billing issues. You cannot have a strong attorney-client relationship if there is uncertainty about your billing relationship.

Your client must know when he or she will be billed for your services and when payment is expected. This is not something that can be sprung upon your client. Many clients will have to make arrangements to coordinate payment. The more advance notice that you provide them, the less friction there will be when you issue a bill and seek payment.

For those clients who pay a retainer fee that is not designed to cover all the potential case fees, you need to be clear that you do not expect the initial retainer fee to cover all the fees. In addition, you need to be clear as to when you will expect the retainer account to be replenished.

During the retention process, you should explain to your clients when and how they will be billed for your services. We realize that very few attorneys look forward to reviewing and issuing bills; nevertheless, it must be done, and it should be done consistently.

We have encountered numerous attorneys who have run into significant ethical and/or collection issues because they issue their bills sporadically. Clients appreciate it when you develop a consistent schedule for your bills to be issued and when you stick to that schedule.

At a minimum, your invoices must make it clear to the client what services have been performed, what the client has been charged, and the status of the client's retainer account. The client's financial status is not a subject that can or should be tiptoed around.

Chapter 13 regarding billing discusses the establishment of your firm's billing and collection policies in greater detail.

Case Status

Your client should always know the status of the case. Ideally, you will provide your client with an outline that sets forth the steps you plan to take in the case and when these steps are likely to occur.

We realize that you cannot predict every step, much less its timing, with certainty. Furthermore, we recognize that the roadmap may change depending on the actions taken by the other side of the case. These caveats should be shared with the client. Nevertheless, the client will appreciate a rough roadmap over being kept in the dark.

As you approach each step in the roadmap, you should contact the clients to let them know that you are getting ready to take the step and to remind them what this step entails and where you are on the roadmap. While each step may be second nature to you, for your client who rarely interacts with the legal system, each step will be a foreign concept. The client will find a brief refresher valuable.

Your client should never feel the need to call your office to find out what is happening in his or her case. We consider a call along these lines a failure to properly manage your client and the case.

Complaints

The absolute last thing you should do when a client complains is disregard or dismiss the complaint. The way you handle a complaint is frequently as important as or more important than whatever triggered the complaint.

You may not agree with the client or you may feel that the complaint is unjustified, but that is clearly not the way the client feels about it. Address the complaint head on. Find out what prompted the client to complain, and then see what you can do to address the client's concerns.

Rather than being upset that the client complained, you should be thankful that the client is telling you what the issue is and giving you a second chance. Plenty of clients will quietly seethe, sharing their frustrations with their contacts, and end the representation without you having any idea of the damage that has been done.

When clients complain, they are telling you exactly what the problem is from their perspective. You are responsible for explaining to them (without patronizing) why their complaint is unfounded or, if the complaint is legitimate, explaining to them how you are going to address their concerns.

These are some of the common complaints we hear about attorneys:

1. My attorney will not return my calls.
2. My attorney will not explain what is happening in my case, or I do not understand what my attorney is saying.
3. I do not understand what I am being billed for or why I am paying for that.
4. My attorney does not listen to me and is not trying to get the resolution I want.

Too many attorneys completely ignore client complaints, hoping that they will simply go away on their own. This avoidance often bleeds into the case. The attorneys no longer want to talk with the clients at all because they do not want to hear the complaint, and this lack of communication leads to missteps in the case, compounding the original problems.

Some attorneys who do listen to the client's complaints are frequently very dismissive of them. We hear attorneys make comments that can be summarized as stating that either the client does not know what he or she is talking about, the client is crazy, or the client has always been a problem. Remember, it is your job to educate your clients about the legal process and to guide them through it.

Team Members and Work Allocation

Let your clients know from the outset who will be working on their case and what each person's role will be. Another common complaint by clients is that they thought they were going to be working primarily with a partner, but all of their interaction with your firm ends up being with an entry-level associate or an assistant.

If other team members are going to work on a client's case, let the clients know as early as possible who else will be assisting them, what role the team members will play, and why you believe this is the best way to structure the representation. Clients should never be surprised when they start receiving messages or calls from a new team member. Again, do not put the clients in the position of calling you to ask what is happening on their case.

Not all the work on the legal matter will be performed by your team. The clients will be responsible for some of the work. At a minimum, the clients will need to provide information to you so that you can provide the most effective legal services.

The clients' role needs to be spelled out at the beginning and updated as the matter progresses. Many clients will have the attitude that they explained the issues at the initial consultation, they hired you to take care of the issues, and that is why they are paying you. You must be clear on what you need from the clients.

Every lawyer knows that he or she cannot provide the best services without input and cooperation from the client. While it may seem intuitive to you, not every client will recognize this. Therefore, you must make it clear that you expect the client to actively participate throughout the case, otherwise you will end up with a client complaining that you are not completing the legal services in a reasonable time period. While the client is complaining about how slow you are, you are waiting for the client to provide the one document that you need to finish the work product. All of this can be avoided with clear and frequent communication.

Technology

Technology is your friend, and it certainly can make client management much easier. Every law firm should have customer relations management (CRM) software to help manage your clients and cases.

CRM will allow you to maintain all your clients' contact information in one place. The software can be designed to remind you to touch base with your clients at each step of their case.

While it may not seem necessary to invest in CRM or other technology to track your clients' contact information or the workflow in their cases when you open your firm, we strongly recommend that you start early. As your client base grows, it will become harder and harder to keep track of everything. Moreover, it is much easier to build a functional and helpful CRM when you do not have much information to input. It will be exponentially harder to build a CRM when you have to input years of data (see Chapter 15 on technology).

Value for Clients

You should take extra time to explain to the clients what you are doing on their behalf. The more the clients appreciate the effort you are putting into their case, the more likely they are to feel as if they are receiving real value for the money they are spending.

This is especially true for clients who do not have much experience with the legal system. These clients have no concept of what it takes to handle a case from beginning to end. They only recognize that they have a legal issue and they hope that the lawyer they hired will solve it.

Attorneys who handle similar cases every day lose sight of the fact that a great deal of effort goes into these cases. It may not feel like much to the attorney who is used to doing the same tasks repeatedly, but we urge you to think back to the first time you did each task. Now imagine doing each task without the benefit of a legal education and without any familiarity with the legal system. This is what your client would be facing if he or she did not have you.

Pro Tip: The "small" promises are just as important as the big ones. Everyone has a friend who is always running a few minutes late. Think about how you feel every time you are waiting for your friend to arrive. Now imagine how you would feel if the person you are paying hundreds of dollars per hour to speak with you cannot be bothered to be on time.

We encourage you to let your client know each task that needs to be accomplished and what it will take to accomplish each one. This will help your client understand what he or she is paying for. You know that your clients are getting value for their buck; however, unless you explain to the clients what they are getting for their money, they may not realize how much value they are receiving.

Keep Your Promises

If you do not take anything else away from this chapter, take this: keep your promises. When you tell clients what you are going to do, make sure that they understand what you mean, and then make sure you do it when you said you would get it done.

Promises about small items are just as important as promises you make about big issues. If you arrange to speak with your client or send your client a message, do not miss the appointed time.

While being late or even forgetting may not seem like a significant issue in the grand scheme of things, it can have a lasting impact on your relationship with your client. These interactions form the foundation of your attorney-client relationship.

When you say you are going to deliver something to your client, do it.

Managing Clients Section of Your Business Plan

We anticipate that your answers to the questions below will serve as an outline for the managing clients section of your business plan. These answers will form the foundation for how your firm will work/partner with its clients.

1. Expectations
    a. What expectations do you have of your clients?
        i. *Cooperation*
        ii. *Communication*
    b. What expectations can your clients reasonably have of you?
        i. *Scope of services*
        ii. *Billing*
        iii. *Communication*
2. How will you share these expectations?
    a. Will the expectations be outlined in writing or orally?
    b. Who will present the expectations to the client?
3. What will your system of communicating with your client be?
    a. When will you share your expectations with your client?
    b. Which team member(s) will share the expectations?
    c. How will your firm communicate with your clients?
4. Who will be interacting with the clients?
5. What values are the clients receiving?
    a. What services are you providing?
    b. How will you explain to the clients that the services have value?

6. How will you make things convenient for your client?
   a. Technology
      i. *Automatic renewals*
      ii. *Online payments*
      iii. *Video conferencing or other remote meetings*
   b. Knowing who the right point of contact is for your client

See the Appendix of this book for sample Flat Fee and Hourly Rate Retainer Agreements that you can customize for your firm's needs.

11

Legal Services: Your Product

Legal services are the product your business provides. How you define your legal services will have a huge impact on how you run your business and your relationship with your client. This definition will include not only the practice areas or types of cases your firm will handle but also the scope of services you will provide within each practice area.

In this chapter we have used decidedly business terms to describe your legal services. There is no question that lawyers owe a greater duty to their clients than most businesses owe to their customers. However, we have purposely used pure business terms to emphasize as strongly as possible the business aspects of your law firm. Failure to run your law firm as a business is often a route to failure for a law firm.

The concept of selecting the practice areas your firm will handle seems straightforward on its face, but a number of factors should be considered when making this decision. On the highest level of analysis, you need to consider what types of cases your attorneys are qualified to handle, what types of cases your attorneys want to take, and what amount of revenue those cases will generate. Different firms will assign different values to these factors.

Practice Areas and Product Lines

The logical starting point is to focus on practice areas in which your attorneys and staff already have experience, ones that they enjoy working on and are qualified to handle. This approach is efficient and requires the lowest investment of human and financial resources.

However, identifying your practice areas, such as family law or trusts and estates, with general categories is only the first step in describing your legal services. General practice areas such as family law encompasses a wide range of legal matters, which we will call product lines. For example, family law could encompass any of the following: adoptions, premarital agreements, custody, visitation, child support, spousal support, property division, settlement negotiations, litigation, protective orders, and others. Each one of these subsections of family law is a different product line.

Pro Tip: Define the legal work you want to do and be specific about it. It is not enough to use a generic practice area name as the description of your legal work. There are too many subparts that require too many different skills to rely on a generic description.

A family law firm could include all or only some of these services, so it is important to be clear about which ones you provide. Without a clear explanation, even other family law lawyers may not know what a "family law" practice encompasses. As you can imagine, if other family law attorneys are not sure what your practice entails, potential clients will understand even less.

You need to define your practice areas with much more specificity both for yourself and for your potential clients. A specific definition of your product lines will help you organize and structure your firm internally in the most efficient way, and it will reduce confusion that your referral sources and/or potential clients may have about what you do.

Scope of Work

Even after you clearly define your product lines, the scope of work within each product line can be defined more narrowly. The actual legal work may entail research, drafting, and/or litigation for each product line. These legal tasks require vastly different skill sets. Not all firms, much less individual lawyers, can competently do all three.

After you decide which product lines and which tasks within them you will handle, the next decision is determining the complexity of the cases you will handle. Will your firm handle simple cases, complex ones, or any case within the scope of work within the product line that walks in the door?

Some of you are probably asking why we are suggesting that you limit the cases you will handle. Because different product lines and tasks within those product lines require different skills, you cannot efficiently build your team without knowing the scope of work you will perform.

Also, different types of clients seek different types of legal services. Narrowing the scope of work you provide will enable you to tailor your marketing efforts to the audience that will want that type of work done.

We acknowledge that you must choose broad enough product lines and/or scopes of business to ensure that there is enough of a market for those services to generate business. However, we are confident that there will not be a shortage of work unless you are wholly unreasonable in the restrictions you place on the work you are willing to do.

Discard that fear that you will be sitting in your office twiddling your thumbs if you do not take every case that walks in the door. This fear can be terrifying, especially when your firm is new and you have no frame of reference. Just remember that for every case you take, you lose the opportunity to take a different case because you do not have the time or resources to handle another case. Make sure you are taking the cases that *you want to work on.*

In larger legal markets, we are confident that there will be enough work for you no matter how restrictive you are in your scope of work. However, even in larger markets, the more narrow your scope of work is, the more limited your pool of potential clients. You will have to become one of the top professionals in your scope of work to generate enough business.

Law firms in smaller legal markets may not be able to place the same restrictions on the scope of work they will perform. This still does not mean that you have to take every case that walks into the door. Small-market law firms should still place limits on their scope of work, but they likely will need to be more flexible as to where the line is drawn.

Expansion of Product Lines

Inevitably after you launch your firm, you will face the question of whether the firm should expand its practice areas, product lines, and/or scope of work. Many people have built very successful firms by focusing on one product line that they perform very well. Those firms have perfected their systems and can efficiently and profitably handle a large number of cases within their product line.

However, firms that limit themselves to only those practice areas in which they already have experience may be overlooking significant market opportunities. The most common way firms expand their practice areas is when they take on cases in different areas at the request of their clients. Sooner or later some of your clients will have legal issues outside the scope of the case you were originally hired to handle. In short, the firm expands to meet a readily apparent demand, and over time, this becomes a full-blown practice area.

The advantage of this approach is that it requires very little financial risk at the outset. You know that there will be cases in this area because your existing clients are already asking for your help in these areas. Furthermore, if your clients are asking you to handle cases that are related to your preexisting practice areas, your team members may feel equipped to handle this legal work with limited training. It will feel like a relatively natural extension to your team members, and as a result, they will feel more comfortable with the transition.

The disadvantage of taking any case that walks in the door that is remotely related to your existing product line is that this practice can lead to a disjointed firm. While the initial cases may be closely related to your existing product lines, over time the cases your firm accepts are likely to stray further from your core product lines. Before you realize it, your firm will be handling cases that are not related to one another and their differences do not permit you to take advantage of any economies of scale. This situation will require greater investment.

Unless the new practice area fits in seamlessly with your existing practice areas, you will be required to establish completely new systems. This is highly unlikely, and we do not encourage you to try to force a new practice area to be handled like an existing one to avoid the costs involved in creating and developing new systems.

With new systems and a different type of work, your team members will need additional training to become competent in the new practice area or you will need new team members. Both of these scenarios are likely to be disruptive, as team members often are uncomfortable with small changes, and this would be a significant change.

If you decide to add a new practice area, you need to be careful to avoid a situation in which you essentially have two separate law firms operating under the same firm name. If the practice areas are kept separate from one another, your firm will lose some of the synergies and benefits that you envisioned when you took the first few cases outside of your original product line.

Even if the practice area is related to the ones you have already established, there will be growing pains. You will have to make an investment in human resources, and you will have to develop new systems and processes for the new product line. At least some of your team will be required to redirect their efforts from the preexisting product lines to new ones. At a minimum, their efforts on the preexisting product lines will need to be replaced. More likely, you will have to replace them and also train them to handle the new product lines properly.

Technology can streamline the time and effort it takes to get up to speed on a new product line. Typically, complementary legal services will have similar processes to achieve the desired legal product. You can and should use your existing processes to the extent possible. Using a documented process within an existing program can generate significant savings, particularly if you can simply customize your existing program to work with your new product line.

We encourage you to always keep your eyes open for opportunities and to keep an open mind about them. Our preference would be to develop a plan to expand your product lines that outlines when and how you will move into them. However, we recognize that there may be times when the opportunity to expand into a new and unexpected product line is irresistible. When that happens, we urge you to develop a plan to outline how you will incorporate the new product line into your firm.

What Is Your Role as a Lawyer: Counselor or Commodity Provider?

Historically, lawyers did not look at providing legal services in terms of product lines and profit margins. Everyone has the vision of the country lawyer who handled whatever legal issue walked in the door or the consiglieri who handled whatever problem arose for his client. Those lawyers viewed their role as one in which their responsibility was to take care of whatever their client needed.

Those old-fashioned lawyers tended to think of themselves as counselors and advisors, and they viewed their job as one in which they guided their clients through their legal controversy or matter from its beginning to its end and often were available to guide their clients even when there was no legal matter pending.

While the lawyers felt that this was their responsibility, they also had the power to define the scope of their legal services however they wanted. There was limited competition among lawyers and no competition from outside of the legal profession, leaving clients without alternatives when they needed law-related work done.

Pro Tip: The best lawyers provide advice to their clients that takes into consideration legal, financial, and emotional considerations. Lawyers who ignore financial and/or emotional considerations may win the case in court but still have an unhappy client if they fail to consider the whole picture.

Yes, we very much want you to view your law practice as a business, but we strongly believe that you can maintain your role as a counselor *and* run a profitable business. Acting as a true counselor and providing comprehensive legal guidance is a smart business strategy. By counseling your clients instead of simply providing a product, you will develop a strong relationship with your clients. Knowing your clients well will allow you to understand the totality of the circumstance, which will permit you to provide them with the best guidance. An added benefit is that your clients are likely to refer additional business to you.

However, we have observed many lawyers who have moved away from this model and toward one in which they provide only a product. While some lawyers still view their product as one in which they provide comprehensive representation, more and more lawyers are specializing, and those lawyers view their product much more narrowly. For example, trusts and estates lawyers may view an estate planning document as the total sum of their product and not include any follow-up in their scope of work.

When lawyers and clients look at their relationship as a purely transactional one in which the lawyer provides only a product, the attorney-client relationship changes substantially. As online legal providers have grown and clients have become more cost conscious, lawyers and clients have started to view legal services as a commodity. From a purely profit-focused business perspective, this approach can be successful, but we do not endorse it.

Lawyers have adapted to the marketplace to provide clients with what they want. While maybe not quite this blatant, it is almost as if law firms put their services on a shelf and let the clients choose the brand and price level they want to purchase.

This model completely ignores what legal services are appropriate for the legal issues and instead focuses solely on cost. The attorney is no longer providing guidance and advice as to what the client needs to navigate the legal matter, but instead the client dictates the scope of the legal services based on what he or she is willing to pay. There is no question that clients have much more knowledge and access to information about legal services than they once did, but very few clients know more than the attorney about what level of legal services is appropriate.

The lawyers who are letting the client select the level of legal services tend to focus on providing the bare minimum necessary to meet the sale conditions that the attorney and client agreed upon. These lawyers do not look to create relationships with clients, and generally speaking, the client is not looking for a relationship with the lawyer. These relationships are strictly transactional.

The transactional lawyer needs to structure his or her office in a manner that will produce and reproduce its legal services as quickly and efficiently as possible. These offices tend to depend on volume to generate a profit. The less it costs the firm to produce its services, the more profit the firm earns on each case.

Every lawyer, even the transactional lawyer, should aim to provide high-quality legal services or at least a good value for what the client pays. A client who feels that he or she received good value for his or her payment will refer other clients or at least will not provide negative feedback. No amount of advertising can overcome a series of poor online reviews.

There are still many "old-fashioned" lawyers on the other end of the spectrum who set the parameters of their representation and how much it will cost. These lawyers tend to define their legal product very differently than the transactional attorney. While the transactional attorneys sees the final product (e.g., document, trial decision, etc.) as the totality of their legal services, the old-fashioned lawyers view the final product as just the last step in the long road of representation.

Providing Legal Services Efficiently

Regardless of how you define your legal services, there are two significant advantages to providing services efficiently. First, the more efficient you are in providing the legal services, the more profitable each case will be. Second, better efficiency will lead to better services and happier clients who will refer additional work to you.

While each case is unique, there are always similarities. The facts of the cases may be different, but each case will pass through some of the same stages. For example, all cases go through some sort of discovery phase. In nonlitigation cases, the lawyer must discover information from his or her client in order to provide the best advice. In litigation cases, the lawyer must discover information from both his or her own client and the other side. Knowing that you will have to conduct this phase, establish a systematic way to gather this information.

Find as many of these similarities as you can in your cases, and develop systems to navigate through those sections of the cases. Once you have systems in place, your team members will be prepared to handle those aspects of the case efficiently. There is no need for them to reinvent the wheel every time discovery needs to be done.

As we indicated previously, carefully defining your legal services will enable you to determine the composition of the team you need to provide these legal services. You can gauge whether you need an attorney, paralegal, or other support team member to perform each task that must be completed. This allows you to hire the right mix of team members, and to find team members who can and want to fill the role you have outlined for them. When you put together a balanced team with members who are all filling roles that they are well equipped to handle, and equally as importantly, expect to be handling, the team will provide peak performance.

Pro Tip: Listen to your client! Always find out what your client believes is a favorable outcome.

As we discuss in Chapter 4 on team building, we strongly recommend building a system first and then hiring team members to fit into your system as opposed to simply hiring talented individuals and trying to build a system around them. Defining your product, legal services, carefully and thoroughly will allow you to build the best team.

Client Interaction

As you prepare to provide your legal services, do not forget about the client's role in this process. Too many attorneys ignore their clients and move forward with whatever they think is best.

We encourage you to think of your client as your partner. You and your client need to work closely together to achieve the best possible result. The first step in your partnership is to *listen* to your client. Remember, it is his or her case. The client is the only one who can tell the lawyer what a successful outcome looks like to him or her. What you think may be a great outcome may not be one from the client's perspective.

Take the time to explain the legal process to the client. Aspects or procedures that feel obvious to you may not be so obvious to someone who does not interact with the legal system on a day-to-day basis. The legal strategies and timing may not make sense to your clients, and many clients view legalese as a foreign language. As the clients' partner, it is your job to guide them through the legal system and translate its language for them. A good guide does not simply say "follow me" A good guide explains what the other person is going to see (before it happens), why that is important, and where the tour will end. We doubt many, if any, of your clients signed up for the mystery tour with a surprise ending.

After you have listened to what your client believes the issue is and what the client wants to accomplish, it is your turn to explain how you intend to get there. There are many different approaches to a legal matter. You should take the time to explain pros and cons of the different options. Make sure that your client is comfortable with the option you are recommending and understands why you made the recommendation. If the client is not comfortable with your approach or style, the client may not be happy with your representation even if the ultimate outcome is what the client stated that he or she wanted.

Of course, we have all encountered clients whose goals are unrealistic or unreasonable. You need to be prepared to let the clients know that you cannot meet their goals as soon as you realize that is the case. It is not a good idea to string these clients along with the theory that you will be able to talk sense into them at some point in the case. This strategy rarely works and usually ends with an unhappy client.

For those clients with realistic goals, explaining your approach entails not only your style but also what legal work needs to be done to accomplish the goals. Your clients need to understand what it will take to get to their goals so that they can make an educated decision as to whether they want to pay for all of that legal work or whether they want to adjust their goals.

We believe that if you treat your client as if he or she is your partner, you will address many of the client complaints about attorney-client interactions. It is important to remember that both you and your client have a great deal to add to the partnership, and you cannot succeed if you do not work together.

Quality Control

Even the best team needs protocols to ensure that the quality of its product meets your standards. In the legal field, the lowest product standard is set by your jurisdiction's ethical rules. At a minimum every team member must abide by the ethics rules and obtain the required training—that is, continuing legal education. We strongly encourage you to strive for more than the minimum.

The first step in your quality-control process should be to explain to each team member what the expectations are for his or her position. Make it clear what you want him or her to do and why. It is extremely helpful to describe the entire legal services process to the team member even though he or she may only be responsible for a small portion of the process.

When team members can see the entire picture, they can understand the value of their role. More importantly for quality control, the team members can understand why it is important that their tasks be done in the manner you describe. Without understanding the big picture, your team members may feel that it is fine to do it their way so long as the task is "done."

It is not enough to explain the expectations to all team members when they start working for your firm or they start working on this particular product line. The oversight and training must be an ongoing process. There is always room for improvement, and over time the process may need to be tweaked to keep up with changes in the marketplace and/or technology. Without any guidance, it becomes very easy for an experienced team member to fall into the rut of doing the same thing day in and day out. The further into this rut your team member falls, the harder it will be to get out and to adjust to whatever has changed.

Rather than letting your team members fall into a deep rut, your oversight process should be consistently and regularly pushing for improvements. This will allow you to make small, incremental changes that your team can handle relatively easily as opposed to periodic wholesale changes in how your system works. For example, it is much easier to teach your team members to upgrade from Word version 2016 to Word version 2019 than it is to have a team member adjust from dictating everything to typing his or her own documents.

Pro Tip: Invest heavily in technology! Your clients expect you to be using current technology, and you will need current technology to provide the best legal services.

Smaller changes are far easier to manage, but by making them regularly, your team will stay on the front edge of the field. Not only will this be much more attractive for your clients, but also it will make it easier for you to attract and retain top end talent.

Regardless of the size of your firm, you should maintain and regularly update a self-made library of forms, memorandums, and so on for your firm. Such a library can be a valuable resource for your team members. In addition, the team members are far more likely to follow the lead that you set in this library than branching out to handle the matter in their own way.

As circumstances change, especially with technology, you may need to revise the process you use to provide legal services to take advantage of what is available. We cannot stress the importance of regular reviews and strategic planning (see Chapter 20 on strategic planning). By looking forward you can ensure that most of your changes feel small and manageable to your team members instead of wholesale changes that feel life altering and extremely uncomfortable to many.

Technology's Role in Legal Services

We have not reached the point at which computers can provide legal advice, but artificial intelligence may be able to do this sooner than you think—a frightening thought that we will save for a future edition of this book.

Meanwhile, technology is the single greatest market disruption in the past 25 years, and its advances continue to disrupt the market on an almost daily basis. For starters, the marketplace for your legal services has expanded exponentially since clients rarely have to set foot into your office to obtain legal services. At a bare minimum, your firm must have the ability to communicate with its clients in a variety of ways—phone, e-mail, and so on. More clients are demanding that communication be done through videoconferencing, texts, apps, and other means. The firms that are able to meet these demands will be in a better position to service, attract, and keep clients.

In the olden days, law firms kept paper files, and the client had to visit the office to review the file. If it has not done so, your firm should be moving to electronic files that can be easily shared with the client. There are numerous programs that allow you to scan everything into searchable PDFs or to securely upload files to a location that you and the client can both access, whether a file-sharing service or a client portal, which comes with many case management systems.

We rarely see law firm libraries any longer. Statutes, cases, and treatises are all available online. Every firm should have access to an online library. Not only is an online library more convenient to access (regardless of whether you are in the office or at the courthouse), but also it will contain the most up-to-date information.

Many jurisdictions allow or require electronic filings, and their courtrooms require that exhibits be displayed through courtroom monitors instead of in paper binders. As our society moves further into the digital age, judges and juries will expect to see everything electronically, and those lawyers who try to display exhibits on easels or in binders will be viewed as dinosaurs.

The number of technology tools available to trial lawyers these days is truly astounding. We have heard from trial lawyers who use devices to maintain real-time communication with their offices and experts during hearings and depositions among other amazing tricks. We strongly recommend that you sit down with your IT provider or attend an upcoming technology conference to see how you can integrate technology into your practice (see Chapter 15 on technology).

Legal Services Section of Your Business Plan

We anticipate that your answers to the questions below will serve as an outline for the legal services section of your business plan. These answers will form the foundation for what services your firm will provide and how they will be provided.

1. What products will your firm provide?
   a. Practice areas
   b. What aspects/segments of each practice area will your firm handle?
   c. If you do not handle some aspects of a practice area, how will it get done?
2. Will you expand your product lines?
   a. Why are you adding a new product line?
   b. What impact will the new product line have on your firm?
   c. What will the timeline for new product lines be?
   d. What steps will you take to create new product lines?
   e. Are there any product lines that you consider to be off-limits?
   f. How will you determine if it is worthwhile to offer new product lines?
3. How will you staff these product lines?
   a. Lawyers
   b. Support staff
4. Are you a counselor or do you provide a product?
5. How will you provide legal services efficiently?
   a. What systems will you have?
   b. How will cases or matters be staffed?
   c. How can you use technology to your advantage?
6. How will you ensure the quality of your legal services?
   a. Training
   b. Supervision
   c. Mentorship
   d. Other

12

Ethics: How to Stay Out of Trouble

Firm Culture

The first and most important step in ensuring that no one at your firm runs afoul of the ethics rules is the culture that you establish. A distant second step is the procedures that you put in place to avoid ethical issues.

Pro Tip: Never underestimate the importance of firm culture. Never think that you have a good firm culture and that nothing else needs to be done. Developing and maintaining your firm culture requires constant attention. It takes a great deal of effort to maintain a good culture, but it takes only a few missteps to ruin your culture.

Your team members will take on your persona when it comes to ethics. Your actions speak much louder than your words. Regardless of what you say to your team members, they are looking to see how you behave when an ethical issue arises.

Legal ethical issues typically do not arise on a daily basis, but when then do, you can be sure that every team member will be watching to see how you handle them. Will you overlook an issue or try to circumvent a conflict if it looks like the conflict will force you to refer a good case to someone else? Will you skirt around the edges of the disclosure rules if it will benefit your client? Team members will assume that they will be doing things correctly if they follow your lead.

Since legal ethical issues do not occur frequently, your team will look for clues as to how you will handle other types of ethical issues in other places. Often, everyday life and office issues can be translated into ethical lessons, and they arise all the time. They range from overarching behaviors such as how you treat other people to more specific actions.

Do you eat someone else's food from the office lunchroom? Do you offer to share the last piece of cake, or do you take it for yourself? Are you fair when you split the check at lunch? Do you treat some team members differently from others? All of these scenarios establish whether it is acceptable for you to do something that benefits only you if the other person does not know about it, cannot prove it, or is not strong enough to object to it. If you do these things, the basic lesson is "do it if you can get away with it."

You probably make dozens of little decisions every day that give your team members a sense of how you would act when a legal ethical issue arises. You must set the example you want your team to follow.

Ensure Ethical Behavior

Do not assume that everyone knows that he or she should behave ethically. Your firm's ethical reputation is too important to let it depend on an assumption. You must make it clear to your team that you expect them to behave ethically.

Do not take ethical issues for granted. What may come naturally or seem like basic common sense to you after years of practice may be completely foreign to a new team member. You cannot afford to assume that your team members will understand how to handle an ethical issue when it arises.

Consider this actual business scenario: Several luxury restaurants and hotels became frustrated with their staff when they were not providing first-class service to their patrons. These restaurants and hotels continued to receive complaints about the service even after their managers repeatedly told their team that each guest deserved top-of-the-line service. When these service providers brought in an outside consultant, they discovered that their servers had never been a guest in a luxury restaurant or hotel, and as a result had no idea what the manager meant when he or she said that they needed to provide first-class service. Without the context and understanding of what first-class service meant, the training the team members had received regarding their specific tasks was insufficient.

Pro Tip: Solo and small firms may not be able to set up internal meetings about ethics. We encourage lawyers in these firms to find mentors or attorneys at other firms with whom you can confidentially discuss ethical issues. It is always helpful to get someone else's perspective to ensure that you do not look at the situation only from the perspective that will give you the answer you want.

The same concept applies to your law firm. Once you have told them, your new team members know that they are supposed to behave ethically, but they may not have any idea what that really means. This is particularly true for those team members who have limited work experience. They may have a textbook understanding of what ethical behavior means, but they may not know how to apply this knowledge when an issue arises in the real world.

Education about Ethical Issues

We encourage you to look at ethical procedures from two perspectives. First, your team members need to be taught the ethical rules. While it is critical to establish an ethical theme for your office, it is also critical to ensure that your team members learn the ethics rules. Second, your team members need to know how to deal with situations in which ethical issues are likely to arise. You cannot plan for every possible ethical dilemma, but you can certainly prepare for the ethical crossroads that arise in every client representation.

Formal Ethics Training

Make sure your team members know that not only is there money in the budget for them to attend ethics continuing legal education (CLE) training but also they are required to do so. Most states require a certain number of ethics CLE credits. There is no penalty for exceeding that minimum. Even though paralegals and other team members may not be required to attend CLEs or a minimum number of ethics CLEs, they should be encouraged to attend. Your entire team should be fluent in ethics rules so that anyone can spot an ethical issue before it blossoms into an ethical problem.

Pro Tip: Do not assume that everyone knows the ethics rules whether or not they have completed law school. New ethical issues and gray areas arise every day. Encourage your experienced team members to share their experiences with the newer team members.

Your firm should require that all team members receive formal and informal ethics training. Aside from your own everyday behavior, spending time and/or money teaching your team members about ethics sends a strong message that ethics are important to you.

Informal Ethics Training

You should block off time for periodic meetings about ethics and be willing to send your team members to CLEs about ethics. These meetings do not need to be frequent (at least annually), but they need to be consistent enough to remind your team that ethics matter and frequent enough to ensure that any trending issues are addressed.

When you do meet to discuss ethical issues, some potential topics could include your firm's ethics procedures, topics that team members have raised throughout the year, or ethical issues that you have seen other firms face. All team members who handle any aspect of a case from conflict checks through the legal work that touches on ethical issues should be at these meetings.

If you are looking for topic ideas or speakers, most malpractice carriers would be thrilled to send a representative to discuss statistics about malpractice and ethical claims or the hot topics in these areas. It may even be possible for your attorneys to get CLE credit for the presentation.

While your actions do speak louder than your words, you cannot ignore your words. Any discussion about ethics should be straightforward and direct. This is not a subject you should joke about. Inevitably, at least one of your team members will not get the joke.

While the ethics meetings and training should focus on the team members that directly provide legal services, all team members should have a basic understanding of ethical issues that commonly arise in your practice. Receptionists, administrative assistants, billing assistants, and other team members who interact with a wide segment of the firm's clients may be able to spot a potential ethical issue—for example, a conflict—before an attorney who is focused solely on his or her clients.

Bar Disciplinary Process

We suggest that you encourage team members to actively participate in your bar's disciplinary process. There is no better way to learn and understand the practical application of ethical rules in your jurisdiction than to play a role in the disciplinary hearings and to decide how the ethics rules will be enforced.

Support those team members by making it clear that their participation in this aspect of the bar is a positive contribution to the bar and is a positive reflection on the firm. When team members see that their or their colleague's participation is valued, it will further enhance the message that ethics are important. In addition, the team member who participates will learn a great deal about ethics and should be required to share his or her knowledge with the rest of the team.

If ethics are important to you, and they should be, you should make sure that all of your team members know that you are available to discuss potential ethical issues. In the real world, ethical issues are rarely straightforward or obvious. The team member will be forced to balance zealous representation, firm and individual goals, client pressures, and convoluted ethics rules.

Case Reviews

We recommend conducting regular meetings among team members to review case strategies. These team meetings can be organized in many different ways, but we suggest that you consider the following three options: (1) case teams, (2) attorneys and paralegals, and (3) experienced and inexperienced attorneys.

Pro Tip: Case reviews are a great way to work a case. Team members reviewing a case together will generate better ideas and strategies, and they will be able to test them from multiple perspectives. Bouncing ideas between team members can be a positive bonding experience. Case reviews can also give you an early warning signal as to whether a team member is struggling.

When there are multiple team members working on a case, the case team should meet periodically to ensure that everyone knows who is responsible for each task and nothing falls between the cracks. Also, periodic meetings provide an opportunity for the team members to bounce ideas off one another.

Meetings that include a collection of attorneys and paralegals in which anyone can ask questions about a current case, changes in the law, and so on can be very productive. These meetings allow team members to get feedback from their colleagues as to how they should handle different situations including, but not limited to, ethical questions. Also, team members who are not working directly on a case may be able to provide guidance or ideas on a case that had not been considered because they will look at the case strategy from a different perspective.

At a minimum, new and/or inexperienced team members should be required to meet regularly with a more experienced team member. These reviews/meetings should be designed to help guide team members through strategic aspects of cases, and these meetings should also be used as opportunities to discuss ethical issues and to guide the team member through any ethical issues that arise. The lessons about ethics are far more likely to resonate with a team member if they apply directly to his or her case.

Business Reasons That Ethics Are Important

Let's take a moment to talk about why ethics should be important to you from a business standpoint even if they are not important to you on a personal level. Most clients looking for attorneys want one that they believe is ethical even if they have doubts about the ethics of lawyers in general or the lawyer on the other side of the case in particular.

Loss of Referrals

As discussed elsewhere in this book, we have found that most referrals come from other attorneys. No one will know better than other attorneys whether you are an ethical lawyer or not. Very few attorneys are going to refer their family member, close friend, business partner, or anyone else they care about to an attorney they think is unethical. In short, acting unethically will prevent you from getting cases from one of the best possible referral sources.

We strongly believe that every lawyer should strive to meet and exceed the highest ethical standards on principle and for the sake of the profession. That said, if that is not enough to motivate you to be as ethical as you can possibly be, then your own self-interest should motivate you. The more ethical you are, the wider the pool of potential clients.

Potential Reprimands

Yes, there are potential clients who want the bar room brawler who believes that all is fair in love and litigation. You have to ask yourself whether these cases are worth it. The clear risk is that the other side and/or the judge reports your behavior to the bar, and at best you spend time and money defending yourself and at worst you are disciplined, suspended, or disbarred.

Karma

The less obvious, but just as real, risk is that the client who is counting on you to act without morals will treat you the same way. You could be dealing with clients who turn their back on you and claim that they never authorized or knew that you would behave this way. More likely, the clients will refuse to pay some or all of their bill and threaten to expose your unethical behavior if you pursue collection. No one case is worth these risks, and after a few of these cases, they may be the only type of cases you can get.

Therefore, if for no reason other than your selfish business interests, act ethically and instill that quality in your team members. This will create a much larger pool of potential clients, far more referral sources, and a greater likelihood that you will find clients you want to work with.

Procedures to Avoid Ethical Pitfalls

Another way to show your team you are serious about ethics is to take the time to establish firm procedures designed to avoid ethical pitfalls. Merely taking the time and energy to put procedures together is a meaningful signal. That said, the procedures themselves should be effective ones and not just for show. Every legal matter has certain junctures where ethical issues could potentially arise.

Pro Tip: Make sure one of the first things you do is to establish a reliable conflict system. Assign certain team members to manage the conflict system to help ensure that the conflict checks are completed consistently and accurately.

Conflicts of Interest

The first pitfall is when a potential client contacts your firm and you must determine whether there is a conflict of interest. Every firm must have a thorough and clear-cut procedure to obtain sufficient information from potential or existing clients to determine whether a conflict exists and how to communicate with clients regarding conflicts.

Unfortunately, one size does not fit all when it comes to conflict checks. Firms that handle complex business matters with multiple parties will need a different system than firms that represent an individual preparing his or her estate plan. Even so, there are a few aspects that need to be addressed in every conflict check system.

Pro Tip: Every firm needs a good conflict system. If for no other reason than financial, we recommend against playing fast and loose with your conflict system. The fees you will earn from a case will pale in comparison to what you will pay to fix any ethical issues. We know one attorney who appealed time and time again to prove that he did not have a conflict in a divorce case he had handled. We are confident that the attorney will regret taking that case for the remainder of his career.

Every team member needs to know when a potential client is crossing the line into sharing confidential information. Team members should not accept confidential information until a conflict check has been performed.

It is important to note that potential clients often attempt to share confidential information in very informal settings, such as happy hour, lunch, or other social functions. When your friend begins to ask you whether his or her business has a good contract claim at a backyard barbecue after a few drinks, your friend does not necessarily realize that he or she may be sharing confidential information, but you need to know that. Ideally, you would stop the conversation before confidential information was shared, and you would limit the conversation to very general legal concepts. However, if confidential information is provided, you need to enter it into your firm's conflict system as soon as possible.

On the flip side, your firm should take steps to let potential clients know that merely contacting you does not create an attorney-client relationship. Whenever possible, warn potential clients not to share detailed information about their case until you have agreed to represent them. Voicemail messages and websites that allow potential clients to send e-mails should instruct the potential clients to leave only the information necessary to conduct a conflict check and warn them against sharing detailed case information.

Pro Tip: How to avoid a client complaint: communicate, communicate, and communicate! Clients appreciate attorneys who deliver bad news far more than attorneys who deliver no news. Keep your clients informed and do it in a timely fashion.

Your conflict system will not be very effective if it is not comprehensive. It needs to include all potential conflicts for each team member and for each legal matter. When you add team members who have worked at other firms, you need to ensure that they bring their conflicts list with them so they can be added to yours. This may be more difficult to do for non-attorneys but remember that you are responsible for your legal assistant's or paralegal's knowledge as well, and their previous experience with a case could create a conflict for you.

It is obvious that the parties need to be entered into your conflict system. However, in most cases, that is just the beginning. For example, in divorce cases you may need to include paramours and/or other family members. Criminal attorneys will need to add co-defendants and/or witnesses. Every practice area has categories of nonparties who present a higher risk of conflict, and there should be specific guidelines for your team as to how these nonparties are reported in your conflict system.

Depending on the conflict, you may need specific procedures as to how you communicate that a conflict exists. For example, if one spouse contacts a divorce attorney, that spouse may not want his or her spouse to know about the meeting. When the other spouse contacts the same attorney to inquire about representation, there is no question that the attorney cannot represent the second spouse. However, the firm cannot divulge why there is a conflict because the fact that the firm met with the first spouse is confidential information that the first spouse did not want shared.

Pro Tip: Solo practitioners should coordinate with other solos or attorneys in other firms to discuss potential ethical issues. If you are not comfortable discussing hypothetical issues with other attorneys, make sure you know how to contact the ethics hotline in your jurisdiction.

Communication

Lack of or poor communication with clients is the most common factor in ethics complaints or malpractice claims. Your firm must have a procedure in place to handle communication with clients. This procedure needs to address (1) how much time can pass before your firm responds to client communications, (2) what and when correspondence and/or information from the other attorney will be shared with your client, and (3) how information will be shared with your client.

There are two critical aspects of client communication. First, your client needs to understand what to expect from you and you must meet those expectations. For example, if you tell your client that all calls, e-mails, or text messages will be responded to by the close of business, do not wait until the next day to respond. Second, you and your team members cannot delay or avoid sharing negative information with clients.

Clients understand that there are risks in their cases, and everything may not turn out the way that they hoped. But clients do not understand when they are not told what happened. Inevitably, the cover up leads to bigger problems. In the best-case scenario, the client is angry and frustrated about the lack of communication, and in the worst case, the delay causes the client to miss an appeal deadline.

How to Handle Ethical Issues

When a potential ethical issue arises, every team member needs to know what to do. There should be at least one point of contact at your firm to answer ethical questions. Depending on the size of your firm, there may be an ombudsman or risk manager who handles these questions. Smaller firms may designate a senior partner or an attorney who is willing to educate himself or herself in these issues.

There will be times when the ethical issue stumps your in house "expert." Assuming that you do not want to discuss your potential ethical issues with an attorney in another firm, you still have two excellent resources.

Most bar associations have ethics hotlines where you can submit questions confidentially and obtain confidential answers. In many cases, you are permitted to rely on these answers in any future ethics complaint or malpractice claim against you.

Also, all malpractice carriers have mechanisms through which you can obtain guidance. The last thing a malpractice carrier wants is for you to do something unethical because it will likely lead to a malpractice claim that the carrier has to defend.

Ethics Section of Your Business Plan

We anticipate that your answers to the questions below will serve as an outline for the ethics section of your business plan. These answers will form the foundation for how your firm will handle ethical issues that arise.

1. What will your firm culture be?
   a. How will you establish a firm culture?
   b. What do you do if a team member acts contrary to the firm culture?
2. What practical steps will you take to ensure ethical behavior
   a. Firm meetings
   b. Malpractice presentations
   c. CLEs
3. Why is ethical behavior important to you from a business perspective?
4. What is the difference between ethical and professional behavior?
5. What procedures can you put in place to help your team members avoid ethical pitfalls?
   a. How will you deal with ethical challenges that your team members face?
   b. What ethical issues are most likely to occur at your firm?
   c. How will you handle ethical issues that arise as a result of your client's behavior?
   d. How will you handle ethical issues that arise through opposing counsel's behavior?
6. Who will provide your malpractice insurance?
7. What do you do when a team member does not act ethically?

13

Billing and Collection: How Will You Get Paid?

Billing and collection is one aspect of law firm management and ownership that lawyers tend to despise. We have yet to find an attorney who relishes preparing bills or collecting fees from clients. No attorney went to law school to learn billing practices, and law schools perpetuate the difficulty by rarely trying to teach lawyers how to bill or collect fees.

Although billing and collection may not be the most enjoyable aspect of practicing law, it is critical to the business side of your firm. Of course, you must perform the legal work you were retained to perform, but all your efforts to represent the client are worthless from a profitability standpoint if you do not get paid for your efforts.

Particularly because very few lawyers want to deal with billing and collection issues, it is vital to have specific procedures and to allocate time each month to address billing issues. Having procedures that spell out how billing and collecting fees will be handled and dedicating time to them will make it harder to procrastinate.

Billing Policies and Expectations

The most important and first step in any billing procedure is to ensure that everyone on your team and your potential client understand the billing policies and payment expectations. Your team needs to understand how the firm expects to be paid for its services and the procedures the firm plans to employ. Nothing will sabotage your firm's efforts to get paid more than a team member misstating your firm's policies or, even worse, making up his or her own payment terms for a particular client.

Clients rarely offer to make payments before the payment is requested. Requesting payment is a much easier and smoother process when the client knows when the request will be coming and why the request is being made. You can accomplish this by establishing the client's expectations about payment as early as possible in the relationship.

Pro Tip: Let your lawyers focus on legal work, and let your billing department focus on communicating with clients about outstanding bills.

Communication with Your Client

Your firm should determine who will communicate with potential clients or clients about billing issues. Those team members need to be well versed in your firm's billing and collection procedures to the point that a client receives the same message regardless of whether the client speaks to more than one person on your billing and collection team. If the client reaches out to a nonmember of the billing and collection team, the client should be quickly re-routed. Everyone in the firm should know how the clients can be efficiently directed to a billing and collection team member.

Who should be a member of the billing and collection team? Many law firms assume that lawyers should be the client's primary contact when billing questions arise. We urge you to reconsider this assumption. We believe that lawyers are far more efficient and effective focusing on the legal work and that your firm would be better served by hiring someone else to focus on billing issues.

Another benefit of having a non-lawyer handle billing issues is that the lawyer and client do not fall into potential conflicts over money. When the lawyer is demanding fees from the client, even if the lawyer does not say it out loud, the client may wonder whether the lawyer is giving his or her best effort while there is an outstanding fee collection issue.

When is the last time you paid your doctor directly? When is the last time you wondered whether your doctor was doing his or her best to treat you while you had an outstanding bill? The separation between the service provider and the person/department handling the money issues is valuable.

We recommend moving the discussions about fees and payment away from your lawyers as soon as possible. Part of your initial recruiting process with potential new clients should be to explain your fee structure. While most firms still have their attorneys explain the fee structure to potential clients, others have begun posting fees and rates on their website or having a billing department explain the fee structure to potential clients.

We recognize that the larger your firm is, the easier it is to have someone other than an attorney discuss fees with a client. That said, the attorney's time is better spent performing work that can be billed to a client. Not only is time spent by an attorney dealing with billing issues rarely billable, but also the attorney who engages in billing discussions often has to spend additional non-legal time smoothing over any disagreements about billing. The firm would benefit if the lawyer spent that time doing billable work and had an administrative or non-billing employee handle the majority of the billing issues.

That being said, the attorney who knows the facts and issues of the case is in the best position to gauge how much the client is likely to incur in fees and costs. Therefore, regardless of who does it or how the fee and cost information is delivered to the client, the attorney must share information with the billing team so that they can set the most realistic expectations possible for the client.

Pro Tip: If your firm is too small to have a designated (non-attorney) team member who can discuss fees with your client, we recommend making as clear a line between your discussion about legal issues and your discussion about fees as possible. Make it clear to the client that you are changing subjects before talking about fees.

As much as we would like to take lawyers completely out of the billing and collection process, that is probably not possible. At some point the client is going to ask the primary attorney to explain the fees incurred or projected. The client likely will have the strongest relationship with the attorney, and therefore, it is only natural for the client to raise issues with the attorney. When this happens, ideally the attorney will be able to re-route the client to the billing department, but if not, the attorney must be prepared to follow the firm's billing procedures.

Pro Tip: Be as realistic as possible with your client about fees. Clients do not appreciate surprises when it comes to their bills, and surprises often lead to complaints and nonpayment. If you think telling a client what the real fees will be at the outset will scare off the client, what makes you think that the client will pay your fees after the legal work has been completed? Setting realistic expectations for your client is far more likely to lead to payment and a satisfied client.

Educating Your Clients about Fees and Costs

After you have determined who will make up your firm's billing team, the next step is to develop procedures for educating your potential clients about your fees and costs. That is not a typo—your billing procedure starts with your potential clients. Before you agree to represent a client, the client needs to understand what you expect to be paid for your services and when you expect payment.

We have encountered attorneys who are afraid to share their fees and how much the case will cost until after the client has hired them because either they are concerned that the client will balk at the potential costs or that the client cannot afford it. This is a recipe for disaster.

In this attorney's best-case scenario, the client pays the fees but ends the representation with a bitter taste because he or she feels duped regarding the arrangement. The worst case is that the client refuses to pay your fees because the client does not believe that he or she agreed to pay what you have billed or the client really cannot afford your fees. The most likely outcome is that the client pays some of the fees, you spend time trying to collect the fees, and both you and the client are unhappy about the relationship.

Fee Payment

Most industries have a general standard for bill payment. Law firms are somewhat unusual in that there is not an industry standard. Firms often having different billing philosophies for different practice areas and sometimes even for different clients. Certainly, there are obvious differences in billing practices between firms that collect fees based on hourly rates, flat fees, or contingency fees, but there is an even more important distinction to be made between firms that collect fees in advance of performing work versus those that collect fees for work already done.

From a cash flow and business management perspective, obtaining fees in advance is a much more efficient approach. Not only does your firm get paid at the same time the work is performed, but also your firm does not have to spend any time, energy, or money trying to track down payment for work that has already been done. Furthermore, when the payment occurs in advance, the chance of you or your client misunderstanding each other's expectations are minimized.

Those firms who perform legal services before they bill for them are extending credit to their clients. If you are going to extend credit to your clients, you must have a reliable way to gauge whether the client is a worthwhile credit risk.

Your firm must have systems in place to assess the client's credit worthiness. Some factors that should be considered when deciding whether to extend credit include the nature of the firm's relationship with the client, the client's solvency, type of case, and likelihood of success, among others. When you are handling cases that depend on a trial decision, merger completion, or some other scenario that is not completely in the lawyer's control, there is a greater risk that the client will not pay the fees owed. For example, even if the attorney did a phenomenal legal job, but the client did not get the desired result—for example, the other company pulled out of the merger, a jury saw the evidence differently, or so on—the client may not be willing to pay the fees owed.

Pro Tip: Whenever possible, we encourage lawyers to obtain retainer fees. Then when you bill a client for work performed, you can immediately transfer the money from your trust account to your operating account. Every day that you have to wait to collect fees for your work makes the money collected less valuable.

For example, say you performed $1,000 of legal work in January and assume that a conservative investment generates a 5 percent annual rate of return. Client 1 pays you promptly, and therefore, you receive $1,000 in January. Client 2 delays and pays you $1,000 in December. The payments made by these clients are not equal in value.

Client 1's payment is worth $1,050. You had the cash and could invest it for the entire year.

Client 2's payment is worth $1,000 at most. Considering that you or a team member spent time trying to collect the fees, the payment is worth less after factoring in the time expended to collect payment.

No matter when you plan to collect fees from your client, the client should understand your expectations from the very beginning. We encourage you to begin setting those expectations with potential clients. Only in exceptionally rare situations will you want to adjust your billing practices for a client, and therefore, if the client is not comfortable with your billing practices, better for everyone to know at the outset before your firm has invested time and energy into the client's case.

At a minimum, as part of the initial consultation, your firm should explain the billing rates for those team members likely to work on the case, how the firm will issue bills, and when the firm expects to get paid. These basic terms should not change from client to client, and anyone on your billing team should be able to present this information to the client.

Tracking Time

The one aspect of billing that attorneys must be responsible for is tracking their time. Of course, this is critical for attorneys who bill by the hour. Those attorneys should track their time contemporaneously.

Pro Tip: Pay whatever it costs to ensure that every billing employee has a licensed billing program on his or her primary computer so that he or she can record time contemporaneously. You will make up the license cost in the first couple of days in time that will not be lost because it was not recorded.

Most billing programs have stopwatches and other easy applications that allow attorneys to easily track their time. We strongly recommend that attorneys use these stopwatch features to ensure that they are accurately recording their time. We are regularly amazed by how much some attorneys overestimate how much time a task took and by how much other attorneys underestimate the time they spent on a task when they do not use timers or record their time contemporaneously.

Make it easy for your team members to track their time. Ensure that all team members have access to your billing program on their preferred devices whether, it be their desktop, laptop, or cell phone. Make sure that there are clocks in the rooms where your team members will meet with clients; timers on the telephones; and timers on billing programs, smartphone billing applications, and so on.

Pro Tip: Send regular invoices to your clients. We recommend at least monthly. We have heard too many horror stories about clients who have no idea what they owe to their lawyer because they have not received an invoice in months or longer. Clients are far more likely to pay off their account balances if they are billed regularly rather than hit all at once with a huge bill.

Even if you are working on cases that will not be billed by the hour, such as flat fee or contingency cases, we strongly recommend that you track your time for two reasons. First, by tracking your time and what you have done on a case, you can demonstrate to the client all you have done for them. Second, you can use the information about how much time you have spent on a case to determine if the case is profitable.

Retainer Agreement

If the firm is going to represent a client, the fee structure must be memorialized in writing that is signed by you and your client. Your firm should have a retainer agreement, engagement letter, or similar document that sets forth the terms of your representation, specifically including the fees and costs that will be billed to the client and when payment must be made. In a perfect world, neither you nor your client will ever look at the retainer agreement again, but if a billing issue arises, you should always be able to refer back to the retainer agreement to see what was agreed upon.

Invoices

We strongly recommend sending invoices to all your clients at least monthly. Invoices should convey both what work has been performed during the billing cycle and how much is being removed from the client's retainer account or how much the client owes the firm.

Simply listing your billing entries on an invoice and hoping your client will understand them is not sufficient. Most of your clients do not deal with law firms or legal matters routinely and probably will not understand terminology in the billing entries that seem detailed and self-explanatory to the lawyer who wrote them. Just because you speak legalese does not mean that your client is fluent in it.

We encourage you to take the time to explain your invoices to your client. For example, if your firm has done a significant amount of work during a billing cycle, particularly work that may not obviously provide an immediate or obvious benefit, such as discovery or legal research, you should send an explanation to the client with the invoice. Clients who recognize the value they are receiving are far more likely to pay their bills in a timely manner and without complaint.

Monthly invoices are probably the most consistent communication your firm will have with your clients. Do not ignore this opportunity to communicate with your clients. Do not make the mistake of only conveying bad information (how much your client owes you) without conveying good information (what you have done for them).

We recommend that you send invoices to your clients even when you are not asking them for a payment. Even clients who have retained you on a contingent fee or flat fee basis should receive regular invoices. The invoices should let the clients know what you are doing on their behalf. Remember that clients will not see all the work you do, and clients who do not work with lawyers regularly will not understand or appreciate what happens behind the scenes unless you tell them.

Pro Tip: Unless you are performing legal work for a flat fee or on a contingency fee, be clear with your clients that their original retainer fee will not necessarily cover all the costs of their case. Do not be shy about asking your clients to replenish their retainer accounts.

Retainer Replenishments

If your firm collects retainers, you must make it clear to the client as to when the retainer account must be replenished. In our experience, replenishing retainers arises most often in two different scenarios. The first is relatively straightforward in that there has been a steady amount of work done on the case and the retainer account is low. In that case, you are probably asking the client to provide the same retainer he or she had previously provided. In the second scenario, the retainer account is running low or is not sufficient to cover a significant expense that you anticipate will occur in the next couple of months. For example, the client's trial is approaching, and as a result, you know that he or she will incur substantial fees. In this situation, you should ask the client to pay a retainer large enough to cover the expected work. Since this retainer is likely to be larger and may create a financial hardship, the client should be given as much advance notice as possible.

When attorneys wait until the last minute to ask for a large payment to be made, the chances of the client making the payment are slim. This often places the attorney in the unenviable position of having to perform legal services without payment because not only did the attorney wait too long to ask for payment but also the attorney also waited too long to be permitted to withdraw from the case.

Now you have to hope that the client will pay you when he or she can afford to pay. In your best-case scenario, your firm will spend time and effort collecting fees—an expense that could have been avoided if you had requested the fee payment in a timely manner. The worst case is that the trial does not go well, and now you are in the position of trying to collect fees from a client who knows that he or she will be paying for an unfavorable result. Even if the lawyer did a fantastic job, the client may not appreciate the work performed and will probably feel as if he or she is not receiving a good value for the payment. Collecting fees in this scenario can be incredibly difficult.

Collection Process

Of course, the ideal situation is to have enough money in the client's retainer account to cover the fees incurred in the case. Unfortunately, even those attorneys who manage their billing procedures extremely well run into situations in which they have to collect fees from clients. Your firm should have procedures in place as to who, when, and how your firm will contact a client to collect payment if the client does not pay an invoice within the time frame set forth in the retainer agreement.

As encouraged previously, the first point of contact should be from a nonlawyer member of the billing team. Any conversations by telephone or in person should be memorialized in a billing file and/or correspondence to the client confirming the payment arrangements that were arranged.

Pro Tip: Do not ignore overdue balances. The longer a balance goes without being paid, the less likely it will ever be paid. Statistics show a sharp drop in collection rates for balances that are 30 days overdue versus those that are 90 days overdue. Two months may not seem like much time, but that is a critical time period for collections. Too many attorneys and law firms get caught up in their current work to put forth the effort to follow up with last month's client. Do not fall into this trap. Create a procedure (see Chapter 17 regarding procedures) to follow up.

The follow up regarding nonpayment should be prompt. Statistics show that the longer a bill is outstanding or overdue, the less likely it is to be paid. You should reach out to your client with the overdue balance within 30 days of the due date, and you should follow up regularly until payment is made or a payment plan is agreed upon.

The partner responsible for the client should be used as a last resort to collect fees from the client. As mentioned previously, if the lawyer is involved in the collection process, you run the risk of creating the appearance or perception that there is a conflict between the attorney and client over money. Also, once the lawyer steps into the picture, there is no one with more authority to address the issue with the client.

Often times, lawyers compound their collection issues by continuing to work on a case while fees are outstanding. Not only are you not getting paid by your existing client and additional work is only creating a larger account receivable but also you are also taking up time that would otherwise be available to work for paying clients.

Admittedly, there are times that this cannot be avoided because of trial deadlines or other scenarios in which the client would be prejudiced. You cannot shirk your ethical duty to your client regardless of the retainer account's status. When we recommend that you stop working for clients who are not paying you, we are not talking about scenarios in which you have an ethical duty to continue working on the legal matter.

Lawyers should think long and hard before hiring a collection agency or pursuing legal action to collect fees from a client. Pursuing aggressive action like this frequently results in the client filing a malpractice claim or ethical complaint against the lawyer.

Regardless of whether the law firm is correct in pursuing its fees, the collection comes at a significant financial and reputational expense. The law firm will have to pay lawyers to defend itself, and malpractice insurance costs are likely to increase. Simultaneously, the law firm's reputation could be damaged by the allegations that the client makes regardless of whether those allegations are true. When you begin any collection action, be careful not to violate any of the debt collection protections.

Methods of Payment

Make it easy for your clients to pay you. Generally speaking, clients are not eager to pay for legal services. They are paying for a service that most did not particularly want in the first place. When they show up with a payment, let them make it!

You should be willing to accept various forms of payment. Most firms accept checks, credit cards, and cash, and so should you. Although your office is not open 24 hours a day, your clients should be able to pay you whenever they want. Many law firms allow clients to pay by credit card through their websites or wire payments to their accounts, and a few are allowing clients to pay through PayPal, Venmo, and other similar options.

We are seeing more clients asking if they can pay with cryptocurrency. While we can envision a day when cryptocurrency becomes a standard form of payment, we are not there yet. There are too many questions as to what happens if you were to receive a payment in cryptocurrency and the next day its value changes. If the value goes up, did you accept a greater payment than you earned; and if it goes down, does your client owe you more money? We are not comfortable recommending that you accept payment in a currency whose value fluctuates so wildly.

We encourage you to consider any methods of payment that are ethical and to make it convenient for your clients to get their payments to you. We can see many changes on the horizon with regard to payment, and we recommend that you keep an open mind and investigate these opportunities as they arise.

Billing Software

We strongly encourage you to purchase a billing program. Even if you are a very small firm with few clients, we do not recommend manually creating invoices.

Billing programs will help you stay organized, track payments, create professional looking invoices, and create reports that can be exported for other purposes such as tax filings.

There is a wide variety of law firm–specific billing software such as Clio, MyCase, Rocket Matter, CosmoLex, Timeslips, Tabs, and PCLaw. This is certainly not an exhaustive list. It is important to research the advantages and disadvantages of each program to find the one that will best serve your firm.

For smaller firms, particularly those without a resident technology expert, we suggest that you place a greater emphasis on choosing software that your IT vendor and your accountant are comfortable working with. Nothing would be worse than purchasing a program that theoretically does everything you need but does not work because you, your IT vendor, and your accountant cannot configure it properly.

Although we recommend that you purchase software that is designed for a law firm, smaller firms can use accounting programs to accomplish the basics of billing. The most well-known accounting program is QuickBooks.

There are alternatives to QuickBooks, but if you are looking for an easy solution, QuickBooks is the way to go. Virtually every accountant and tax preparer is well-versed in it and therefore can help you set up your program to prepare the reports you will need. Also, given its popularity, it will be easy to find help if you have any difficulty with your program.

Choosing billing and/or accounting software is an important decision. We encourage you to determine what you need the program to do for you, research the options, and talk with your IT vendor to ensure that the software you choose is the right one. For research, we recommend that you read the ABA's *Solo and Small Firm Legal Technology Guide* written by Sharon Nelson, John Simek, and Mike Maschke.

Billing and Collections Section of Your Business Plan

We anticipate that your answers to the questions below will serve as an outline for the billing and collections section of your business plan. These answers will form the foundation for how your firm will bill clients and collect fees.

1. What are your billing policies and expectations?
2. Who will communicate with clients about billing issues?
    a. Billing department
    b. Lawyers

3. How will you track your time?
4. How and when will you educate your clients about your fees and costs?
5. How will you get paid for cases?
    a. Flat fee, hourly, contingent
    b. Will you have different fee rates or structures for different clients?
6. Retainer agreement
    a. Scope and terms
    b. Retainer fee
    c. Replenishment of retainer
7. How will you invoice your client for fees and costs incurred?
    a. Timing
    b. Delivery method
    c. Technology
8. Collection
    a. Who will handle your collections?
    b. What do you do when a client refuses to pay or cannot pay?
    c. What options does the client have to make a payment?

See the Appendix of this book for a sample Client Billing Invoice that you can customize for your firm's needs.

14

Finance: Budgeting and Managing Your Money

Pro Tip: Remember that you are not only a lawyer but also a business owner. Budgeting is a critical role that all business owners must learn to understand. Business owners do not have to be budgeting experts, but they need to understand how budgets work and what the budgets are telling them about their businesses.

It is important to remember that your law firm is a business. Producing a good product or providing top-notch legal services will only get a business or law firm part of the way to being successful. There are countless stories of businesses that have a wonderful product but still go out of business. Frequently, those businesses go belly up because they cannot manage their finances.

Budgets are the most effective and efficient means of measuring whether your firm is maximizing its resources. Budgets will enable you to identify where there are opportunities to increase your profits. Additionally, budgets will allow you to develop plans that you can actually afford to implement.

We often find lawyers who do not take the time to create budgets for their firms. This is an incredibly big oversight. We hear two primary reasons that lawyers avoid creating budgets. First, most lawyers did not go to law school to crunch numbers and really do not enjoy the task. As a result, it gets put at the bottom of the to-do list, and never gets done. Second, lawyers figure that they are working hard, clients are paying fees, and the rent is getting paid, and therefore, there is no urgent need to track the money that closely. In recent economic downturns, a lot of lawyers learned the hard way that this is not a great strategy.

Budgeting Generally

You must recognize that all budgets will contain projections and that projections are not always going to be accurate. Many lawyers use the excuse that it does not make sense to spend much time budgeting when you cannot be certain that the projections will be accurate.

It is somewhat ironic that attorneys take this attitude toward budgeting when this is effectively the same approach that every attorney takes when he or she goes to trial. No attorney can predict a trial outcome with absolute certainty. Good attorneys advise their clients on the risks of trial and the range of likely outcomes before trial based on their knowledge of the circumstances, but no one guarantees an outcome.

The best budgets are developed with the same strategy. Take all of the available knowledge to determine the range of potential revenues and expenses, and create a budget based on what you believe to be the most likely outcome.

Expenses

We prefer to start building our budget by outlining expenses before projecting revenues. Tracking and predicting most expenses is easier than predicting revenues because in many ways, you have more control over your expenses than revenues.

When it comes to expenses, you choose whether to incur an expense and/or what level you are willing to pay. We suggest building the expense side of your budget by dividing the expenses into three categories: (1) absolutely required, (2) those that you feel are required, and (3) discretionary.

Absolutely Required Expenses

Given all of the changes in the way that modern law firms are structured, the "absolutely required" category has very few expenses other than your bar license dues and malpractice insurance. Even with malpractice insurance, you have some control over its cost, as you can choose between options with different deductibles, levels of coverage, and so on. To the extent that there are any other expenses that you are required to incur to practice law, they should go into this category.

Pro Tip: Keep an open mind regarding the expenses that you feel are required. Locking yourself into an expense could have a big impact on the overall direction of your firm. Do not incur an expense just because the firm down the street is incurring the expense. Make an independent judgment as to whether the expense is worthwhile.

Feel Required Expenses

The bulk of your expenses are likely to fall into the second category where you feel that the expense is required. As we have stressed throughout this book, there are many creative ways to structure your law firm. Since you have discretion as to how your law firm is structured, we argue that the expenses necessary to operate your law firm are not absolutely required.

You could always opt to change your firm structure, eliminating the need to incur an expense that you felt was necessary in the previous structure. For example, as technology improves and more firms turn to virtual offices, expenses such as rent that law firms have traditionally considered to be absolute requirements are becoming more discretionary.

For this reason, it is critical that you take the time to determine what your firm needs as opposed to simply copying what someone else has done.

The expenses that commonly fall into this second category are salaries, benefits, insurances, rent, utilities, cleaning services, phones, computers, software, supplies, marketing, and so on. Although you must pay salaries, namely your own, we include salaries in this category because there is so much discretion regarding the amount.

We urge you to keep an open mind regarding these expenses. Just because your firm has always incurred these expenses in the past does not mean that you have to keep incurring them for posterity's sake. Two easy examples of expense changes in the past decade are the significant reduction of Yellow Page advertisement costs and legal book purchases. One reason to create and review your budget is to ensure that there is a good reason to continue incurring the expense.

Discretionary Expenses

The final category of expenses is discretionary. These are the items that you want and think would be valuable for your firm but are neither mandatory nor necessary to operate your firm.

This category contains a mixture of expenses that you will not incur until you have more resources and other expenses for which there is a base amount that you view as necessary, but you would like to increase the amount of the expenditure. For example, most firms conclude that they have to spend some amount of money on marketing—for example, on a website or bar associations—but there are other expenses associated with marketing, such as conferences and social functions, that they would like to do but are clearly discretionary.

Many attorneys assume that they will buy these discretionary items if there is enough money left over at the end of the year to buy them. This plan often falls apart when the partners look at the year-end profit and decide to distribute it to themselves rather than spending it on a discretionary expense for the firm, or the opportunity to benefit from the discretionary expense has already passed by.

The best way to put yourself in position to purchase a discretionary item is to plan for it. While your current-year budget may not allocate any expenses toward the discretionary item, putting the expense into the budget as a line item will raise awareness and compel you to look for ways to fund the expense in future years.

Fixed Versus Variable Expenses

Expenses that recur regularly are called fixed expenses. These are the easiest expenses to project and plan for in your budget. Many of these expenses will likely be governed by contracts, and therefore, you will know exactly what the obligations will be.

Common fixed expenses include rent, insurance premiums, and salaries.
Common variable expenses include bonuses, credit card fees, and marketing expenses.

You may not be able to predict other fixed expenses as precisely, but to be included in the fixed expense category, the expenses should fluctuate within a relatively small range. Expenses such as utilities and legal research costs typically fall in this category.

Variable expenses are usually harder to predict because the amount and timing are less consistent. That being said, there are different degrees of variable expenses.

For some variable expenses, you will be able to estimate the amount but not the timing. For example, you can obtain cost estimates for a new computer or desk, but it is harder to predict when you will need to incur the cost. When budgeting, we recommend that you insert these expenses into your budget using your best estimate as to when the expense will be incurred. If you are uncertain about the time estimate, the best time estimate will be to use the manufacturer's estimated life expectancy.

Since you will never know in advance when your computer will crash and need to be replaced, the only way to budget for this expense is to estimate when you will need to replace the computer. The safest approach is to find out the unit's life expectancy when you purchase it and use that timeline.

If the computer does not crash, there is some discretion in this, as you may choose to purchase a new computer earlier, or you may hold onto an older one that still works (maybe not as quickly or as efficiently as a new model) for a longer period. If you base your budget on the life expectancy, you will most likely be in good shape financially when it comes time to purchase the new equipment.

For other expenses, the amount may be a wildcard, but timing may be easier to gauge. Your budget should contain your best guess as to the expense in the time period that you expect it to occur. For example, you may offer all of your team members the opportunity to attend an expensive out-of-town seminar, but historically not everyone has attended. The cost will fluctuate year to year based on where the seminar is located and how many team members attend. You should include an estimate based on an average of how many team members have attended in past years and historical costs of the seminar.

We recommend that you project the significant variable expenses on a monthly basis even if they will occur only annually or even less frequently. By inserting a monthly cost into your budget, you can save money so that when the expense occurs, you can pay it from your reserve. It is easier to save on a monthly basis than annually. The alternative to saving enough money to pay for the unpredictable expense is being forced to take funds from other expense categories, such as your salary, that month or to borrow funds when the expense payment is due. Inevitably, you will need funds for the variable expense at the least opportune time. If you have not planned for the expense, you face the risk of a shortage in income when you can least afford it and/or you are forced into unfavorable financing terms.

Revenue

Predicting revenue can be tricky even for firms who have been operating for many years. Many variables both inside and outside of your firm may impact your revenue.

Outside variables that you have no control over could have a significant impact on your revenue. It is difficult, if not impossible, to predict when most market adjustments (think subprime mortgage crash or natural disaster) will occur. If we could predict these events, we should be picking lottery numbers regularly.

While you may not be able to predict when an event will happen or even that certain types of events will happen, you can estimate the impact such a market event will have on your firm revenue. Once a market event has occurred or the marketplace has been trending in one direction for some time, it will be necessary to revise your budget estimates to take into consideration the current information and circumstances.

There are some market forces that you may not be able to control but you can predict. For example, if your practice is based on defending individuals who use marijuana, you can see the trend to decriminalize and/or reduce prosecution of those cases. Your revenue will decrease unless you shift into other product lines.

When your firm first opens, you have no track record, and therefore, your revenue projections are likely to be educated guesses. The more effort you put into turning those "educated guesses" into "informed predictions," the better off you will be.

For those of you who are starting a new firm, talk with other practitioners about their experiences. While many attorneys may be reluctant to tell you what they earn, they are far more willing to share information about how many cases you can expect to have and/or how much revenue an average case will generate.

With a firm that generates its revenue through hourly billing, the following factors are critical in estimating revenues: billable rates, collection percentages, and number of hours that each billable team member will bill.

We encourage you to look at billable rates and collection percentages together. It is misleading to say that your billable rate (or expected revenue) is $500 per hour if you only collect 75 percent of the fees you bill. From our perspective, in that scenario your expected revenue is really $375 per hour, and this is what needs to be reflected in your budget.

Pro Tip: Be honest about your collection rates and what they mean to your bottom line. We can recall one conversation in which an attorney was boasting that his hourly rate had just gone up to $450 per hour. In the next sentence, he told us that he collected about 60 percent of what he billed. To us, his hourly rate is $270. Not nearly as impressive.

Billable Rate

It is relatively easy to predict billable rates for many attorneys because they either set their hourly rates at the beginning of each year or rarely change them. As a result, the billable rates are relatively stable throughout the year.

We recognize that there are many attorneys who vary their billable rates by client and/or the type of work they are doing. These attorneys need to estimate how often they will adjust their hourly rates or how much of each type of work they plan to do. It is important for these attorneys to determine what their average hourly billing rate is both for all cases and for each type of case they handle.

In many respects, this analysis is the most important aspect of budgeting for attorneys whose billing rates fluctuate. Frequently, these attorneys assume that they are doing well because they are very busy handling legal matters. As a result, these attorneys do not focus on what type of work they are doing, only that they are working. The problem is that they may be allocating the majority of their time to lower-paying cases, leaving them with limited time to handle more profitable work. By taking the time to prepare a budget, these attorneys can determine how to allocate their time to achieve their profit goals.

Collection Rate

As mentioned previously, an accurate estimate of your collection rate is essential to gauging what your true revenue will be. As with all projections, they get easier and more accurate once you have historical data to give you some guidance. Even if you do not have complete confidence in your projections, it is still worthwhile to make projections. At a minimum, the projections should reflect your collection goals, so long as they are reasonable.

You can safely assume that your collection rate will be higher if you focus on obtaining retainer fees before performing the legal work. The less effort you place on obtaining retainers, the lower your collection rate is likely to be. Furthermore, more experienced attorneys tend to have higher collection rates because they are better equipped to identify and weed out deadbeats, and they have much more practice collecting fees.

Certainly, the ideal scenario is that your projected collection rate is accurate. However, the value in projecting it even when you are not confident in it is that you have a benchmark to measure yourself against at the end of your budgeting period. If you are not meeting your goal, you can use the budget to determine what additional resources need to be allocated to improve the collection rate.

Billable Hours

The hardest revenue variable to predict for team members who bill by the hour is the number of billable hours each billable team member will bill. You can set billable goals for each team member, and provided that those goals are reasonable, you can use those goals for your revenue projections. When you first open your firm, it is hard to predict whether you will be able to meet those goals. The longer your track record is, the more confidence you can have that you will meet the billable goals.

Even harder than predicting revenue for an attorney who bills by the hour is the attorney who handles only contingency cases. Attorneys who handle contingency cases can and should predict revenue based on their own historical averages. For those attorneys who have not tracked their own performance or for new attorneys, find information regarding case averages from other attorneys or insurance companies.

Pro Tip: Budgets are a great tool to remind you to check to make sure you are staying on top of your expenses. Seeing how much a particular supply cost adds up over the course of a year will motivate you to periodically check to see if there is a less-expensive provider.

We realize that revenue projections for contingency attorneys can be thrown off by a particularly good or bad result. This might be an even bigger issue for attorneys who limit their practice to huge cases that take multiple years as opposed to attorneys who grind out car accident after car accident. Attorneys who really go all in on bigger cases should be budgeting for multiple years at a time.

Periodic Review

Ideally, your budget should project your finances for several years. The first year should be detailed, and your expectation should be that the projections for the upcoming year will be pretty accurate.

While you are optimistic that your research will produce accurate estimates in the future years, you must recognize that those projections will be less reliable. For this reason, it is critical that you review and revise the budget periodically to update it as more reliable information becomes available.

We strongly recommend breaking down your budgets, especially for the upcoming year, into monthly or at least quarterly segments. The smaller time periods will allow you to identify and plan for the cash flow fluctuations that your firm will likely experience.

We recommend that you review your budget either monthly or quarterly to see how close reality is to your predictions. If your predictions are not accurate, you can and should make adjustments for the remainder of the year. In addition, you should revise your entire budget at least annually.

A side benefit of the regular reviews is that it can help you identify whether someone in your firm is embezzling money. Sadly, every year we hear of a law firm in which someone within the firm misappropriates funds. Reviewing the budget will not protect you against all forms of embezzlement, but if your actual expenditures start to exceed your expense projections by a wide margin, that should raise a red flag and trigger an investigation.

Cash Flow Management

Most law practices have cycles when they are likely to have more work. For example, trusts and estates or tax practices may be busier in December when clients are looking to take steps to minimize their tax liabilities. Or family law practices may be slower in December when families want to focus on the holidays rather than their divorce cases.

Cycles like these are important to recognize because they will have a significant impact on the timing of your firm's revenues. A monthly budget should identify which months you predict will be high- or low-revenue months.

This becomes a bigger issue when you have a slow-revenue month coupled with a high-expense month. Continuing with the family law firm example, many will experience low revenue in December/January but will still pay year-end bonuses in December. By budgeting, these firms can anticipate where there will be cash flow difficulties and plan ahead to address them.

We do not recommend distributing all of the firm's profits after a particularly good month when you can predict a shortfall in the near future. If you have a good budget, not only will you know that an upcoming period is likely to have a shortfall but also you will have a rough idea of how much the shortfall will be. This information will enable you to make solid financial decisions as to how much you can afford to distribute without putting yourself in a position of having to scramble to overcome a shortfall.

Pro Tip: It is critical that you understand the peaks and valleys of your cash flow. Most law firms cannot count on the same level of income each month or quarter. If you plan properly for the valleys, you can arrange for less-expensive ways to navigate the slower months. Knowing the difference between a great month and one in which you expect higher revenue can save you from overextending yourself.

For firms that have significant surpluses, the finance department should have a plan as to how those surpluses will be invested until their distribution. Your firm may be able to increase its savings by investing it wisely.

Planning for big ticket expenses in advance will allow you to avoid major cash flow crises. When you budget for big ticket expenses that occur infrequently, you can save for them rather than having to borrow to pay for them.

While you may not be able to avoid debt altogether, planning for and saving for large purchases will enable you to avoid or minimize the need for debt. There may be times when incurring debt is the best option, but ideally you will be in a financial position to choose whether to incur debt, not to be forced to take out debt because that is the only option. Inevitably, when you are forced into using debt, the terms will not be favorable.

Startup Expenses

Your budgeting should begin well before you open your firm. Since you have not opened your firm yet, presumably there are no revenues to predict. Once your firm opens, the budget should include your revenue projections.

The adage that you have to spend money to make money is absolutely true when it comes to hanging your shingle. You will have to incur certain expenses before your firm opens its doors. These expenses are likely to be substantial capital expenditures, such as rent, furniture, computers, phones, copiers/scanners, and so on.

The best practice is to start researching and predicting expenses as soon as you decide to open your own firm. Developing a timeline as to when you will incur the expenses is just as important as estimating the amount. If you need to borrow funds to get started, you should work closely with your banker or lender to customize when the borrowed funds are made available to ensure that you can purchase what you need when you need it. However, you do not want to receive funds earlier than you need them because the longer you have the funds, the more costly (extra interest payments) the money becomes.

One question that will arise when you start your firm, and continue throughout your ownership, is whether to lease or purchase. A surprising amount of office equipment can be leased. Leasing equipment can be a great way to avoid a large lump sum expense, and most leased equipment comes with service options (yes, you pay for them), but the owner has an incentive to ensure that its equipment is up and running. However, buying the equipment may be cheaper but may come with more headaches such as arranging for servicing on your own.

Emergency Funds

Every firm should have savings set aside for an emergency. Since you are not likely to have excess revenue when you first open your office, it will make sense to borrow more than you plan to spend immediately for this purpose. Your firm will be incredibly vulnerable when it first opens, and having emergency savings will enable you to overcome an unexpected setback without crippling your startup efforts (see Chapter 21 regarding emergency planning).

Every budget should include savings to create an emergency fund until you have set aside a sufficient amount. We recommend that your emergency fund contain funds sufficient to operate your firm for several months.

We confess that the first draft of this book, which was written before the coronavirus disease 19 (COVID-19) crisis, recommended that you have enough emergency funds to cover at least two months. We now suggest that two months is the bare minimum, and three to four months is preferable.

We encourage you to include your own salary when calculating what it would cost to operate the firm, but you could stretch your emergency funds by reducing or eliminating your salary for a short period.

Budgeting Software

Do not underestimate the value of good budgeting software. While you may not review or use the budgeting software as often your billing or word-processing software, it is a vital tool in evaluating the firm's performance.

QuickBooks and Quicken are two of the most widely used budgeting software programs. However, these are certainly not the only programs that will track your income and expenses. Before choosing a program, consult with your accounting team to ensure that they will be able to easily access the information that you accumulate and it will be in a format that is compatible with what they need to do.

One decision that you will face is whether to purchase a standalone budgeting program or one that is integrated into other programs. There are numerous programs designed specifically for law firms that combine budgeting, bill paying, expense tracking, and billing into one program.

The all-in-one programs can be significant time savers. The different tasks within the program are synchronized to work well with one another. On a practical level, you and your team will have to enter the data only in one place, and it will be auto-populated into the other sections of the program.

If you purchase individual programs to accomplish each task, the data entry will take much longer. The advantage of this approach is that it will be easier for you to upgrade when improvements are made. Typically, updates are made more frequently to individual programs than the ones that merge several programs together.

The downside of using one program that does everything is that it becomes very difficult to transition from that program when there are advances.

We urge you to take the time to investigate which software will work best for you. As part of this investigation, you should consult with your IT department or vendor and your accountants. The program that comes with all of the bells and whistles will be useless if your IT vendor cannot operate it or it produces information in a format that your accountants cannot use (see Chapter 13 regarding billing and Chapter 15 regarding technology).

Finance Department

All businesses should have a strong finance department that works collaboratively with all of the other firm departments. As we mentioned in Chapter 4 regarding team members, this is one of the critical roles that someone in your firm must fill.

The finance department plays a critical role in any firm planning decisions. You cannot develop an effective plan without knowing whether the firm can afford to pay for it.

In addition to budgeting and planning, the firm's finance department must take care of the basics such as balancing the checkbook, paying bills, accepting payments, and tracking retainer accounts. Your firm must implement systems and procedures to handle these repetitive day-to-day tasks.

We strongly recommend that you restrict check writing or account transfer authority to very few team members. Also, expenditures over a certain amount should require authorization from at least two people.

All employers feel that their finance department and the people they see every day can be trusted. However, every year we see a story in the bar disciplinary news about a lawyer being sanctioned because his or her long-time team member made unauthorized withdrawals from client funds. There must be a system of checks and balances.

It is critical for every team member to understand that client money held in the firm's retainer account is not the firm's money. That money belongs to the client until the firm earns it.

Finance Section of Your Business Plan

We anticipate that your answers to the questions below will serve as an outline for the finance section of your business plan. These answers will form the foundation for how your firm manages its money.

1. Budget
    a. Revenue
        i. *Projecting revenue*
            1) How many cases will you have when you open, in three years, and in ten years?
            2) How much revenue does each case generate?

ii. *Tracking revenue*
  1) How do you track the money coming into the firm?
  2) How do you determine how much revenue each case generates?
  3) How do you track cycles or cash flow fluctuations?

b. Expenses
  i. *Projecting expenses*
    1) Fixed expenses
    2) Variable expenses
    3) Extraordinary expenses
  ii. *Tracking expenses*
    1) Fixed expenses
    2) Variable expenses
    3) On a per-case or per–team member basis

c. What are your key indicators of financial success?
  i. *What is your definition of financial success (years 1, 3, and 10)?*
  ii. *How do you use the budget to measure success?*
  iii. *How do you use the budget to achieve your definition of success in future years?*

d. What software will you use for your budgeting?

2. Startup revenue and expense considerations
3. How will you manage your firm's finances?
   a. Will you take out debt to start your firm or to fund its operations?
   b. Does your firm have cash flow cycles that need to be considered?
   c. What will you do with any profits?
4. Who is going to handle the financial aspects of your business?

See the Appendix of this book for a sample Budget Spreadsheet that you can customize for your firm's needs.

15

Technology: Staying on the Cutting Edge or Keeping Up

Understanding how to *utilize* and *apply* technology in your law firm will have significant impact on whether you will be able to run a successful organization. Notice how the words *utilize* and *apply* are emphasized here.

We are not stating you need to master technology yourself, write or decipher code, or understand all the mechanics of the technology you are utilizing. However, it is critical that you understand how technology can impact your firm and where you can get the best value.

There is no question that technology permeates every aspect of your firm. We are no longer in an age where lawyers simply use computers as fancy typewriters. Technology used and applied wisely can transform your firm and give you a significant competitive edge.

Who Is Technology Designed to Impress?

The best technology will provide benefits to your clients and your team members, but this will not always be the case. We strongly recommend that you consider the impact technology will have on both your clients and your team members.

Pro Tip: Consider how your team members and your clients will react to your technology choices. You need to please both of them.

When you are deciding what technology to purchase, you should consider whether your client will find it useful. Will the technology reduce the time or cost to perform your services? Will the technology enable you to provide a better service?

Equally as important as your client's perspective on technology is the impact it will have on your team members. Certainly, new (and younger) team members will expect a certain level of technology. No one wants to work at an ancient computer terminal or one with a slow Internet connection.

Challenges of Technology

We recognize that technology changes incredibly fast. You may have been on the cutting edge yesterday but are behind the curve today. Just when you start to feel comfortable with the software you purchased a year ago, a new version becomes available.

The challenges of keeping up are even greater when you are dealing with an unfamiliar field. We rarely encounter attorneys who are skilled in technology. At best, some attorneys consider technology a hobby. Due to this lack of interest and/or familiarity with technology, it takes even more time and effort to keep up with new developments.

Given the rapid changes in technology, we seriously doubt that most attorneys can keep up with the changes on their own. As you are well aware, there are numerous college programs, certification courses, and other education programs designed solely for learning about specific aspects of technology.

You must develop and manage a comprehensive technology plan for your law firm. Unless you are a technology buff or have enough resources to hire a team member who focuses on technology, we strongly encourage you to get help from an expert in this field.

There are countless IT companies who focus on servicing law firms. These companies are familiar with the hardware needs of law firms and the software programs law firms use. Once you find this company, you need to develop a relationship with them that allows you to consult with them periodically about what you will need in the upcoming quarter or year.

While we firmly believe that all successful firms keep up with technology advances, firms on the cutting edge of technology can dominate the market or fall flat on their face. As with all technology, the innovators are gambling that the technology they choose will become the standard.

For those who want to be on the cutting edge, you run the risk of choosing the Lumia instead of the iPhone. Most of you are probably asking what the Lumia is. It is Microsoft's attempt to enter the smartphone market.

We encourage you to always be looking forward to see if you can be on the cutting edge, but at a bare minimum, you need to keep up with advances in technology.

Utilizing Technology

Technology is great, but contrary to what some techies would likely argue, it is not always the answer. The first decision you have to make is when you want to use technology and when you want to use an old-fashioned method to accomplish the task.

For example, some attorneys use calendar applications that allow clients to book their meetings online in time slots provided by the attorney. This impersonal system could save the attorney, team members, and clients significant time, and therefore, money. Other attorneys and clients will find the lack of personal contact to be a turn off.

Consider how your clients would react to this method of scheduling and whether it would appeal to them or not. Saving time and money by streamlining the scheduling process will backfire if you lose clients as a result.

Technology is extremely effective for repetitive tasks. Many lawyers overlook the similarities and repetitive nature of certain aspects of their cases. We understand that each case is different, hence the phrase "case-by-case basis," but there are functions that must be done in each case that are repetitive. Properly designed technology can save a significant amount of time and money.

While we are not there yet, artificial intelligence is making huge strides. Before long, artificial intelligence programs will help attorneys complete a wider range of tasks. Firms who are looking to be on the cutting edge of technology should monitor the developments in this area.

Pro Tip: New technology comes out every day. You need to constantly monitor what is being offered. You cannot make a technology purchase and think that you have solved that issue for the next year, much less the next few years. Reviewing your technology options should be an assignment that never ends.

Applying Technology

Purchasing the newest and coolest technology is only the first step. The world's best technology is useless if you and your team do not know how to use it.

Whenever you purchase technology, you need to budget for the time and money it will take to get your team up to speed on the technology. Do not purchase new technology if you will not have the resources to train your team to use it.

Technology becomes even more frustrating for nontechnology buffs when they cannot get it to do what the salesperson promised it would do. This frustration can lead to a dangerous cycle of the firm decision makers refusing to invest in new technology because the previous purchases never lived up to their expectations, when, in fact, the former technology did not live up to expectations because team members never learned how to use it properly. This cycle is a trap that you need to avoid at all costs.

Efficiency and Productivity

One of the most valuable advantages of technology, particularly from the client's perspective, is your ability to perform certain tasks faster. When you can complete a task faster, it tends to lead to savings. The easy saving to spot is the fact that tasks that take less time to complete typically cost the client less.

The less-obvious savings are the savings that a faster conclusion to the case generates. From the client's perspective, the sooner the legal matter is resolved, the sooner the clients can return their complete focus to their own goals. Very few clients would list spending their time and money on litigation as one of their goals.

Technology has made the greatest strides in administrative functions. Instead of having to carry around a physical file that may consist of boxes of documents, technology enables you to put a huge amount of data on a single tablet or on your phone.

The mobility of your case file allows your team members to work on the case and access the entire file wherever it is most convenient, such as the courthouse, client's office, or expert witness's office. In addition, it is very easy to transfer portions of an electronic file to whomever needs it.

File management software allows you to keep all correspondence, documents, and other case-related materials in one place. Without this software, different aspects end up saved in different programs, and multiple team members may not be able to access all of them.

This software is absolutely critical for efficiency when multiple team members are working on the same case. In the old days, a team member would have to have the physical file in his or her possession to access the entire file, and when one team member had the file, no one else could use it. File management software organizes the file electronically, making the entire file available to every team member who is working on a particular case and enabling multiple team members to access the file at the same time.

There are various programs that scan documents easily and place them into your file management systems. New programs such as Scanbot allow you to use a smartphone to take a photograph of a document and turn it into a PDF. Once a document is scanned as a PDF and added to the electronic file, any team member (regardless of location) can access the document instantly.

Other programs such as HotDocs allow you to maintain a directory or library of paragraphs or sections that you can access and insert into a document. Building the directory at the outset is time consuming. However, once you build the directory, you will be able to draft documents much faster.

Voice recognition software is another tool attorneys can use. In effect, attorneys can dictate what they want written without the need for an assistant to turn the recording into a document. This is a prime example of how technology can advance to enable attorneys accomplish tasks at a lower cost.

The key to voice recognition software is patience and consistency. Taking the time to train the software about you and the language you use in your documents will pay dividends in the future, but there is a learning curve.

More and more firms are using technology to enable clients to access their case files remotely through portals or other avenues. Rather than having to meet with your client and pull the parts of the file that the client wants to review, the client can access whatever part he or she wants and whenever without requiring your assistance. This will improve the client's opportunities to help in his or her own representation, and it will reduce the time your firm spends on tasks that do not move the case toward its conclusion.

Performance

Earlier in this chapter, we discussed how technology can make your process more efficient, and therefore, it becomes less expensive to produce your legal services. Technology can also improve the quality of your legal services.

Technology has made the greatest strides in courtroom presentations. Through advances, it has become much easier and cheaper to present evidence in formats that are visually attractive for a judge or jury to view.

Evidence presented electronically or through video can be easily changed to match the testimony almost instantly as opposed to hard copies of documents that cannot be edited on the fly. Until recently, only the largest and wealthiest firms could afford to provide evidence in this fashion.

Before long, this technology will be affordable for all firms. Furthermore, many courts already encourage the presentation of electronic evidence. It will not be long before the courts prohibit hard copies of documents and require them to be submitted electronically.

Virtual Hearings

Coronavirus disease 19 (COVID-19) forced many courts to hold virtual hearings and many attorneys to handle not just hearings but other matters virtually that ordinarily would have been in person such as client meetings, depositions, and firm meetings. Even when COVID-19 restrictions are lifted and the world returns to something close to "normal," we anticipate that virtual actions will not go away.

There is a wide variety of software available to conduct videoconferences such as Zoom, GoToMeeting, WebEx, and many others. The features on these programs are slightly different, but all serve the same general purpose.

There are two features we encourage you to consider. First, it can be very helpful if you can share your screen. This will enable you to share documents with all the meeting participants so everyone is literally on the same page and everyone can see any edits or notes you are making in real time.

Second, some of the programs have waiting rooms so that you can place meeting participants in the waiting room until you are ready to have them join the other participants. This feature can allow you to place opposing counsel and the opposing party in another "room" while you and your client have a discussion.

If you are a litigator, you should obtain the software your local courts are using. Not only will you need it for your hearings, but also using it for all other matters will make you more proficient with it.

Pro Tip: Never underestimate the need for security. Your clients value your ability to protect their confidential information above all else. The best security programs and measures are only as strong as their weakest link. Be certain that everyone in your office receives extensive training on your security measures.

These programs are inexpensive and relatively easy to use. Your clients are going to expect you to be familiar with them, and many clients may find that the advantages of being able to jump onto a videoconference from wherever they are and not having to deal with traffic or any other logistical issues of getting to your office are greater than the advantages of meeting in person.

Security

Technology can be a double-edged sword when it comes to security issues. When applied properly, technology can enable you to protect client confidences more effectively than in the past. Passwords, restricted access, and encrypted correspondence are all inexpensive tools that you should have.

On the flip side, the more mobile devices your firm uses, the more likely one of them will be lost or stolen. It certainly feels as if we read a story every few weeks about how someone lost control of a laptop that enabled a nonauthorized user to access thousands of credit card or social security numbers.

You have a duty to preserve your client's confidences, and it is imperative that you purchase whatever technology is necessary to do this effectively. In addition, you must have set procedures in place regarding the use of this technology.

If you plan to allow team members to load firm and/or client information on their personal devices, we encourage you to implement a policy that addresses how this information will be handled when the team members leave the firm and/or change devices. We recommend that there be an agreement that allows your IT team to clean the device.

Clients need to feel safe and secure when they leave confidential information with you, and this information must actually be safe and secure.

A written IT security policy is essential in this day and age. Your team must be trained properly, and the policy should be communicated to your clients. Security is a shared responsibility, and all parties who have access to sensitive data must do their part.

Technology Plan

Every law firm should have a technology plan. Technology will play a critical role in the success of your firm today. Your ability to keep up with advances in technology will play a critical role in your firm's ability to remain relevant. We cannot overemphasize the importance of technology in the success of your firm.

Below we have addressed several aspects of technology that we believe every firm should consider. This is not intended to be an exhaustive list of technology decisions that you will face, nor is this list tailored to the specific needs of your firm.

Computers

A good place to start for your firm's technology is with the type of computer your firm will be using. You can choose to use a desktop, laptop, tablet, or any combination of these three. Core factors to consider are where you want your employees working, preference in computer styles, operating system capabilities, and productivity and security issues.

Some firms prefer desktops because it ensures the employees are working at the office and they can minimize security issues. Desktops come with more power/memory at a lower cost than the other options discussed below.

When selecting a computer, consider the operating system the computer uses and if it has the capability of working with your firm's chosen software packages. For example, Dell computers typically use a Windows-based operating system. In the past, many law firms had to use PC options because most legal software programs would only run on Windows, which was not an option on Apple computers.

Apple computers were touted as having more design, visual, and marketing capabilities than business functions. Recently, Apple has opened up its operating system to provide for Windows-based capability, which in essence provides two computers in one.

Computer monitors are normally bought separately from the desktop. Using just one monitor is the exception now rather than the norm for desktops, particularly given the relatively low cost per monitor. We highly recommend using two or three monitors with the desktop. The extra monitors will significantly increase your productivity.

Laptops are portable and provide you with the capability of taking your office with you. Laptops typically have only one monitor, which is usually smaller than a desktop monitor. However, laptops can be docked when they are in the office, and additional monitors can connect to your laptop just like the desktop.

Normally, desktops come with more memory and power at a lower cost (see the Solo and Small Firm Legal Technology Guide series written by Sharon D. Nelson, John Simek, and Michael Maschke) than laptops, but you can add memory to the laptops with an additional investment. Laptops do present additional security issues because they are portable and if stolen put your firm's data at risk.

Computer tablets such as Apple iPads and the Microsoft Surface Pro product line now compete with laptops because they are lighter to carry and can give you the same memory capability as a laptop.

Laptops come with more memory at a lower cost than tablets. With an additional investment you can add memory to your tablet so that it provides the same memory capability as a laptop.

Tablets are better suited for attorneys who are often out of the office as part of their duties (e.g., presenting in court, depositions, marketing to referral sources, prospective clients, and so on). Visual presentations are easy to demonstrate on tablets and can be done over a coffee table.

Whichever style you choose, we recommend you consult your team members regarding their preferences. You may want to have a general policy for one type of computer across the board because it may be easier to manage and maintain one type of hardware. However, you may be able to accommodate some individual preferences such as monitor sizes or designs, keyboard or mouse styles, wireless keyboards or mouses, and so on. These small accommodations may go a long way to improve morale and efficiency without costing much.

Smartphones

You can expect most team members to use smartphones in addition to computers. We cannot remember the last time we encountered an attorney who did not have a smartphone. Smartphones perform virtually all of the same functions as a laptop but at a fraction of the size.

The term "smartphones" is somewhat of a misnomer. They are really computers. Certainly, they provide the ability to make phone calls, but they also enable attorneys to correspond by e-mail and text, scan and review documents, prepare documents with voice recognition software, and conduct research.

Pro Tip: If you are providing your team members with mobile devices or encouraging them to work on their personal devices, be aware that your team members' "office" may be located somewhere that you would not approve of. Your team members may choose to text colleagues while driving, write e-mails to your clients on the subway where someone can easily look over their shoulder, make client calls from a noisy restaurant, or any number of other locations that you do not consider appropriate for work.

While virtually every firm we encountered provides a computer for each team member, many law firms do not provide smartphones for their team members. We found that more often the team member purchases his or her own smartphone, and the law firm grants the team member the ability to access work e-mail and case files from it.

When team members purchase their own smartphones, there are several concerns that should be considered. First, when team members purchase their smartphones individually, the team members will likely end up with different phones, either iPhones or Androids. Different devices will have different capacities and will require different maintenance and upkeep. Second, since the smartphone is a personal device, you can expect the team member to use the smartphone for personal uses. These uses may create greater security concerns.

Phones

Your firm's phone system is essentially another computer network. The options and features available with modern phone systems seem endless. The first step in choosing a phone system is to determine which features matter to you.

We recommend that you choose a system that gives you the option to have direct lines (even if you do not use them) and individual voicemail boxes. Another useful feature is an app that enables you to disguise your smartphone to make it appear as if you are telephoning from your office phone system.

Printers, Copiers, Scanners, and Paperless Technology

Virtually all law firms still have printers and copiers, but these machines are now used more often as scanners and means of saving documents electronically. Most law firms are going "paperless" because lawyers do not need to physically print documents anymore.

Courts are moving toward paperless systems, as litigants can file pleadings and other documents electronically. Many contracts can be signed electronically through programs such as DocuSign, and some jurisdictions now permit electronic copies of contracts to be filed instead of original documents.

As the prices for printers, copiers, and scanners decrease, most firms can afford to purchase individual devices for each work station. Individual devices tend to be smaller and slower than larger machines. However, the team member will save time if the device is located within arm's reach rather than having to get up and walk to a copy room every time he or she needs to use the device. Also, the individual device offers the holdouts in your office the opportunity to print documents they want to review without interrupting every else's work flow.

Whether or not your firm has individual devices, we recommend that you have at least one larger device. These are typically networked devices that can e-mail any documents that are copied or scanned to any users designated. Also, the speed of larger devices can be very helpful for large copy/scan jobs.

The amount of paper used in the legal industry is too much for us to bother quantifying. Continuing at this pace with paper will cause you to incur needless storage costs, and it will have a detrimental effect on the environment that can be avoided by going paperless.

Software Packages

Now that you have chosen your hardware, you need to choose your software. We recommend that you choose software in the following categories:

1. Contact management software
2. Productivity software
3. Document assembly software
4. Case management software
5. Document management software
6. Security software
7. Billing and accounting software
8. Subscription issues

Do not be overwhelmed by these categories. You will not necessarily have to choose eight different programs. Many of the functions above are consolidated into a few programs. However, as you evaluate these choices, you need to ensure that the features of the software will accomplish what you want.

Contact Management Software

A good marketing strategy utilizes a strong contact management system. These systems make it easy to capture, store, and access basic information for all your contacts, including referral partners, prospective clients, clients, colleagues, and other professionals.

This software replaces the Rolodex of the past. Not only do you have people's contact information but also you can add notes and key data about your contacts in the software. You can sort and find information quickly, and in addition, the programs will analyze the contact information to discern patterns.

Productivity Software Packages

An example of a current productivity software package is Microsoft Office, which has programs for your e-mail, calendar, word processor, and spreadsheets. You will be utilizing these types of programs to communicate with prospective clients, referral partners, your team, and opposing counsel.

When choosing your productivity software package, it is important to consider on which devices it will be installed and whether the programs will be compatible with your team members' smartphones. As team members become more and more mobile, you will get the most bang for your buck if the productivity software is able to travel with your team members.

E-mail

E-mail has replaced the phone as the most common form of communication for attorneys. Not only is it important to choose a reliable e-mail system, but also you should utilize an e-mail system that will save e-mails in a client file.

It should be easy to access all of the e-mail correspondence in a case whenever you open the client's electronic file. Given how frequently you will use e-mail, it is important to investigate the e-mail system to ensure that it will work well with your other software packages.

Calendaring

The days of a desk calendar are over. Everyone should have a good electronic calendaring system that clearly sets forth his or her schedule. The calendaring program should allow you to share your calendar with team members, and it should permit you to grant the authority for certain team members to add meetings to your calendar.

You should be able to invite team members to attend meetings through your calendar, and likewise, they should be able to invite you. When these invitations are issued through the calendaring system, the meeting details should appear on everyone's calendar.

Make sure that the calendaring program has a reminder feature that will work for you. Many programs will issue e-mail or audio alerts or popups to remind you. Proper use of the reminder feature will help you meet deadlines and attend meetings or calls in a timely manner.

A good calendaring system used properly will go a long way toward reducing the risk of an ethical complaint. You can use a calendar to manage your return calls, meetings, and other client interactions to ensure that you are always responding in a timely manner.

Pro Tip: For larger firms, document assembly software can help standardize your documents to ensure that the important points are always covered even if an inexperienced team member is preparing the document.

For smaller firms, document assembly software can make you more efficient. This will save you from searching for a recent example or starting from scratch. However, the advantages of the software may not outweigh the costs of the program itself and the time it takes for you to build the prototype. Smaller firms should look closely at the cost/benefit analysis of these programs.

Voice Recognition Software

Another productivity software to consider is voice recognition software. This software has advanced dramatically over recent years, and high-quality dictation software is available at reasonable costs.

This software requires an initial investment of time to train it to recognize your voice and for you to become familiar with its functions. Once you make this relatively small time investment, dictating your letters, pleadings, contracts, and so on or preparing notes or memorandums of client meetings with voice recognition software can save a tremendous amount of time.

Document Assembly Software

Document assembly software can provide huge time savings when you are preparing documents. Whether you are drafting documents whose only significant difference is the client's specific information or you are inserting background information about your client into several documents, these software packages can streamline this process.

You should not have to spend time creating a document that will not vary much from client to client, such as an engagement letter or cover letter, from scratch. Proper use of document assembly software can make this task an easy one once you draft the first one.

Pro Tip: Every modern law firm should have a document management system that allows all appropriate team members access to client or work files. Electronic files enable multiple team members to work on a file at the same time from multiple locations.

Many practice areas will create multiple documents for the same client, and each of these documents will require the same specific client information. You can use document assembly software to autopopulate your client's information into all of these documents simultaneously rather than having to type the information into each individual document. Not only will this save time, but also it will reduce the chance that you will make an error.

Many document assembly software packages can be integrated with your contact management software to further streamline the process.

We are not big fans of cutting and pasting. You may be able to get away with that for a certain number of cases, but over time, things get missed or some items do not get cut that should have been cut. Not much irritates clients more than receiving a draft document to review and finding another client name in several locations instead of their own name.

Case Management Software

Selecting your case management software is probably one of the most important decisions you will make. Good case management software can lay out the tasks required for each step of the case and integrate with your document assembly system to generate the required documents at each step of the case (e.g., meeting agendas, client documents, and firm documents), provide you with the exact status of a case at a glance, and provide a list of follow-up items and checklists for closing the file.

Document Management Software

Your document management software is your virtual filing cabinet. As law offices become paperless, your document management software will become increasingly important. Your whole organization will use this structure as its home base.

We urge you to take the time to design your document management software to store documents logically and functionally in a way that you and your team members can easily and quickly access whatever you need. The document management system can be organized in many different ways.

For example, you can structure your electronic files to place correspondence, notes, contact information, pleadings, agreements, contracts, and so on in different files. An alternative is to create electronic folders that match the various stages of a case, such as client acquisition/intake, engagement, delivery of services, and closing the file.

Storage

Every firm will have to decide whether to store its data on a server at the office, on an off-site server, or in the cloud. Some attorneys use a combination approach of a server at the office with an off-site backup system.

More and more law firms are becoming comfortable with the concept of storing their data in the cloud. There is research on both sides of the argument, and it comes down to what you are comfortable with for your firm and your clients.

Security Software

Every law firm must have security software. Remember that you are responsible for maintaining your client's confidences. Typical security software includes programs designed to thwart viruses, malware, and ransomware.

If your team members are going to access your computer systems remotely, they should do so through VPN. Furthermore, everyone should be required to use two-factor authorization to gain remote access to the network.

Billing and Accounting Software

Billing software should be user friendly and make sense to you and your team. The last thing you want to spend time doing is keeping track of your time. Your billing program should make it very easy for you to enter time for each client, list the tasks you performed, and track the time you spent on each task.

There are several programs that now integrate billing and accounting programs. These make it very easy to track time, issue bills, and transfer funds from your retainer account to your operating account.

We realize that very few attorneys enjoy the tasks associated with billing and accounting. For this reason, it is even more critical that the billing and accounting software be user friendly. The fewer challenges you and your team face when performing these tasks, the more likely that they will get done and done well (see Chapter 13 regarding billing).

Subscription Issues

There are various cost structures for software programs. Some programs will require you to purchase the program at the outset and to purchase a new version when you want an update.

It is becoming more common for programs to require ongoing subscription fees per user. One advantage of the subscription fees is that these programs may automatically update as part of the fee package.

Make sure to ask the scope of the subscription and if there are any termination fees associated with the subscription. Then make sure to incorporate these fees into your budget projections, as they can rise quickly if not monitored properly.

Help Choosing the Right Technology

This book just touches the tip of the iceberg when it comes to technology options and decisions. We recommend utilizing consultants to help you choose the right technology for your firm. Technology is one of the most important investments you will make.

For more information about technology issues in the legal field, we recommend that you read the Solo and Small Firm Legal Technology Guides written by Sharon Nelson, John Simek, and Michael Maschke. These books provide clear and practical advice for attorneys making technology decisions for their firms.

Technology Section of Your Business Plan

We anticipate that your answers to the questions below will serve as an outline for the technology section of your business plan. These answers will form the foundation for how your firm will decide what technology it will use and why.

1. What technology does your firm need?
    a. To provide your products
    b. To implement your systems
2. Who is going to deal with your technology?
    a. Installation
    b. Maintenance
    c. Updates
3. Will the technology provide convenience?
    a. For your clients
    b. For your team members
4. How will you secure your files and client confidential information?
5. How will you use technology to communicate with your clients?
    a. Will clients have remote access to their files?

16

Systems: What Systems Do You Need?

Pro Tip: Yes, it's broken record time: WRITE down your systems! While it takes a great deal of time to write down the systems the first time you do it, you will save time every single time afterward.

Reliable business systems enhance the chances of producing predictable results. Leanmethods.com has a great definition of a business system: "A business system is designed to connect all of an organization's intricate parts and interrelated steps to work together for the achievement of the business strategy."

Successful lawyers have successful systems behind the scenes that allow them to run their firms efficiently and to provide clients with what they need, when they need it, and in a timely fashion.

From our perspective, your systems are the framework that forms the foundational structures that support your firm. After you put your systems in place, you can develop procedures to streamline the individual steps in each system.

Creating Your Systems

The first step in creating a system is to take a step back to determine the result you are aiming to achieve. Every system should be designed to enable your team to reach your ultimate goal.

Once you know what the end goal is, you can determine how you will get there. It is not enough to identify the end goal and hope that you will be able to achieve it. You will need to develop the steps you and your team members will take to reach your goal.

As we have emphasized throughout this book, we strongly encourage you to put your systems and each step in your system in writing. We realize that writing down your steps will require longer hours up front when you are building your systems. This time spent will be well worth it when your systems allow you to exponentially leverage your time in the future.

Your systems will not be reliable if they cannot be repeated. Writing down the system will greatly increase the likelihood that your team members will follow the steps you outline and achieve the results you are seeking. The goal is to organize the steps within your system in such a way that the delivery of your services to the client and the execution of your projects are efficient and consistent.

Pro Tip: Solo practitioners should establish systems. The creation of a system will compel you to consider different options and choose the best one. Having a system will allow you to repeat the steps instead of having to reteach yourself how to do a task each time.

As an alternative to creating your own system, you can utilize an established, proven system. There are collaborative networks in specific legal areas that have mentors and systems already in place. For example, the National Network of Estate Planning Attorneys™ is a collaboration of estate planning attorneys who having specific training programs, established processes, case management systems, and mentors to assist those entering the field.

Rather than creating the wheel yourself, you can leverage the resources of network for a membership fee. However, you still have to put in the work of customizing the steps and tasks to fit your particular practice.

Purpose of Systems

Some attorneys keep the process to themselves so that only they know all the steps. These attorneys are missing the point. Communicating your system to your team will enable you to delegate tasks efficiently. This is how you move from wearing many hats to wearing only the hat(s) that you were made to wear and enjoy wearing!

Your systems should be designed to show your team how you want tasks accomplished and, more importantly, lead them to your ultimate goal. If your team follows the systems you put in place, the outcomes should not only be predictable but also be outcomes that you want.

Systems provide a foundation for communicating key information to your team. The stronger the communication, the higher the likelihood of a successful practice.

If you do not have systems in place, you run the risk that your team will start from scratch each time. This approach will likely make each project take longer. In addition, each time you start over, your team members may handle the project differently, leading to different results.

Measuring the Effectiveness

Developing your systems is only the first step. The next step is measuring their effectiveness. Once you put your systems in place, they should be measured in two fashions: (1) Is your team following the standards you set forth in your system? (2) Is the system still effective?

Team Performance

Documenting your process and communicating it to your team establishes a baseline of what you expect. You must follow up with your team members to determine if they are meeting those expectations.

If they are not meeting them, you have to investigate why the lapses are occurring. The most common cause of implementation failures is poor communication by a team leader to the rest of the team. Often, the team leader will not explain either how the specific task needs to be done and/or what the end goal is. You need to be certain that your team members understand what you want them to do.

Other reasons that systems fail include an inability of the team member to perform the task you have assigned or a general lack of capacity. When you develop a system and assign tasks, you must be realistic about what your team members can competently do.

Pro Tip: If something is not being performed in accordance with your expectations, address it immediately. Do not ignore or delay facing the issue. You can address the issue with one-on-one meeting(s) or regular team meetings to keep the project on track. Being proactive will increase the likelihood of success and efficiency.

We recommend developing systems first and then finding team members who can perform the tasks you want to accomplish. If you do not develop your system to fit the skills of your team members, you will likely end up with a system that does not lead to the goal you truly want to achieve.

Regardless of whether your system is the best in the world, it will not be effective if your team does not have the capacity to execute it. You must be prepared to fully staff the positions and roles you envision in your system, or you need to redesign your system.

System Effectiveness

We encourage you to quantify the effectiveness of your systems. Measuring the effectiveness of a system or reviewing key business indicators is a basic function of a chief operating officer. Although this statement may seem obvious, many attorneys fail to realize that they are the chief operating officer of their firm. If you are in this role, you need to take an intentional step back from working on your legal matters to work on your business.

There are always ways to measure the effectiveness of a system. These measures could include any of the following: how much time it takes to finish a project, how much new business resulted, and how happy your clients were with your work.

Some measures can be performed with the data you already have. For example, you can measure how many hours it takes to perform a specific legal project or how many months/years it takes to conclude a legal matter.

You may need to seek information to determine the effectiveness of other measures. When it comes to client or team satisfaction levels and other intangible measures, you will need to gather information either from interviews or surveys to obtain reliable feedback.

Attorneys who rely on their instincts alone as to whether a system is working well often end up with systems that work but inefficiently. Your instincts (and your clients and team members) will let you know if your system is a total failure, but your instincts will not be able to tell you if you are missing ways to save time or money.

Getting Feedback on Your Systems

You should review your systems regularly to determine what is working, what is not working, and what adjustments are necessary. We encourage you to get input from internal and external sources.

Internal Feedback

Your team will provide the internal feedback. If you want meaningful feedback, you must create a safe environment for your team to provide candid feedback.

If your team members do not feel comfortable being honest with you, they will comment only on the portions of the system that are working well. While this feedback is valuable, it is incomplete.

Pro Tip: If you do not believe you can obtain meaningful feedback internally due to the size of your firm, we recommend discussing your systems with members of other firms to get their feedback. Even though they do not work in your firm, they can provide an inside perspective that you cannot get from a client or vendor.

No system is perfect, and all systems can be improved. If your team does not feel they can tell you when a system is not working or how it can be improved, their feedback will not be very valuable.

Pro Tip: Do not be scared to get feedback even if you think that it might be negative. All feedback can be helpful. Even an unhappy client will appreciate that you value his or her input enough to ask for it.

In a best-case scenario, your team members will feel comfortable coming to you whenever they see something that needs to be changed. Even in the best-case scenario, many team members will not take the initiative to come to you.

For this reason, you should establish specific times throughout the year when you solicit feedback. In effect, you want your team members to review your systems and offer suggestions.

The more involved your team members are in the discussion and development of your systems, the more likely they are to buy into them. Communication with your team is critical in achieving smooth systems (see Chapter 5 regarding reviews).

External Feedback

Most of your external feedback regarding your legal work and the customer-facing aspects of your firm will come from clients and former clients. While some clients will volunteer feedback both good and bad, many others will keep their thoughts to themselves.

The clients who volunteer their thoughts are a gift that you should not ignore. These people are providing you with valuable information regarding your systems. Positive feedback confirms that you have created a good system.

Negative feedback cannot be ignored. Even if you think that the feedback came from an irrational client, you need to investigate. Sticking your head in the sand and hoping that the issue will fix itself is not a good strategy. Take advantage of the feedback to determine if your system was not properly implemented on that occasion or if there is a fundamental problem with the system.

We understand that reliving a negative result or client interaction is not an enjoyable experience. However, analyzing how you reached a poor result or interaction will likely provide you with more valuable information than analyzing positive results or interactions.

Most clients do not volunteer their feedback. In order to reach these clients, we suggest that you conduct a closing interview or ask them to respond to a survey. Ask them what went well, what did not go so well, and what should be improved.

One way to get a broader sample size for comments is to create a Client Advisory Board consisting of a sample set of your clients. When creating a Client Advisory Board, you must be careful to put together a group that is representative of your clients as a whole.

The advantage of a Client Advisory Board that meets a couple of times a year is that you will receive detailed feedback from those clients. The possible disadvantage is that you will be receiving feedback from a limited number of clients, and you may be missing important feedback from other clients.

With regard to your operating systems that clients may not be able to observe clearly, you can obtain external feedback from mentors or coaches. You can gain a great deal of information by bouncing ideas off someone who is not directly involved in your business.

Mentors or coaches can give you some tips that help you create or improve your systems. Getting a fresh perspective can lead to innovative approaches and strategies that may not be apparent to you.

As we gain more experience in our field, it becomes easier and easier to do what we see other firms doing. A mentor or coach can be a great way to break that cycle and broaden your options.

Adjusting Your Systems

You should always strive to improve your systems. No system is perfect, and there is always room for improvement.

That being said, adjustments to your systems should not be done without a good reason. Too much change or too many changes without an underlying rationale will create confusion and reduce the confidence your team and anyone who interacts with your system has.

Whenever possible, we recommend making small changes on a regular basis rather than overhauling the entire system. Small changes are much easier to implement, and your team members are far more likely to buy into them.

As much as we encourage you to consider all the feedback you receive, we recommend that you resist the urge to make changes simply because one client is unhappy. Make sure that there is a good basis for any adjustment rather than a knee-jerk reaction to something you heard.

Implementing Your Systems

Once you have created and written down your system, it is time to train your team. It is astounding to us the number of times we have seen attorneys draft a memo on their new system, e-mail it to their team, and then complain that the system did not work. The best systems are the ones in which you and your team share the same vision. This does not happen organically. You will have to take the time to explain the purpose of the system and why it is an effective approach.

The training sessions should make the ultimate goals clear, and they should explain why a particular approach to each task was chosen. Of course, the training should also teach the team members how to accomplish the tasks they will be responsible for performing.

Certainly, there are attorneys and business owners who feel as if there is no need to explain why they are doing something. Their philosophy is that their team members should do whatever they are told as long as they are receiving a paycheck.

This approach is unlikely to elicit the best performance. Furthermore, team members who do not understand why a system is being used will not be able to provide useful feedback as to how the system can be improved even if they wanted to do so.

Team members who understand the "why" are far more likely to "buy in" and feel invested in the outcome. Those team members will perform at a higher level and will actively participate in reviews designed to determine how the system can be improved.

Systems Section of Your Business Plan

We anticipate that your answers to the questions below will serve as an outline for the systems section of your business plan. These answers will form the foundation for determining what systems your firm will have and how they will be implemented.

1. What systems will your firm have?
    a. Marketing
    b. Client workflow
    c. Billing
    d. Client relations
    e. Data protection
    f. Human resources—training
    g. Other systems designed specifically for your firm
2. Who will create the systems?
3. How will you measure the success of the systems?
    a. Internal feedback
    b. External feedback

4. System updates
   a. Who will be responsible for updating the system?
   b. How often will the system be updated?
5. How will the systems be integrated into your firm?
   a. Will your partners approve each system development or update?
   b. How will you train your team members on the systems?

17

Procedures: Developing Procedures for Your Firm

Establishing consistent procedures will help you implement your firm's core values. We have found that certain tasks such as communicating with clients, answering the telephone, and many others as set forth below are fundamental to all law firms, and having a reliable system for these will keep your firm on track and out of trouble.

Also, in the never-ending pursuit of efficiency, procedures will enable your team members to accomplish tasks in a more efficient manner. Efficiency leads to more satisfied clients, happier team members, and higher profits.

Pro Tip: Developing procedures in solo and small firms is just as important as developing them in larger firms. Having established procedures that you can repeat without having to start from scratch is a huge time saver. Once you have established the procedure, you can focus your time and energy on other matters (e.g., billable work).

We strongly recommend that you determine what procedures your firm needs. When making this determination, there are several factors to consider including, but not necessarily limited to, the following: (1) importance of the task, (2) number of team members who will be involved in completing the task, and (3) how often the task will be repeated.

Importance of the Task

The more important the task is to you, the more likely you should have procedures in place to dictate how it will be done. In a perfect world, your firm will always work cohesively toward your mission.

As we have discussed throughout this book, it is critical that each team member understands your mission. However, even if the team member understands the mission, he or she may not know how to achieve it without guidance. When you provide guidance in the form of a procedure, the team member is far more likely to get close to your vision of the mission.

Number of Team Members Involved

The more team members who will be involved in completing a project, the greater the need for a procedure. Think about this as if you were operating a factory production line. No factory production line lets each team member freelance how his or her aspect of the production will be completed. Each team member follows specific instructions to ensure that the task is done the same way each time.

All production lines are far more efficient when the first person in line completes his or her task in the same manner each time. This enables the next person in line to start in the same place each time and to approach his or her task in the same way each time.

If your team member does a repetitive task differently each time, there will be a greater variance in the quality of the final product. The variance increases exponentially based on the number of people involved in completing the project. Even if each person is only off target by a small margin, by the time you reach the end of the production line, the product could look very different from your plans.

Most administrative tasks that your law firm needs to accomplish can be done in a factory line fashion. Even some aspects of legal services can be done in a factory line without losing the personal touch and/or turning you into the provider of a commodity instead of a legal counselor.

Repetition

The more often your team members have to do the same task, the greater the value a procedure will provide. The old adage that there is no need to reinvent the wheel each time applies here.

The investment of time and energy to develop a procedure for a repetitive task will pay huge dividends. Furthermore, a good procedure will help your team members do the task well and also quickly.

Training

Well-developed procedures will significantly reduce the time you will spend training new team members. Although we expect you to take the time to teach all of the procedures to your new team members, they are not likely to retain everything you say. Having written procedures that the new team members can refer to will be invaluable in the training process and a huge time saver for the team member primarily responsible for the new team member's training.

Creating Procedures

Every firm should have some procedures in place on day one. There are certain tasks that you know are important, will involve multiple team members (or at least involve multiples roles even if they are all performed by one person when you first open), and will be repetitive.

Before you open your doors, take the time to sit down and map out how you want these tasks to be handled. The last thing you want to do when your first potential client calls in is to fumble through answering the call or performing the conflict check.

Once you are up and running, we encourage you to write out procedures for each repetitive task you encounter regardless of how small or insignificant it seems. We realize that this will be time consuming, but that investment of time and effort will be worth it in the long run.

Rather than having to figure out how to do a task every time it comes up, you can point to your procedures manual. This can be an incredible time saver for tasks that recur weekly or monthly—essentially long enough between times to forget how it was done the last time.

Procedures for those tasks that are done more frequently (e.g., daily or even hourly) can also provide significant savings particularly when it comes to training new team members. While it may not seem like much, learning to scan and save client documents in your system (in the right place!) may be stressful and frightening to a new team member. Being able to point him or her to a procedures manual that serves as a reference can minimize some of this stress, reduce the learning curve, and minimize the time that another team member will have to spend training the new team member. In addition, it will greatly increase the odds that all your team members scan and save client documents in the same manner. If most but not all team members use your document management system/procedures, you are inviting a catastrophe.

Pro Tip: We suggest that you consider developing short how-to videos similar to the do-it-yourself videos you can find regularly on social media sites to explain individual procedures. Some team members will have an easier time learning your procedure if it is presented in a video format.

Not only will these manuals help to ensure that your standards are being met, but also they can be used in human resource issues. To the extent that a team member does not understand why he or she is being disciplined, you can point to any discrepancies between the team member's performance and the procedure manual.

Of course, your procedure manual should be updated regularly. There will be times when you want to change the way a task is done, whether because of new technology or new firm strategies, or because someone has discovered a more efficient method to accomplish the task.

Availability of Procedure Manual

The procedure manual should be available to every team member and easily accessible electronically so it can be accessed remotely. There are no state secrets in the procedure manual. While there may be procedures as to how sensitive and/or confidential client or firm information should be handled, the procedure manual should not contain any private information.

Depending on the size of your procedure manual, it may make sense to break it into segments so that team members can easily find the particular procedures they use most often. However, there is no reason that a team member should not be able to see the procedures that other team members use. There will be times when seeing the big picture (i.e., seeing what other team members are doing) will cause the team member to better understand why it is more efficient in the long run for the team member to perform his or her task pursuant to the procedure.

Who Creates the Procedures?

All team members should have input into the procedures. The team members who actually perform the tasks will be in the best position to know what will really work as opposed to what looks good on paper.

Although everyone should have input into the procedures, not everyone should have a say in what the end product should look like. As the owner, you should retain control over what the end product will be and its quality level.

Common Procedures

From our perspective, every firm should have procedures for the following tasks:

1. Answering the phone
2. Transferring calls to team members or voicemail
3. Greeting clients
4. E-mail protocols and signatures
5. Running a conflict check
6. Retainer agreements
7. Scheduling/calendaring
8. Opening and closing files
9. Copying and scanning documents
10. Saving documents (how they will be titled and where they will be saved)
11. Organizing case files and client documents
12. Delivery of correspondence by e-mail, mail, or hand delivery
13. Delivery of pleadings or other filings to court
14. Recording billable time
15. Securing your computer (e.g., periodic password updates, powering off, etc.)
16. Securing correspondence outside the firm
17. Office cleaning
18. Reserving conference rooms or other common areas
19. Supplies (requests and orders)
20. Service calls
21. Requesting and paying filing or other case-related fees
22. Locking and unlocking the office

This is not an exhaustive list. Furthermore, every firm should develop additional procedures that are tailored to its specific needs.

Following are samples of a few of the common procedures we identified. We anticipate that you will adjust these procedures to match your firm's goals and objectives and to consider what is feasible for your firm given its resources.

Answering the Phone Protocol

Always answer calls with *"Good Morning/Good Afternoon, [firm name], how may I help you?"*

If the caller asks to speak with a specific firm team member, reply with *"Let me see if [he or she] is available. May I ask who is calling please?"* This will enable the team member to determine whether the call should be taken.

If the team member is not available, reply with *"I am sorry. [Mr. or Mrs. firm team member] is unavailable [or out of the office] at this time. Would you like to leave a message in [his or her] voicemail?"* Whether the caller leaves a voicemail message or not, get his or her name and send the team member an e-mail with the caller's name (and message). If you take a message, be certain to get a return telephone number even if the caller states that the team member already has the number.

Always get the **name** and **telephone number** for the caller, even if you think that we have the number, if he or she doesn't want to leave a voicemail. Write down **all** messages no matter how silly/trivial they seem to be.

When the [firm] team member is unavailable, **always** e-mail the team member with the name and number of the caller even if the caller does not want to leave a message, and if the caller leaves a voicemail message, it should be noted in the e-mail.

If the caller wants to leave a message with you, make the subject line of your e-mail: **TM – [Caller's Name], [Phone #]**. Then put the message in the body.

Example: To: Team Member Subject: TM – Joe Smith, 703-111-2222

If the caller wants to go to voicemail, put him or her through to the correct voicemail box and make the subject line of your e-mail: **VM – [Caller's Name]**. Nothing needs to go in the body of the e-mail for a voicemail message unless there is additional information to pass along.

Example: To: Team Member Subject: VM – Joe Smith

If someone calls in while you are on the other line, ask the current caller to hold one moment, take the other call, and immediately ask the other caller to hold. Finish the original call and then take the call on hold.

It is very important that we relay telephone messages, voicemail notification e-mails, and package delivery e-mails right away.

Greeting Clients

1. Greet clients immediately.
2. If you are on the phone, please finish the call or ask the person to hold.
3. Offer a drink (water, soda, coffee—10 flavors, tea—3 flavors) to anyone who comes into the office. If soda, ask if he or she would like soda in the can or in a glass. Bottled water is for clients only. If the visitor would like coffee or tea, ask if he or she would like cream or sugar. Coffee or tea is served in the plain black coffee cups.

4. Ask the client to have a seat and let the appropriate team member know *immediately* that the client is waiting.
5. If the team member is on the phone when client arrives:
    a. Pass him or her a note stating that the client (name included) has arrived.
    b. If the team member's door is closed, please send the team member an e-mail.
    c. If you still do not hear anything back from the team member, knock on the door or have someone else knock on the door.
    d. Please repeat steps above until you can ensure the team member knows of the client arrival.
    e. If you are unable to do this because you are busy, ask another team member to do steps a, b, or c.
6. Check the Microsoft Outlook Calendar to see which conference room will be used for the meeting.
7. Ask the team member if he or she would like you to put the client in a conference room. Either way, please make sure the table is clean and the chairs are straight in the conference room prior to its use.

Potential New Clients

Please note that the procedure set forth below is for a family law firm. The information sought from Potential New Clients and the information necessary to run a conflict check will vary greatly from practice area to practice area.

When people call in, you can usually tell if they are a Potential New Client because they will say things like, "My friend told me to call . . . " or "I was referred by . . . " or something along those lines. You might get a pushy person who says, for example, "I need to talk to Team Member X right now" and doesn't (or won't) give you any details.

Before you know if you can put someone through to an attorney, you need to be sure there is no conflict for the firm. In that case, say, "Can I get your name?" If the name is not familiar and you are not sure if the caller is a client or what the relationship to the firm might be, ask, "Have you spoken with Team Member X before?"

If the caller says no, go straight into gathering Potential New Client information for a conflicts check (the sheet will be at the front desk on a clipboard).

If anyone objects to giving this information to someone other than the attorney, explain that you need to do a quick conflict check to be sure no one in the firm has had anything to do with any of the parties involved in the matter. Explain that it is standard practice for all law firms and will only take a moment. Most people are amenable to this (and if they are not, that is a red flag).

General Information on Potential New Clients:

1. We do not offer free consultations.
2. Initial consultations are billed at the attorney's hourly rate (see bottom of Potential New Client Intake Sheet).

3. Team Member X schedules new client appointments.
4. Potential New Clients are not billed for the initial telephone conversation with the attorney.

Our number one goal is to connect the client with an attorney while he or she is on the line.

If the caller indicates that he or she is a Potential New Client, fill out the Potential New Client Intake Sheet completely. See Attached Potential New Client Intake Sheet.

Standard Conversation:

OK, before I connect you with Mr. or Ms. Attorney, I need to get a little bit of information from you so that we may perform a conflict check. This is simply to verify that no one here at the firm knows anything about the matter for which you are calling.

Are you able to provide that information now?

If no:

Would you prefer that we send you a link to provide this information online OR is there a better time to call you back?

If yes:

Can I please get your full name?

May I have your spouse's full name?

[Please get a maiden name for a female party.]

Can I get the best number to reach you?

Is that a cell, home, or work number?

May we leave a message at that number?

Is there an e-mail address that the attorney can use to contact you?

May I ask how you were referred?

I'm going to ask a few questions just so I can give the attorney a little bit of information before [he or she] speaks with you.

What county do you live in?

Have there been any court filings, or have there been any court dates set?

How many children (ages)?

Do you know if your spouse or other party has an attorney?

OK, I am going to place you on a very brief hold while I run a conflict check. I will be right back with you.

Once you have completed the Potential New Client Intake Sheet, place the Potential New Client on hold and ask the requested attorney if he or she is available for a Potential New Client phone call.

If the attorney is available, tell the attorney it will be a few minutes while we run the conflict check.

RUN CONFLICT CHECK

Post-Conflict Check Conversation

Conflict: YES

If there is a conflict, then:

I note there is a conflict in our system, so unfortunately our firm will be unable to assist you. If you would like, I can call you back with referrals to other attorneys in the area.
If the client asks why there is a conflict, then:
I am not permitted to provide the reason other than to note that there is a conflict. Would you like me to provide you with a referral?
Conflict: NO
If the attorney is AVAILABLE:
Mr./Ms. [attorney] is available, and I am going to connect you for a brief conversation with him/her. Before I do, I want to inform you that you will not be billed for this brief conversation, but he/she may recommend that you come in for a consultation. That consultation is billed at his/her hourly rate, which is $______. He/she can discuss the specifics of that consultation with you. You'll be in good hands with Mr./Ms. [attorney].
If the attorney is UNAVAILABLE:
"Specific Attorney"
Mr./Ms. [Attorney] is out today/this morning/afternoon. I will make sure to let him/her know that you called and that you are waiting to hear from him/her. However, if you would like, I can also check to see if another attorney in the firm can speak with you now.

Implementing Procedures

Having a procedure is a very strong first step, but it is only the first step. You have to implement the procedures and follow them.

The procedures will need to be explained to each team member to ensure that he or she understands them and "buys in" to using them. Regardless of how great your procedure is on paper, it will not be worth much if each team member is executing the procedure differently.

Team members are far more likely to implement the procedures in the manner you intended if what you want them to do is clearly defined and they understand why you want it done a certain way. We cannot emphasize enough how important it is for your team members to understand the "why."

The most common reason procedures get sidetracked is that a team member unilaterally decides to do his or her task differently than you requested. Although you could argue that the team member should not deviate from the instructions, you do want to encourage your team members to look for more efficient ways to accomplish their tasks.

The scenario in which a team member has a good intention—that is, the team member wants to find a better or faster way to do the task—will often end in frustration and aggravation for all involved if the team member does not understand why the task needs to be done a certain way. While the team member may be able to do the individual task faster, the next team member in line will not be able to finish his or her task nearly as quickly. If the initial team member understands why you want the task done a certain way, the team member will only look for shortcuts that will not put the next team member at a disadvantage.

We encourage you to schedule regular procedure refreshers. These refreshers can be used to remind team members of how you want the procedure to be performed. At the same time, this can be an opportunity for team members to discuss ideas to improve the procedure. The bottom line is that periodic reviews of the procedures will lead to greater efficiency and better quality control.

For more information about procedures, we suggest that you read the Law Office Policy & Procedures Manual series from the American Bar Association.

Procedure Section of Your Business Plan

We anticipate that your answers to the questions below will serve as an outline for the procedure section of your business plan. These answers will form the foundation for determining what procedures your firm will have and how they will be created.

1. What procedures does your firm need?
    a. Phone scripts
    b. Filing procedures
        i.Physical files
        ii.Electronic files
    c. Storage space
    d. Customer relationship management system
    e. Emergency procedures
2. Who will create the procedures?
3. Procedure updates
    a. Who will update the procedures?
    b. How often will they be updated?
4. How and when will procedures be delivered to team members?

See the Appendix of this book for a sample Training Guide and Procedure that you can customize for your firm's needs.

18

Office Environment: What Does Your Office Look Like and How Does It Operate?

The office environment sets the stage for your clients and your employees. The first decision you need to make about your office is whether your office environment will be designed to attract clients and/or to attract and retain employees. While your goal may be to balance the interests of both constituencies, costs and other considerations often lead to most firms prioritizing one over the other.

Location

The office location itself will send a message to prospective clients who you anticipate will meet with your team members in person. For those firms who will interact primarily with their clients remotely, the office location will matter much more to your team members, assuming that they are not working remotely.

Different location characteristics will appeal to different sets of clients. This is why you need to investigate what will be most attractive to your prospective clients. Generally, people are most comfortable with environments that are similar to their own environments.

When the general counsel for a large corporation that is housed in a downtown skyscraper goes looking for a law firm to represent the corporation in an upcoming litigation matter, most general counsels will feel far more comfortable in another downtown skyscraper office building than in an industrial park in the outer suburbs. It is not an accident that white-collar law firms looking to represent corporate clients have offices in downtown business districts where corporate headquarters and decision makers have their offices.

Prospective clients who are looking for personal legal services may prefer to meet with someone closer to where they live or at an office that is easy to reach. Attorneys who represent individuals instead of businesses may find it easier to attract clients if their offices are located in the suburbs or near transportation hubs such as subway stations or highway interchanges.

On the other end of the spectrum, there are many firms whose clients will rarely, if ever, visit the firm offices. There is no reason to purchase office space intended to impress these clients, and therefore, those firms should focus on what will appeal to their team members. These firms are often located in places that are either easy to reach or in locations that offer amenities that their team members will appreciate. These firms can arrange for meeting spaces that are convenient for their clients on those rare occasions when they need to meet in person.

The location choice for many firms will not require them to choose between pleasing only clients or team members. On some level everyone appreciates an office that is easy and convenient to reach or is in a location they will have to go to anyway. For example, criminal defendants often need to make multiple trips to the courthouse. When their attorney's office is located nearby, they can make the most of their trip by visiting their attorney at the same time. In addition, the proximity to the courthouse makes life more convenient for the attorneys who make frequent appearances in court.

Office Quality and Style

Within a particular area, your firm is likely to have a wide variety of building choices and office styles. Office buildings are typically rated A, B, or C. These ratings can provide you with a basic starting point to evaluate your options. The ratings will place buildings in general categories based on their appearance, building quality, and amenities. Of course, the rental rates correspond to the rating level, with A-rated buildings being the most expensive.

Clients and team members know that fancy buildings with restaurants, gyms, and concierges are more expensive than other options. Will your clients be impressed that you can afford such space, or will they fear that they are paying for your office space rather than your legal expertise? Do your team members want a fancy office with lots of amenities or only a functional space where they can work? If you rent a high-end space, will your team members fear that they are not getting paid as much because the firm's resources are going to pay rent? These are critical questions you need to answer when you are choosing your building.

Pro Tip: Solo practitioners must remember that they are not the only people that must be happy with the office quality and style. The office must be designed with clients and other guests in mind.

There is no question that the neighborhood and building set the stage and give everyone the first impression of the firm, but the firm's office itself is even more important. Clients and team members recognize that factors outside of the firm's control may play a significant role in the neighborhood or building where the office is located, but the firm has almost complete control over the appearance and environment within its own office. This is where your firm can truly express itself and let everyone know who you are.

Clients' Perspective of Your Office

There is no detail that is too small to research and analyze. Let's start by looking at the office from your clients' perspective. The ease or difficulty of the commute to reach your office can play an enormous role in your clients' disposition when they come for a meeting.

Accessibility

If your clients have driven to your office, the ability to park somewhere convenient can have as much of an impact on their disposition as the commute. There is not much that is more frustrating than reaching your destination and then having to circle the block for 20 minutes until a parking space opens up. If you need a reserved parking space, your clients probably need one as well. In addition, even though the parking may not technically be your responsibility, we believe that you have a duty to your clients and team members to ensure that they are parking somewhere that offers reasonable safety features, such as an attendant and good lighting.

Once the clients arrive at the office, it must be accessible for all. You must ensure that your office is compliant with the Americans with Disabilities Act. Furthermore, if your clients tend to be elderly or disabled, your office needs to be designed to make these individuals comfortable. There must be ramps, elevators, guardrails, and so on to make your office easily accessible.

Entering Your Office

Now that your clients have arrived, parked, and reached the door to your office, will the door to your office allow them to see inside or will the clients have to open the door to see what they are getting themselves into? Doors that allow your clients to see into the office before they enter are welcoming. The clients can see where they are going, and there is an impression of transparency as you have nothing to hide.

When clients enter an office through an opaque door, they have no idea what to expect until they are already inside and the impression is that they will not be able to find out what is going on unless they investigate for themselves. For anxious clients, this may add to their anxiety.

The door plays an important role in your office security. Glass doors that allow your team members to see who is approaching or entering the office will give your team members a chance to prepare themselves to address whoever is approaching. For those practice areas in which you may be dealing with clients who may not be at their best or mentally unstable, such as divorce or criminal defense, the style of the door should be given extra consideration.

Pro Tip: Your client forms a first impression of your office long before he or she meets the attorney. The more positive that first impression is, the more likely that client relationship will get off on the right foot.

Many firms are moving to locked doors that can be opened only by a buzzer or remote system after the team member verifies that it is safe to open the door. While a locked door provides the highest level of security to your team members, it is the least welcoming approach for your prospective clients.

Lobby/Reception Area

After your clients open the door and walk into your office, they will enter the one part of your office that they will see every single time they visit it. Some firms skimp on the lobby because the firm decision makers do not spend nearly as much time in the lobby, if any, compared to the time they spend in their offices. However, the lobby plays a critical role in your clients' first impression of the office. We recommend allocating resources to making this a comfortable, efficient, and welcoming space.

This does not mean that you must have the most opulent lobby. You must balance the costs of allocating space for the lobby and money for its furnishings against other needs of the firm. We have seen firms whose lobby areas range from huge and opulent areas with plush couches to small spaces that feel like you are standing at a fast food counter waiting for your number to be called.

When deciding what your lobby will look like, you should consider how long your clients are likely to be waiting. Perhaps it is not intuitive, but we believe that the firm's philosophy regarding how long clients will wait before being met by the team member they are scheduled to see is an important part of the office environment. It certainly sends a signal to your clients as to how much of a priority they are to you.

Offices where clients have to wait for their appointments to begin will feel very different than ones in which the clients go almost immediately from the door to their meeting. When you walk into an office where clients are required to wait, it can feel as if there is a bottleneck in the lobby area. Not only will those waiting clients get the impression that the team member values his or her time more than the clients' time, but also it will prompt clients to wonder where they fit in the firm's pecking order.

Clients who are moved quickly from the office door to their meeting space will not question their importance to the firm. Those clients will feel as if they are the firm's top priority during their scheduled time.

As technology takes over many firms, firms are moving away from traditional receptionists who sit at a desk waiting to greet the next client. Many firms are allowing clients to enter an unstaffed lobby and have either a doorbell or a bell that the clients ring to notify someone they are present. This approach saves money but also tells the clients that client service is not your top priority.

Even those firms who are no longer staffing the waiting area with a team member typically have a receptionist desk. These desks tend to fall into one of two general categories. The first is a normal office desk, and the second is a raised desk that looks like a battle station that the team member is using to defend his or her territory. The battle station can be intimidating, and certainly will give some clients the feeling that they must conquer the greeting team member to advance into the office. The more standard office desk is usually lower and does not require a seated person to look up at the team member behind it.

The desk can symbolize your firm's thoughts about the attorney-client relationship. Desks that put the clients on the same level as your team members can imply that your firm members and the clients are on equal footing and that you are teammates or partners in the legal matter. Firms that literally look down at their clients may give the impression that the lawyer is the most important person in the relationship and that the clients should be subservient to the attorney. Be aware of the subtle and subconscious signals your firm is sending to your clients.

While clients are sitting in the lobby area, you have complete control over what they see and hear. This is the perfect opportunity to put promotional materials about the firm or its team members in the clients' line of sight. These promotional materials can include brochures that explain what the firm does, articles written by your team members, and awards or plaques recognizing your firm's accomplishments. Seeing these accomplishments will remind your clients that they made a good choice in selecting your firm. Within reason, do not pass up opportunities to reinforce your clients' positive thoughts about your firm.

In addition to materials regarding your firm, there should be other options such as noncontroversial magazines or newspapers. Some firms have opted for televisions. If you are going to have a television in the lobby, you need to ensure that it is not so loud that it distracts team members or clients who are not watching and that the content is something that will not offend anyone.

You should carefully consider what type of chairs you will have in the lobby. For most firms, the chair choice will be more about style than substance. However, certain types of firms need to be certain that their chairs are suitable for the majority of their clients. For example, trusts and estates firms whose clients are likely to be older and may have more disabilities will need chairs that are easy to get in and out of.

Greeting Your Clients

When your clients walks into the lobby, will there be a person there to greet them? An empty reception desk with a bell for the clients to ring for service screams that your firm has streamlined its process to the point that it will provide only what is absolutely necessary. Some clients will interpret this to mean that your focus is only on what truly matters in the legal case, while others will see this as a sign that you provide only the bare minimum.

The greeting your team member provides to your clients should be choreographed. Ideally, your team member should strive to accomplish three things: (1) provide the clients a warm welcome, (2) make the clients comfortable, and (3) steer the clients to the person they are scheduled to meet.

Efficient offices will have a system in place that will let the receptionist know which clients are scheduled to visit the office so they can be greeted by name (see Chapter 17 regarding procedures). This simple pleasantry can go a long way toward making the clients feel valued. Your team member can make the clients feel comfortable by offering them a drink and ensuring that they have somewhere to sit while they wait. Once the clients are situated, the team member should promptly notify whoever the clients are scheduled to meet. These simple and inexpensive steps are very effective ways to make your clients feel valued and important.

Most clients will have to wait a few minutes in even the most efficient offices that strive to connect clients with the person they are scheduled to meet as quickly as possible. What will they do while they wait, and what will they see and hear during that time? Your firm should have a system in place to guide your clients through this interaction.

After the clients have been welcomed and the person the clients are meeting has been notified, the next step is to ensure that the clients are comfortable. At a minimum, there should be somewhere for the clients to sit and relax.

Pro Tip: Use your office décor to create an image for your guests. Your guests are developing a perception in their mind as they look around your office whether you want them to or not. You may as well take the time to design the office to lead them toward an image that you want them to see.

The team member who greets your clients should offer them something to drink, and you should consider having snack food in the lobby area. If you are going to offer drinks or food, it should be something easy to eat and something that will not be messy. Food and drink often puts people in a better frame of mind and can send the message to the clients that everything is not strictly business related. Although this appears to be a small gesture, sharing something to eat or drink with a client can help develop more of a personal rapport.

Many firms overlook the importance of the team member who greets clients. This team member is likely the first person your clients will see and interact with, and therefore, this team member is incredibly important in the clients' first impression of the firm. This team member must project the image you want for your firm.

Just consider the different impressions that the following two scenarios provide. Scenario 1: A firm has a team member who is sitting behind a desk, working on his or her computer or organizing documents; this team member stands to greet clients when they enter the office and wears attire that is either as formal or casual as that of the attorney the clients are going to meet. Scenario 2: A firm has a team member sitting at a desk reading a paperback novel with his or her lunch items spread out on the desk; this team member looks up when the clients enter the office and by his or her outfit appears as though he or she is heading to the gym. The team members in both scenarios may have the same skills and accomplish the exact same tasks equally well, but your clients will have very different impressions of your office.

Common Areas

Aside from the lobby seating, reading materials, and greeting, you need to consider what colors the walls will be and what artwork will be visible in the hallways, conference rooms, and other common areas. The artwork and wall colors will say a great deal to your clients. Even the clients who are not art aficionados can distinguish between contemporary art and historical paintings.

Contemporary art may give clients the impression that your firm is on the cutting edge, whereas the firm with historical pictures may signal that your firm is traditional and will do things by the book. Similarly, a lobby with bold colors or a bright accent wall will say something completely different than a lobby painted eggshell white.

Many firms who have a team member in the lobby to greet clients will also ask that team member to answer the firm's telephone calls. It is critical that this team member answer those calls professionally and efficiently without saying anything confidential that someone sitting in the lobby may hear. Moreover, the team member answering the phone cannot make any comments or facial expressions about the caller, as the clients observing this will wonder what the team members are saying behind their back.

Pro Tip: Make sure that your team members who have offices near the reception area or walk by that area keep their voices down and do not accidently share confidential information or unflattering commentary about a party or opposing counsel with everyone who happens to be sitting in the lobby.

Certain clients may feel self-conscious sitting in a lobby area. They may feel this way because the type of case is sensitive, the clients are recognizable, or the clients are simply anxious or particularly private. To the extent that you can anticipate when clients may feel this way, your firm should move these clients immediately into a conference room even if the team member the clients are meeting with is not ready yet. These clients will appreciate the privacy of a conference room even if they have to wait.

Your firm should establish a policy as to whether team members will meet with clients in conference rooms or individual team members' offices or if the team member will have discretion to choose. Generally, meetings that take place in conference rooms feel a little less personal and perhaps a little more sterile. The tradeoff is that the firm will have more control over the environment. Your firm should give the same care and consideration to the chairs, tables, artwork, and so on in the conference rooms, and for that matter all of the common areas, as you give in the lobby.

Whether in the hallway or in an individual office, files cannot be left around. In an abundance of caution, the outside of a file or box should contain only the clients' initials. Client files should be kept neatly in file cabinets, assuming your firm has not already transitioned to electronic files.

Any files clients do see need to be neat and organized. The last thing that you need clients to see is a disorganized or scattered client file. If they see that you keep someone else's file in that manner, they will reasonably assume that there is a good chance their file may end up looking the same. Office doors should not be left open when team members are on client calls and other clients are walking by.

Regardless of whether the meeting space is in a conference room or an individual office, the minimal requirement is that the space be functional. You and your clients need to be able to accomplish whatever is on the meeting agenda. As more and more firms shift to electronic files, this means that the team members must be able to access the electronic files from the conference room.

Technology in the Office

These days, the functionality of an office often is directly proportional to its technology. Modern clients expect firms to maintain a certain level of technology, and they are looking for signs throughout the office that your computer, phone, and other systems are current models. Client expectations regarding technology are likely to fluctuate depend on your practice areas. For example, intellectual property clients will probably expect more sophisticated technology than criminal defendants.

Setting aside certain cases and clients, technology probably will have an even more significant impact on your team members. Your team members will use the technology day in and day out. At a bare minimum, the technology must meet the basic needs of your team members. However, more sophisticated technology may make it easier for your team members to do their job, and as a result, make your firm more efficient. Furthermore, younger team members in particular tend to be attracted to newer and more sophisticated technology.

Virtual Offices

Up to this point, we have assumed that your firm will have a physical office, but more and more law firms are doing away with physical offices as technology enables team members to work remotely and to meet with clients either by telephone or through videoconferences. There are certain practices in which the attorneys never need to meet with their clients, and some of those firms have done away with physical offices completely. When firms rarely meet with clients, they can use virtual offices or rented space for meetings and work remotely the rest of the time.

A virtual office will establish a significantly different atmosphere than a traditional physical office, especially for your team members. While functional, it becomes more difficult to build interoffice relationships and comradery when colleagues do not see each other.

You can build relationships online. Younger team members who grew up interacting with their friends electronically and online may be more comfortable with these relationships than older team members who are more familiar with face-to-face interaction.

Technology now provides the ability to appear as if you are in the office even when you are not physically there. Phone apps and remote computer logins are just two ways that you can use technology to make it appear to clients that you are calling or e-mailing from your office when you are elsewhere. When used properly, these tools can offer a great balance for team members who do not want to be in the office every day versus clients who expect them to be available at all times.

Pro Tip: Even attorneys who work in brick and mortar offices will need to be prepared to conduct virtual meetings. Every day, and particularly after the coronavirus disease 19 (COVID-19 crisis), more and more clients demand virtual meetings.

Virtual meetings have exponentially increased what can be considered office space. Now the background of every videoconference with clients is part of your office. We strongly recommend that you pay careful attention to your background.

Avoid setting up a videoconference in which the viewer can see people walking in the background, miscellaneous household items, or private areas of your home. We encourage you to have a basic background without much movement or too many items to distract from the conversation.

Law firms who frequently work with clients who have great difficulty getting to an office should consider creating a "mobile office" in which the law firm team members go to the clients with the tools needed to conduct the meeting. Clients who are elderly, disabled, or injured would greatly appreciate this effort.

Physical Offices

For those firms with physical offices, you have to decide whether to allocate more space to individual offices or common areas. The trend in modern office spaces is to make individual offices smaller and to allocate more space to the common areas such as conference rooms, kitchens, and war rooms.

Larger common areas make it easier and more convenient for your team members to collaborate on projects. Arrangements in which each team member's office, including the senior partner's office, is roughly the same size send a signal that each team member is valuable. Even if each team member's role does not truly carry the same value, similar office sizes can reinforce the theme that each role is important and necessary for the office to run efficiently and it encourages teamwork.

Old-fashioned firms tended to provide senior partners or rainmakers with larger and more elaborate offices. These offices were clear symbols to clients and other team members as to where these valued team members stood in the hierarchy of the firm. When clients met with these team members, they assumed that the firm's best was handling their matter. Bigger and/or nicer offices for the senior attorneys or the firm leaders gave younger or less experienced team members something to aim for as a reward for their efforts.

The ability to have private conversations with clients, whether in person or by telephone, must be considered when designing your office space. Although it may save space and money, we do not recommend cubicles or open areas for any team member who will be discussing confidential information with a client. Any team member who will be discussing confidential information must have ready access to a space that provides privacy.

Lighting is another aspect of offices that is receiving far more attention these days. Studies show that natural light is healthier than artificial light. Very few office layouts provide everyone with a window office, but you can use glass partitions on the walls of the window offices and in the hallways to enable as much natural light into the office even if it is not direct light.

Pro Tip: Solo and small-firm owners need to remember to set appearance standards for themselves not based solely on what they like or feel comfortable wearing. You need to consider how clients and other guests to your office will view your appearance.

One of the most direct benefits of having an office environment that your team members like and enjoy is that there will be far fewer sick days, and your team members will have a more positive attitude about being in the office. Fewer sick days translates directly to more production. While far more difficult to quantify, positive attitudes about the office will lead to higher efficiency and productivity.

An even more valuable result of having an office that your team members enjoy is that it will be easier to retain your team members. There are few things that are more costly and disruptive than replacing a team member and training a new one.

Appearance Rules

Another aspect of office atmosphere that will leave an impression on both your clients and your team members is the office dress code. Certainly, consideration should be given to what your clients expect of their attorneys. Corporate clients may expect formal business attire, whereas startup companies may be more comfortable with business casual.

At a minimum, all of your team members should be dressed professionally. The determination as to what professional means should be viewed from the client's perspective of what professional means.

It should be noted that it is much easier to enforce a dress code that requires formal attire such as what would be appropriate in a courtroom than business casual. Business casual and other broader descriptions can open the door to a wide range of interpretations. As a result, if you tell a team member that his or her attire does not meet your definition of appropriate, the team member may take that as a personal attack on his or her judgment and/or style.

Your team members are likely to have dress code preferences. The dress code may play a large role in the type of team member who is interested in working for your firm. Over the past two decades, firms have gone from almost strictly business suits to casual Fridays to business casual and back to more business attire. You will need to balance the desires of your team members with client expectations.

Even more sensitive than clothing is whether you will establish guidelines for tattoos, jewelry, hair styles, and so on. These aspects of an individual's appearance are very personal, and your team members may feel very strongly about them. This situation often creates more friction when the tattoo or jewelry is religious or designed to honor a deceased family member and the team member cannot imagine anyone objecting to this homage to his or her religion or family member. While not offensive, the tattoos or jewelry may not display the image you want for your firm. Team members may struggle to understand why you do not want these images displayed. For this reason, it is very important to establish a firm policy that you apply uniformly.

Individual Offices

We have touched on many aspects of the office that will impact team members throughout this chapter. However, there are a few aspects that are specific to team members and do not carry over to the client perspective.

When you are furnishing your team members' work space, remember that they are likely to spend approximately 2,000 hours per year in the space you are allocating to them. Make it a space they want to have and that they enjoy being in (see Chapter 22 regarding wellness).

This starts with making it comfortable. There are a number of office products suppliers who will send someone trained in ergonomics to your office to help evaluate if the team members' space is set up in the best way. While these ergonomics experts want to sell office products to you, there is no obligation to buy anything, and they can and do provide valuable guidance.

This guidance includes identifying specific chairs, keyboards, mouses, or other equipment that will make the office space comfortable for your team members. The last thing you want is for team members to constantly have a sore back or neck because the height of their office monitor is not properly adjusted or for the team members to develop carpel tunnel syndrome because their mouse is the wrong size. These are easy and relatively inexpensive fixes.

Not only should the office space be comfortable but also it should promote an efficient work flow. This means that all team members should have the tools or equipment that they use frequently at their fingertips. Do not make team members walk down the hall to a printer or scanner if they are printing and scanning all the time. The cost of purchasing an individual device will pale in comparison to the cost of lost time and team member irritation.

We recommend allowing team members to have some flexibility in how their individual office space is decorated. The amount of flexibility depends on how often clients or other non-team members will see the space. Of course, the flexibility cannot be so broad as to allow a team member to put up something that a client or other team member may find offensive, but certainly, team members should be encouraged to put pictures that they like in their space, pick their own screensaver, and so on.

While firms can establish guidelines for what an individual team member's office can and cannot have in it, all individual offices will take on at least some of the team member's personality. The personality may come out in family pictures, artwork, screensavers, or a number of other ways. The advantage of showing some of this personality to a client is that it may enable your team member to build a stronger individual bond with the client.

You must pay careful attention to what your clients will see as they walk through your offices on their way to a conference room or individual office. The most important consideration is to ensure that clients cannot see or hear confidential information about other clients.

Team members who are comfortable in their office space and who can conduct their work efficiently will be happy team members. Happy team members are far less inclined to leave, and they will boost office morale.

Why Office Environment Matters

We recognize that some of you may be thinking that none of this stuff really matters. Instead, you may be thinking that what matters is the legal service your firm provides to your clients. While the legal service you provide is very important, it is far from the only factor that clients consider when evaluating their experience with your firm. Many clients cannot accurately evaluate the quality of the legal services, but they can confidently evaluate your office's appearance and how they were treated.

To quote Maya Angelou, "I've learned that people will forget what you said, people will forget what you did, but people will never forget how you made them feel." This quote is absolutely applicable to law firms. We have met with numerous clients who needed follow-up work on their cases but did not return to the firm that they had worked with previously even when that firm had done a fantastic legal job because they did not "like" the experience or had developed such little rapport with them that they forgot who their previous firm was.

Many of you will have prospective clients who will meet with multiple firms before deciding which firm they will hire. The prospective clients who are willing to take to the time to meet with several firms probably did not even call to make an appointment until they had already confirmed that your firm can provide the legal services they need. When the prospective clients knows that all of the potential firms can handle their legal needs, they will choose which firm to hire based on the ancillary factors. The tipping point may very well be the feel the prospective clients get from the office atmosphere.

With regard to your team members, many of them will choose to take your job offer and/or stay at your firm based on the office environment. Assuming the compensation they are being offered from different firms is in the same general ballpark, office environment will be a critical factor they will consider.

The primary focus of this chapter has been to emphasize the impact the style of your firm's physical space may have on your clients and team members. For the most part, every office will have the items that we discussed in this chapter. For example, everyone with a physical office will have a door, chairs, and so on. We strongly recommend that you consider the message these items will send and that you choose styles that will be most attractive to your clients and team members.

Office Environment Section of Your Business Plan

We anticipate that your answers to the questions below will serve as an outline for the office environment section of your business plan. These answers will form the foundation for how your office space is designed.

1. Who is your office environment designed to please?
    a. What aspect of your office will be important to your clients?
    b. What will your office need to have to attract and retain team members?
    c. Are you trying to convey a message through your office space?
    d. Is it more important for you to have a functional office or one whose appearance is pleasing?
2. Factors to consider regarding your office environment
    a. Location
    b. Office quality and style
    c. Client's perspective of your office
    d. Greeting your client
    e. Common areas in the office
    f. Individual offices
    g. Technology in the office
    h. Ergonomics

3. Office space
   a. Virtual offices
   b. Physical offices
4. Will your firm have rules about your team members' appearance?
   a. Dress code
   b. Hair styles
   c. Tattoos
5. Why does the office environment matter to you?

19

Business Versus Profession: Which One Are You?

We view our law firms as businesses that provide professional services. Market forces will encourage you to provide high-quality legal services to attract clients and encourage you to provide them efficiently.

Throughout this book, we have encouraged you to think of your law firm as a business that provides legal services. We recognize that there are certain ethical responsibilities and fiduciary duties that you must meet as lawyers. This does not mean that you cannot operate your law firm like a business so long as you meet these obligations.

In fact, running your firm as a business should produce more favorable results for your clients while meeting your ethical and fiduciary duties. Let us explain. One of the main goals of a successful business is to produce high-quality goods and services efficiently. Quality legal services includes the following:

1. clear and effective communication with your client and related parties;
2. clear internal steps and protocols that will produce a high likelihood of success of your client's goals;
3. a well-organized, efficient team that knows how to communicate with one another as well as with the client; and
4. a well-organized support system for the team that provides them with the livelihood that satisfies them and will encourage them to stay and grow with your firm.

The more efficient your team is, the more impact you will have on your clients' lives in a positive matter, and you will reach more of your ideal clients. You are providing more, not less. The market will reward this achievement.

Furthermore, running your law firm like a business does not mean that your sole goal is monetary profit. There are many necessary and valuable aspects of legal representation that simply cannot generate significant profits.

A Lawyer's Definition of Success

Everyone who opens a law firm wants the firm to be successful. However, we find that many founding members of law firms cannot define what "successful" means to them. Defining success should be one of your very first tasks.

Financial Success

Without question, many attorneys open their own firms or enter the legal field with the goal of earning financial rewards. The legal profession can be financially rewarding, and certain practice areas and/or firm models can lead to greater riches than others.

There is no doubt that some attorneys define financial success as earning as much money as they can. However, when you take a deeper look at financial success, there are other attorneys who define financial success as earning enough money to handle the types of cases or clients the attorney wants to represent.

Case Satisfaction

Many attorneys define success by how many individuals they can help as opposed to how much money they can earn. The only financial goals these attorneys have are to earn enough money to keep their firm open and to maintain a standard of living that feels comfortable to them.

We have encountered attorneys who work with disabled or indigent clients whose goal is to help as many clients in this situation as possible. Other attorneys want to handle important legal issues such as civil rights, tenant rights, or cutting-edge issues that have no precedent.

Reputation

Some attorneys define success by how the legal community views them. Their peer reviews are far more important than any financial reward. As a result, these attorneys are likely to gravitate to cases that will give them an opportunity to showcase their skills regardless of whether the client can pay the attorneys' fees.

A Business's Definition of Success

At first glance, particularly if you think business defines success solely in terms of dollars, a business's definition of success may appear to be very different than an individual's definition. However, we encourage you to define success from a business perspective as running your firm as efficiently and effectively as possible.

By focusing on efficiency and effectiveness, you will be far more likely to achieve your goals regardless of what they are. Running your firm as a business should produce more favorable results for your clients and meeting your ethical and fiduciary duties.

Quality

Businesses are focused on providing products its consumers find valuable. Therefore, the higher-quality legal services you provide, the higher your client's level of satisfaction and willingness to pay your fees.

When you start focusing on the quality of your product, you must start looking at how you produce your legal services. This leads straight into our model of establishing and implementing thoughtful and detailed plans, systems, and procedures.

The Right Cases

Your plans, systems, and procedures should enable you to screen potential cases in a manner that results in you handling the types of cases you want to handle. The business model of targeting the audience you want to reach and helping those clients you want to represent will not necessarily mean that you are looking to maximize your profits. It will lead you to the cases that you need to have to reach your definition of success.

Rate of Return

At the conclusion of every case, you should be asking yourself whether that case was worth it. This review should help you improve your screening techniques and increase the odds that you will represent clients or take cases with the issues you want.

Answering whether the case was worth it requires you to develop a system to measure each case's rate of return. Rate of return can be measured in many different ways, but it is critical to establish a form of measurement that makes sense to you.

Of course, the rate of return will be influenced significantly by your definition of success. An attorney who values dollars over all else will find that representing an indigent client will have a very low rate of return, whereas, an attorney who values a thank you and fairness in the legal system will probably determine that representation of an indigent client will have a much higher rate of return.

Businesses want to handle the cases that provide the highest rate of return. The key to making your law firm operate like a business and simultaneously allow you to attain your definition of success is to carefully and thoughtfully determine how you will measure the rate of return on each case.

Business Model

We view the business model as one that requires you to streamline and improve your processes to increase your rate of return. We cannot emphasize enough that this does not necessarily mean that you are increasing your profit margin in terms of dollars.

We also cannot emphasize enough that if you run your law firm like a business, you will put yourself in a position to accomplish more of your goals. From our perspective, running your law firm like a business means that you do things as efficiently and effectively as you can. You invest time and money into creating systems and procedures that accomplish this.

The more efficient and effective your law firm runs, the more clients you can assist with the same resources. The more clients that you represent, the more you earn, the more people you help, the more enhanced your reputation becomes, or the more of however you define success.

Shareholders

Public businesses have shareholders. We encourage you to think of your team members and your clients as shareholders. When you start to think of these groups in this manner, it will change your behavior in a positive way.

From a team member perspective, if you start to consider them shareholders, think about how you might treat them differently. If team members could vote to remove you from an officer role, you would keep them educated about firm decisions and you would involve them in important decisions. These actions alone would likely reduce turnover, increase morale, and lead to more thoroughly considered decision making.

If clients were your shareholders, they could vote on the direction of the firm, what cases should be taken, and whether you should get paid and how much. In this scenario, you would endeavor to ensure that the cases you were taking fell within the firm's mission and that you were providing a valuable service.

Ethics

A smart business would require the highest level of ethics. Ethical businesses attract better team members and more and better clients. When a business engages in unethical behavior, it can be a public relations disaster.

For this reason, we find that the concern that operating your law firm like a business will negatively impact your ethics to be unfounded. No law firm wants to be known as the firm that cannot properly manage client confidences, will not meet deadlines, or will not effectively communicate with clients.

Market Forces

Most businesses assume that the market will weed out the inefficient or ineffective entities. The same principle applies to law firms. Law firms that do not provide value do not stay in business for long and certainly do not prosper.

The market, whether it is the legal community or your pool of potential clients, will learn whether your firm offers quality representation at reasonable rates, how it feels to be represented by your firm, and whether your firm meets the expectations it sets for itself and/or clients. Ultimately, the market will dictate how close you come to reaching your definition of success.

Your strategies, plans, systems, and procedures will determine how the market views you. Law firms that focus solely on the current cases they are handling will not develop processes that will direct the firm toward their goals. Law firms with a business model will develop these processes and are far more likely to achieve success.

Business Versus Law Firm Section of Your Business Plan

We anticipate that your answers to the questions below will help you determine how your firm defines success. These answers will help you understand the ultimate goals of your firm so the remainder of your business plan can be designed to meet those goals.

1. Are you a business that provides legal services?
2. How do you define success?
    a. Winning a case
    b. Helping a client
    c. Reputation
    d. Profits
    e. Making money off a case
3. From a business perspective, how do you measure success?
    a. Was it the right case to take?
    b. What was your return on investment in the case?
    c. How do you measure return on investment?

20

Strategic Planning: Short- and Long-Term Goals

Pro Tip: Make sure that you leave time to plan. If you do not allocate specific time for planning, sooner or later the entire year has gone by before you realize that you did not make any plans. Even a very good year can be a better year with planning. Planning allows you to focus on what you really want to do and helps you do it efficiently.

We recognize that an hour spent planning is an hour not being billed. The long-term financial advantages of having a strategic plan will far outweigh the short-term loss of revenue.

We strongly recommend that you plan your firm's direction. Not only should you develop plans, but also you should set short- and long-term goals designed to keep you and your firm on track and focused.

Too many firms float along aimlessly, hoping that things will work out for the best. In a best-case scenario, these firms operate inefficiently but survive. In a worst-case scenario, these firms are disjointed and make very little money.

Strategic Planning

From our perspective, strategic planning means that you determine what your goals are and how you will achieve them. In the context of strategic planning, we are not talking about day-to-day goals. Your strategic plan should set forth your vision for the future of your firm.

Strategic plans should be detailed. For example, it is not enough to state that your plan is for your firm to handle high-dollar cases in the future. A good strategic plan will outline why those cases will be beneficial, what you will do to attract those cases, how you will equip your firm to work on those cases, and so on.

Creating a Strategic Plan

This is where you take time to work *on* your business instead of working *in* your business. Start by visualizing the future and try to make it as clear as possible in your head.

Allocate Time

We understand that you cannot bill your clients for the time you spend creating strategic plans, and as a result, many attorneys do not see the value in allocating time to planning. However, if done properly, a strategic plan will generate far more value over time than what you would have gained by spending that day working on client matters.

We urge you to dedicate time to strategic planning. This type of planning is not something you can do well by squeezing in a few minutes here and there between meetings.

The most effective strategic planners allocate hours or days at a time to develop their plans. Depending on your personality, you may prefer to brainstorm ideas individually or in a group. Both approaches work well, but if you are going to meet with a group, we recommend that you have a meeting agenda and timeline.

While some planners are able to focus within their office, most people will find too many distractions there. We have encountered individuals who schedule "thinking days." These individuals do not go to the office on their thinking days and frequently turn off electronics so that they can focus solely on planning.

Written Plan

As we have emphasized throughout this book, your strategic plans should be written down. Your team members can follow a written plan. A rousing and moving speech about where your firm is headed will feel great, but it will not have the lasting effect of a written plan.

Your written plan should include not only goals but also a timeline for execution of your goals. Projects tend not to be completed when there is no deadline, and long-term plans that will require a great deal of work over an extended period of time will be even harder to accomplish without deadlines.

What Does a Strategic Plan Cover?

Many strategic plans are designed as comprehensive plans, but strategic plans can also address individual aspects of your firm. In addition, a strategic plan may cover the next year or the next ten years.

As silly as this sounds, part of your strategic planning will be to decide what type of plans you need. Will you have a separate strategic plan for each firm department—marketing, finance, technology, legal services, and human resources? We recommend that you have plans for each of these departments and any other major departments within your firm. Furthermore, you may want to develop multiple strategic plans within these departments to accomplish specific goals. There is no hard-and-fast rule as to what your strategic plans must cover.

Periodic Review

Your strategic plans should be living documents. Rarely, if ever, does a plan work out exactly as intended. You must be prepared to adjust your plans as circumstances change.

At a minimum, we encourage you to review your plans on a quarterly basis. You should review your key business indicators. Common business indicators include gross revenues, profits, number of retained cases, number of leads, hours worked, and hours billed.

Key business indicators provide the vital "health" statistics of your business. These common business indicators probably will provide useful information for every firm, but they are not the only indicators that will be valuable. You should develop indicators that will help you measure whether your firm is on a path toward your definition of success.

We tend to think of the quarterly reviews as maintenance. It takes only a few hours to review your key business indicators and to gauge whether your firm is still on track. If the quarterly reviews are your maintenance plan, you should conduct a thorough review and planning session at least annually.

The annual review should be designed to look at the business as a whole. This is an opportunity to measure the success of the plans you have already implemented and to determine what, if any, adjustments should be made to your plans. In addition, this is the time to develop new plans.

Retreats

We think that off-site meetings or retreats can be extremely effective. It is much easier to focus on your strategic plan when you leave your office and all of its distractions behind. An off-site retreat can do wonders for firm morale and shows your commitment to the team and the business.

Pro Tip: Solo and small firms should schedule retreats even if only one or two people will attend. Get away from your everyday environment where all you can see or hear are tasks that need to be done. Find a space that will allow you to strategize without interruption or distractions.

One of our colleagues takes a "thinking day" every quarter. He turns off all of his electronic devices and finds a place where he can plan without being disrupted by everyday distractions.

Your retreat space does not need to be at a fancy resort or an expensive location. Ask your banker or friends in the legal community if you can borrow their conference room for the day.

Many firms go on retreats that can accurately be described as boondoggles. Certainly, a fun location can increase the firm morale. We are all in favor of enjoying yourself, but we urge you to set aside time and mental capacity to determine your firm's path forward.

Regardless of where you conduct the retreat, there should be a clear agenda of topics that need discussions and/or decisions. All attendees at the retreat should have the agenda and any associated materials well in advance so that they can actively participate.

You should consider soliciting agenda items from your team to ensure that you discuss areas that require attention.

We lean toward viewing the firm retreat as a time to look at the firm as a whole and determine strengths, weaknesses, and future direction. This approach is a more comprehensive review of the firm's health as well as a time to set future goals.

There are times when it makes sense to use a retreat to focus on a limited number of issues or even a single issue. When one issue will be instrumental in the future of the firm, a retreat may be the perfect opportunity to give it the attention it needs.

Implementing Your Strategic Plan

Drafting your strategic plan is only step one. You and your team must actively work to implement it for it to become a reality. We recommend that you establish a series of short- and long-term goals to implement your strategic plan.

We believe the most effective approach is to develop your long-term goals first. The long-term goals will reflect your vision for your firm. Your short-term goals are intermediary steps designed to cumulatively lead you to your long-term goals, which will lead to the execution of your strategic plan.

Setting Goals

The more detail you use to describe your goals, the more likely you will be to achieve your goals. The added levels of detail will create a clearer picture of what you want to accomplish.

We encourage you to write down why each goal is important to you and why the goal will move your firm forward. You and your team members will strive harder to achieve a goal if everyone can understand where it will lead you.

Whenever possible, the goals should be quantifiable. For example, instead of stating that your goal is to add more attorneys, the goal should be to increase the number of attorneys by 50 percent within a specific time period.

You should determine and write down what it will take to reach your goal. This should include the resources you will need and how you plan to accomplish the goal.

Also, as you are setting your goals, we recommend that you identify what obstacles you will face. You should outline how you plan to overcome or circumvent these obstacles.

Long-Term Goals

From our perspective, long-term goals are goals you hope to achieve more than one year from when the goal was established. We encourage you to look at multiple time periods, such as three-, five-, and ten-year periods.

Setting long-term goals requires you to have an open mind and a willingness to project what will be possible. Envisioning firm dynamics, market conditions, and so on five to ten years into the future is certainly not an exact science. Of course, the longer into the future that you look, the greater chance that your projections will be off target.

Too many attorneys do not set long-term goals because they lack confidence in their ability to predict the future, and they assume that as a result their long-term goals will be farfetched. We can assure you, you will make mistakes in your predictions. Just because your predictions will not always be accurate does not mean that you should not establish long-term goals.

Instead of avoiding long-term goals, you should review them at least annually. When you review your long-term goals, you can adjust them as you gather more information and the target date for completion gets closer.

We cannot overestimate the importance of having long-term goals. These goals will shape the direction of your firm, and they will focus your team on establishing the tasks that must be accomplished to execute your business plan.

Pro Tip: Get input from as many team members as you can. However, if you seek input from your team members, be prepared to include some of their thoughts and strategies in your plans. You do not have to accept everything your team suggests, but if you ignore everything your team proposes, your team will not feel valued and you certainly will not receive any productive feedback the next time you ask.

Short-Term Goals

We view goals that can be accomplished in less than a year as short-term goals. Short-term goals will enable you to build momentum toward completion of your long-term goals and strategic plan. Short-term goals should be designed as steps to reach long-term goals.

Since short-term goals must be completed within a year or less, they should be smaller in scale and require fewer resources than your long-term goals. An important aspect of setting goals is to ensure that they are realistic.

One huge benefit of short-term goals is that you and your team can see positive results on a regular basis. Reaching a goal will provide positive energy to your team.

Seasonal or Very Short-Term Goals

You can also set seasonal or very short-term goals. These goals should be achievable in three months or less. Setting this type of goal will help unify the team behind something tangible that will lead to quantifiable results that can be achieved in a relatively short period of time.

As you learn the rhythm of your firm, you will likely find that there are certain times during the year when things slow down, and therefore, your team will have more capacity to take on new tasks. This is the perfect time to put a seasonal goal in place.

Who Designs the Strategic Plans and Goals?

You and your team leaders should take the lead in designing the strategic plan and setting your firm's goals. However, we strongly encourage you to find ways to involve your team members in this process or at least solicit and listen to their input.

You will rely on your team members to implement your plans and goals. The more your team members have faith in or "buy" into the plans and goals, the more effort they will put into making it a success. Team members are far more likely to believe in a plan or goal if they played a role in developing it.

The team members in the trenches will be able to provide invaluable practical advice as to what is achievable. A strategic plan or goal will be worthless if it has no realistic chance to succeed.

Consultants can provide valuable insight for strategic plans. While they may not understand certain dynamics within your firm, they can provide objective feedback.

Attorneys certainly have been trained to identify legal issues and to develop a plan to solve the issue, but attorneys often have frighteningly little training or experience in identifying business issues, much less solving them. A good consultant will have the training attorneys lack and a career full of experience addressing business issues.

Solo and small firms who do not want to engage a consultant should talk with other lawyers at similarly situated firms. Talking with other lawyers will provide all of you with a great opportunity to discuss what strategies have worked or failed and why. Also, the other lawyers will be able to provide feedback about your potential strategies from perspectives that you had not considered.

What Strategic Plans or Goals Should You Have?

Every firm should have an overarching strategic plan that is designed to set forth the firm's direction, long-term goals that identify what you intend to accomplish, and short-term goals that lead to your long-term goals.

We recommend that you also develop strategic plans and goals for each department within your firm. These smaller plans and goals must be prepared in conjunction with your overarching strategic plan and designed to work toward your long-term goals. These goals can range from monetary goals such as profit, revenue, and cost control to non-monetary goals such as growth or reputation enhancement.

Strategic Planning for Your Business Plan

We anticipate that your answers to the questions below will serve as an outline for your strategic planning section of your business plan. These answers will form the foundation for how you develop your strategic plans.

1. What strategic plans will you have?
   a. Overall strategic plan
   b. Individual department plans
2. What time frames will the plans cover?
   a. Plan for year one
   b. Plan for year three
   c. Plan for year ten
3. When will you review your plans and goals?
4. How will the plans be updated or modified if circumstances change?

5. What are key indicators that matter to your firm?
    a. Size of team
    b. Revenues
    c. Expenses
6. What investments will you need to get to your plans for year three or ten?
7. Who will be responsible for creating your strategic plans?
    a. Internal
    b. External
8. How will the strategic plans be implemented?

21

Emergency Planning: How to Handle the Extraordinary

Coronavirus disease 19 (COVID-19) reminded the world that a pandemic can disrupt many functions of your firm simultaneously. The pandemic presented major challenges to the two primary emergencies that your firm may face at the same time.

The pandemic caused human resource emergencies. Key team members became sick and unable to work. Shutdown orders prohibited other key team members from following their normal routines. Simultaneously, the shutdown orders either required offices to be closed or prevented team members from accessing them.

Emergencies come in all shapes and sizes. For the purposes of this chapter, think of an emergency as any circumstance that could disrupt your firm's ordinary operation. The goal of your emergency plan should be to create alternative systems and procedures that will enable your firm to continue operating as close to full capacity as possible regardless of the circumstances.

The first step in developing an emergency plan is to investigate what emergencies you might face. The question you need to answer is what could happen that will impact your firm's ability to function.

Human Resource Emergency

Replacing a key employee, even on a temporary basis, can make it difficult to carry on business as usual. The smaller your firm is, the more critical each team member becomes.

Sooner or later, a team member will get sick, take a leave of absence, or otherwise be unable to perform his or her duties for an extended period of time. It is one thing to continue operating when your team member goes on a week-long vacation, but it is another situation altogether when your team member is out of commission for a month or two.

Every firm must plan for this scenario. A team member's absence is not a matter of "if" this occurs, but rather "when" (see Chapter 22 regarding wellness). Although there is not much you can do to prevent a team member from becoming sick, firms may want to consider protocols that minimize the risk of losing multiple team members at one time. Depending on how many key team members your firm has, you may consider protocols that prohibit multiple team members from traveling in the same plane, car, and so on.

Pro Tip: A written guide is absolutely critical for a solo or small firm. In smaller firms, the firm's critical functions are often performed by one individual. If that individual becomes incapacitated, you do not want someone else to have to learn everything from scratch. A written guide would enable another team member to manage the critical tasks with minimal disruption. Without a guide, the team member who steps in may actually spend more time learning how the incapacitated team member did things and trying to follow his or her system than someone might spend opening a brand new firm with whatever systems and procedures he or she thought made sense.

Any plan designed to address a human resource emergency must cover at least two things. First, the plan must understand the team member's role and responsibilities; and second, the plan must identify who will cover the missing team member's responsibilities.

The team member's title is not enough to describe his or her role. Your plan needs to include a written description of the team member's responsibilities. Ideally, there should be a written guide that explains how *all* of the team member's duties are performed, but at a minimum, there must be a written manual detailing how to complete the team member's critical/essential duties (see Chapters 16 and 17 regarding systems and procedures).

The most efficient way to prepare this guide is to have each team member write down the tasks that he or she performs with detailed explanations of the steps taken to complete each task. This should be a living document that your team members create as part of their day-to-day responsibilities.

Having a guide that tells you how to perform your team member's duties is a great start, but you still need someone to carry out the steps. Your plan should identify who this person will be. If it is one of your existing team members, there should be some cross-training done to make the replacement team member more comfortable covering the other team member's responsibilities. This must be done as soon as a replacement is identified, and cross-training must be refreshed periodically.

If you are in a very small law firm, you may need to plan for an outsider such as a temp to fill in for your missing team member. The last thing you want to do is to try to figure out where you will find a temp after your team member is out of commission. Determine where you will locate the temp before one is needed.

Internet and Cable Problems

Given how reliant modern law firms are on their computer systems, any disruption in service can cause serious problems. Take a moment to consider how helpless you are without access to the Internet.

Most firms conduct all of their legal research online, and most of their correspondence with clients and opposing counsel is done by e-mail. Many courts require submission of pleadings electronically. What would you do if your Internet connection failed minutes before your brief was due?

Regardless of how much you invest in your Internet and cable connections, all systems can malfunction. Most law firms are no longer designed to function offline. You should have a backup arrangement in place that will tide you over until you can fix whatever the problem is with your primary connection, and it is imperative that you have the means to restore your systems as soon as possible.

Unless you have a technology expert on your team, you should have an arrangement in place with an IT service to be on call. Finding a service, much less getting them to respond quickly, will be difficult if you do not have a preexisting relationship.

On the plus side, Internet and cable problems tend to be short-term emergencies. Nevertheless, you should have a plan in place that will allow you to continue performing essential functions until the systems are restored.

Pro Tip: Test your team members' awareness of malware. Our IT provider sends at least one test e-mail per quarter to each team member. The e-mail looks like a phishing e-mail or has an attachment that looks like malware. If a team member opens the fake message, the IT provider is notified and can then show the team member why he or she should not have opened the message or attachment. A list or demonstration of what to look for and avoid is always helpful, but regular testing is a great way to reinforce the tips.

Computer Hackers

As firms move toward electronic files and virtual offices, they become more reliant on their computer systems. Cybercriminals have taken notice, and they recognize the value of the confidential information law firms store on their computer systems.

Hackers have started taking law firms, businesses, and even governments hostage. They access the computer system (often through malware opened by a team member) and lock the firm out of it.

Once the cybercriminal has hacked into your system, you cannot access your own files. The hacker has the ability to copy, delete, or distribute a client's confidential information and/or your firm's private information. The cybercriminals will agree to restore your access to your own system for a fee. Although most cybercriminals keep their word and restore your access to your computer system once the ransom is paid, counting on the honor of a hacker is not a sound business practice.

We recommend that you invest heavily in a top-notch security system. However, no security system is foolproof. No matter how sophisticated the security system is, a lapse in judgment by a team member who opens an attachment with malware will allow a hacker to circumvent your security system.

You need to discuss cybersecurity regularly with your team. Make sure your team members know how to identify suspicious material. Additionally, you may want to place restrictions on what websites can be accessed on your firm's computers.

Every firm should back up its entire computer network frequently. The backups will enable you to resume operations with the least amount of lost work product.

Many insurance companies now offer insurance against cyberattacks. The insurance policies often cover your liabilities and the costs of restoring your service, and they will investigate how the computer breach occurred. Even though this is a relatively new form of insurance, many companies offer this coverage with a variety of different benefits.

Destruction of Your Office

Even though many firms now have virtual offices, most law firms still operate in a physical office. The destruction of your office could be catastrophic. Offices are not immune from fires, floods, and other destructive events.

Not having a physical location will hamper your ability to operate, but this is a temporary setback. You can always find new office space.

The real risk is the loss of your client files and your firm's business files. These cannot be easily replaced. Again, the most effective emergency plan is to keep a backup copy of all important files or records offsite.

Remote Operation

If your firm cannot operate from its primary office or your team members are not permitted to come to the office, as occurred with COVID-19, you need to have a contingency plan in place to enable your firm to continue functioning. Modern technology has made it much easier for law firms to continue operating from a remote location.

If you are working from a remote location, you must take steps to maintain not only the ability to function but also security precautions. The goal is to create a virtual office that mirrors the physical office so that your employees can be just as productive at home as they were sitting at their office desk.

Working Remotely

Many emergencies will require your firm to operate without its primary office. In a perfect world, you will be able to continue operating in such a manner that your clients do not realize you are not sitting at your desk. Modern technology makes this much easier than it sounds (see Chapter 15 regarding technology).

Telephones

There are numerous apps that allow you to turn your cell phone into your office phone. If you make a call using the app, it appears to the call recipient that the call came from your office. When someone calls your office line, the call will be routed to your cell phone.

The app technology is not perfect, as there may be a delay of a few seconds before the call picks up, and these calls tend to drop more than typical cell phone calls. If you are not comfortable using an app or you are not pleased with its reliability, you can always forward your calls from your office to another phone line.

Most lawyers today have their own cell phone. As a last resort, you could use your cell phone to conduct business. We say as a last resort because this would require you to share your personal contact information with clients, opposing counsel, courts, or witnesses. We encourage you to keep your personal and business lives separate to the extent possible.

E-mail

Every day more legal correspondence is conducted by e-mail. Your team members should be able to access their e-mail remotely.

Your system should provide a way for your team members to access their e-mail accounts securely through the Internet. If you can reach your e-mail account through the Internet, as long as the entire Internet does not crash, you will have a means of communicating with your team, clients, and so on by e-mail.

Another option to consider is allowing your team members to load their e-mail account on their mobile device(s). Many lawyers already have their e-mail routed to their cell phones.

Videoconferences

Although videoconferences are not a substitute for in-person meetings, they are the next best thing. Your law firm should be able to conduct videoconferences, enabling you to meet with your clients even if your office space is not accessible.

Considering that every teenager with a cell phone has figured out how to use FaceTime and videoconference with friends, there is absolutely no justifiable reason for you to tell a client that you cannot conduct a videoconference.

There are a wide variety of videoconferencing platforms available such as Zoom, GoToMeeting, WebEx, and Google Hangouts. All are relatively user friendly. These programs allow you to share your computer screen so everyone on the videoconference can review a document together.

As you research which videoconference platform will work best for you, we encourage you to look closely at the security features of each. The platforms have different security levels, and you want to be sure that your confidential information remains confidential.

Computers

Your team members will need access to the firm's computer systems to perform their tasks. Assuming that your server is functioning, everyone should be able to access the computer system remotely.

As you decide which computers to purchase, you should consider purchasing laptops or other mobile devices for your team members. If your team members are using firm-issued laptops or mobile devices, you can install security measures to ensure that the team members are safely accessing your system. This approach may require additional costs at the outset, but it will seem like a bargain if an emergency arises.

Another option is to establish secure connections that allow team members to use their personal devices to enter the firm's system. This approach may not cost the firm as much, but it could result in far less efficient results. You are depending on each team member to have sufficient equipment of his or her own, and more importantly, that he or she has implemented the proper safety precautions.

Regardless of what strategy you implement to establish remote access, we strongly recommend that you train each team member. Training your team members to work remotely when it is not necessary may seem like a waste of time and energy, but any cost will pale in comparison to the cost of your firm being inoperable when an emergency strikes.

While you are training your team members, this can and should serve as a system test. You will need to know if your team members have sufficient Internet speed, proper wiring, Bluetooth connections, equipment, and security (firewalls and access).

We recommend that you have all of your emergency procedures in place and the equipment necessary to implement them in advance. However, we recognize that the cost of purchasing this equipment may seem too high when you may never use it.

If you decide not to purchase everything, you must at least map out how and where you would obtain the equipment you would need for an emergency situation. This will save you invaluable time if an emergency strikes and will allow you to focus on other immediate concerns.

Financial Emergencies

We strongly recommend that you establish an emergency reserve (see Chapter 14 regarding budgeting). Every firm should have enough money held in reserve to continue operating for three to six months. In a perfect situation, your emergency fund should be sufficient to cover all of your firm's expenses for that time period. At a minimum, it should be sufficient to cover a significant portion of the partners' income and all other essential expenses.

Any emergency circumstance identified in this chapter, and many other circumstances, can strain your firm's finances. Emergencies often create a dual strains. Recovering from the emergency often will require additional funds to put your firm back in its ordinary working order. At the same time, the emergency will likely make it difficult, if not impossible, for your firm to maintain its projected revenue levels.

Whether or not your firm has cash emergency reserves, you should consider maintaining a line of credit in case additional funds are necessary. Banks are happy to open lines of credit when your firm is functioning at full capacity, but they will be reluctant to open a line of credit when you are in the midst of an emergency.

For this reason, you should consider opening a line of credit when things are going well. Most banks charge a fee to maintain the line of credit even if you do not borrow any money against it. The fee associated with the line of credit will feel like a bargain when you need funds to keep your firm going.

Review of Expenses

When an emergency strikes, you may be faced with some very difficult decisions. Your firm may not be able to afford to continue paying all the expenses it had been incurring.

Your budget should already identify which expenses are essential and which ones are nice to have. Having made this distinction, it will be much easier to determine which expenses can be cut in a financial crisis.

However, your emergency plan should go into further detail. It should identify the order in which you will eliminate expenses. Most emergencies will not require you to eliminate all discretionary expenses immediately. Therefore, you will need to make choices.

Those choices should be made long before the emergency hits. Not only will it be difficult to find time to think through your choices in the midst of an emergency, but also your decision making is far more likely to be impacted by the current circumstances. These decisions may allow your firm to function from day to day, but they may not leave your firm on the best footing when it emerges from the emergency.

Review of Human Resources

The sad reality is that cutting discretionary expenses may not reduce your expenses as much as they need to be reduced. Most law firms spend more on human resources than any other expense. Therefore, the only way to make meaningful expense reductions is to reduce the size of your workforce.

Your emergency plan should identify several different human resource plans depending on how much you need to reduce your expenses. The first step in this exercise is to rank how essential each team member and each team role is.

The next step is to determine whether your team members can perform the critical functions if they have a reduced schedule. In a best-case scenario, you will not have to lay off staff. Instead, you could reduce their hours or place them on furlough. Keep in mind that furlough does not automatically mean that someone will not work until the furlough is over. Furloughing someone can also mean going from a five-day work week to a four-day work week.

Unfortunately, there will be financial crises that cannot be overcome without reducing your workforce. Having a plan that identifies each position within your firm from most essential to least essential will allow you to make the best business decision as to which team member must be laid off. In no way will this be easy.

It is important to know in advance how much you will save with each layoff and how much it will cost you. The obvious savings are salary, compensation, and benefits. There will be other savings as well such as fewer supplies and overhead.

However, you cannot ignore the costs associated with a team member's departure. We presume that each team member provided value to your firm, otherwise he or she would not have been part of your team. You need to know what that value is so you can accurately gauge the cost savings of laying off this team member.

Team Input

As you put together your emergency plans, we encourage you to obtain input from all of your team members. This input will help you create the best possible emergency plan.

From a practical standpoint, your team members may be in a much better position than you are to differentiate between what functions are absolutely necessary to keep the firm operating and those functions that are important.

Your emergency plan must account for those functions that are absolutely necessary and then try to accomplish those that are important. In an emergency situation, your resources will be limited and you will not be able to continue all of your operations. Therefore, you will have to make some difficult decisions regarding which functions will continue.

If you have not reviewed and discussed the outcomes of those difficult decisions with your team members, there could be resistance to your plan at the worst possible time—when the emergency hits and you are trying to implement the plan. Engaging and involving your team members in the creation of your emergency plan and explaining how and why certain functions will be supported over others will go a long way to obtaining buy-in from all your team members.

Practice and Training

All emergency plans should be practiced. The more comfortable you and your team are with the plan, the more efficiently you will be able to put it in place. We realize that no firm will be able to change from the way it has functioned for years to a new "way of life" instantly, but practice and training will reduce the learning curve.

Think of your training as a fire drill. Every elementary school has periodic fire drills to remind students of how they should exit the building. Your firm needs to have fire drills to train its team members how they will function when they cannot access the building.

Emergency Planning for Your Business Plan

We anticipate that your answers to the questions below will serve as an outline for the emergency section of your business plan. These answers will form the foundation for how your firm prepares for emergency scenarios.

1. What emergencies might your firm encounter?
2. How will you pay your expenses in an emergency?
    a. What expenses are essential?
    b. What expenses are discretionary?
3. What are the essential roles, and who are the essential team members?
    a. What is the value of each team member?
    b. What would a furlough plan look like?
    c. What is the order in which you would lay off team members?

4. What arrangements have you made to operate remotely?
    a. Telephones
    b. E-mail
    c. Videoconferences
    d. Computers
5. How will you train your team members to be ready for an emergency?

22

Wellness: Taking Care of Yourself

We firmly believe that your human resources are your firm's most valuable assets. The more efficient and effective your team members are, the more valuable they are to your firm and your clients.

Pro Tip: Take care of yourself! Even though most jobs in a law firm do not require long-distance running, lifting heavy weights, or any other physical feat, physical fitness will lead to more productivity.

Firms routinely spend time and money educating their team members to improve their skills and value, but they often overlook other opportunities to improve a team member's value. Healthy team members will be more productive team members.

For this reason, we encourage you to look for ways to either maintain or improve your team members' wellness. We urge you to take care of yourself and your team members physically and mentally.

We are not medical experts. This chapter includes common sense advice for taking care of your team. Since we doubt many of you are medical experts, you should encourage your team members to consult with their own medical providers for specific guidance.

Work/Life Balance

We subscribe to the theory of "working to live" as opposed to "living to work." Of course, life is not this clear-cut, and there are gray areas between these two theories. Each of you will have to determine what approach will work best for you individually.

Many professionals struggle to establish a good work/life balance, and attorneys certainly struggle with this issue. We urge you to take control of your schedule and to establish a work/life balance you find comfortable.

Proper Time Management

Taking control of your time will alleviate many of the issues that lead to stress. Taking control over your day, week, and month puts you in the driver's seat and not at the mercy of every client's whim.

When attorneys schedule a work meeting on their calendar, the expectation is that the attorneys will attend the meeting. In fact, attorneys almost always attend meetings they place on their calendar.

However, we rarely encounter attorneys who schedule personal time on their calendar. We encourage you to budget time for yourself and place it on your calendar to preserve this time. Common examples of personal time are family time, hobbies, exercise, and social functions, but personal time could include anything you enjoy.

Make sure to protect your free days and/or free time, and do not allow yourself to get sucked into work issues during those times. You need that time to recharge. Furthermore, what is the point of your vacation if you work throughout the vacation only to come home to work more when your "vacation" ends? (See Chapter 7 regarding time management.)

Physical Wellness

Physical fitness and mental acuity go hand in hand. Attorneys do not need to be world-class athletes, but better fitness will help generate better performance.

On one level, individuals who are in better physical shape have better stamina, which can lead to sharper mental abilities for longer periods. On another level, individuals in poor physical shape are often less comfortable in their clothes, chairs, and so on, and those aggravations distract them from their work. These individuals are also more prone to depression due to their harsh self-image.

Rest

It is no secret that attorneys work long hours, and even longer hours when a deadline approaches. Sleep is often the first casualty of these long hours.

Since elementary school, we have been taught how important sleep and rest are to your performance. There is no question that you can survive a day or two with less than optimal sleep, but attorneys frequently turn a day or two into a week or two, and then it just becomes the norm. Over time, lack of sleep will catch up with you.

You need a reasonable amount of sleep in order to function at your best. Studies show that seven to nine hours of sleep per night reduces stress and the risk of depression. Sleep also improves both your mental sharpness and your physical health.

We encourage you to budget time for sleep. As silly as this may sound, having a sleep plan will help you actually get the sleep you need without making you feel as if your sleep is cutting into time you need to accomplish a task.

Exercise

As we said at the outset of this chapter, attorneys do not need to be world-class athletes. The most basic way of looking at exercise is that it improves your heart and lung capacity.

The more your heart and lungs can handle, the less energy you expend on routine activities such as walking from your car to your office or from your desk to the coffee machine. The less energy you spend on these everyday activities, the more energy you have to focus on your work responsibilities.

Regular exercise can help reduce the risks associated with many diseases including high blood pressure, stroke, diabetes, depression, anxiety, types of cancer, and arthritis. The stressful nature of most legal jobs places attorneys at risk for high blood pressure, anxiety, and many other physical ailments. Exercise can reduce these risks.

Pro Tip: Make your workspace comfortable—you are going to spend a ton of time there. Pay a few extra dollars to set up the office the way you really want it. The more comfortable your office is, the more willing you will be to work and the more efficient you will be. Your ability to work comfortably and efficiently will far outweigh the extra costs to equip and design the office.

Exercise goes hand in hand with sleep. A good exercise routine typically leads to a better sleep routine. These two factors can go a very long way in improving your work performance.

Calendaring your exercise will help you achieve better physical health and will also help increase efficiency with the rest of your calendar. For example, we budget time throughout the week for morning bike rides (either indoor or outdoor). In order to be able to ride the bike for an hour, you need to plan the rest of your day accordingly.

Once you get in the habit, you will eventually find yourself becoming more motivated for the physical activities. If you prioritize the physical activities, it is easier for the rest of your day/week to fall in place because success in one area will spread to other areas of life.

Office Ergonomics

Attorneys spend a lot of time at their office, so the office environment should be one that is conducive to relieve stress and physically helps you stay healthy.

Standing desks (or convertible desks) are more common (and less expensive) now and can help alleviate back pain or poor posture from leaning over a computer all day. Similarly, certain keyboards and monitors are easier on the hands and eyes, respectively.

We urge you to meet with an ergonomics consultant for recommendations regarding your office equipment. An ergonomics consultant can help you choose chairs, desks, and equipment for individual team members to make their workspaces as comfortable as possible.

Furthermore, the ergonomics consultant can provide guidance as to how your existing equipment should be set up. For example, your team member may have his or her monitors too high up, forcing the team member to look up all day and creating easily avoidable back and neck pain.

Whenever we mention buying ergonomic office equipment, the first response is always a complaint about its cost. We acknowledge that some office equipment can be expensive, but we urge you to look not only at the cost but also at the benefits.

For example, an ergonomic chair costs an extra $1,000, but it makes it possible for an attorney to bill an extra 30 minutes per day because the attorney is more comfortable.

The chair will have paid for itself in a matter of days or weeks at most, and then it will pay dividends for years.

Organized Work Space

A clean office helps reduce the clutter in your head as well. Do not let files pile up around your desk. The only file on your desk should be the one you are working on at that moment. When you finish the immediate task, the file should be returned to its long-term storage location.

Having a desk covered in files often causes the team member to become discombobulated. The team member starts on one task but is distracted by another file and the tasks associated with that file, and soon there are multiple tasks partially completed and nothing gets finished.

Going paperless will reduce the paper clutter at your team member's desk. However, without a clear and reliable file management system, going paperless will only move the clutter from the top of the desk to the team member's computer.

Mental Wellness

The American Bar Association and many state and local bar associations have significantly increased their efforts to improve lawyer wellness. In particular, bar associations are developing programs to combat substance abuse and mental health issues.

Pro Tip: Get help when you need it. Watch your team to see if anyone needs help. There are countless resources available.

Substance Abuse

Substance abuse runs at high rates for attorneys. Many attorneys do not know how to deal with the common issues related to their high-stress profession. When faced with real-life challenges such as tight deadlines, client demands, and handling negative results, too many attorneys self-medicate with drugs or alcohol.

Most state bar associations have committees designed to help attorneys who are struggling with substance abuse issues. These bar groups are designed solely to help the attorney get the help he or she needs and not to punish the attorney. Typically, everything associated with these groups is anonymous and/or confidential.

Talking to your physician is also an option. Substance abuse is a medical condition, and your physician can guide you to the right specialist to help combat the addiction. Physicians are sworn to confidentiality as well under Health Insurance Portability and Accountability Act (HIPAA) privacy laws.

Of course, we would love for every attorney to avoid substance abuse issues by taking preventative action. However, this is not realistic. The key for attorneys who face substance abuse issues is to seek treatment before they commit legal errors that lead to ethics and malpractice claims.

Mental Health

Many attorneys internalize their work stress until it impacts their mental health and in the worst-case scenario causes a mental breakdown. Attorneys suffer from depression, anxiety, and a host of other mental health issues at high levels.

Pro Tip: The best way to recharge is to completely disconnect from your work. Not forever but for a brief period, let your clients know that you will not be available. Checking e-mails, texts, and voicemails periodically while you are "away from the office" does not allow your brain to fully recharge. The natural inclination is to think that if you deal with a few small things while you are out of the office, there will be a smaller mountain of things to do when you return to the office and it will be easier to transition back to work. The mountain may be smaller, but by checking in on work consistently, it will feel as if you never left. You will be more productive in the long run by taking a block of time to truly recharge.

More bar associations are recognizing the need to help attorneys suffering from mental illness rather than punishing them for the acts that arise as a result of their mental illness. Again, the key for an attorney is to seek treatment before the illness causes the attorney to commit ethical and/or malpractice violations that lead to the loss of his or her ability to practice law.

Depression is caused by many different factors. We have found using the core concepts discussed in this chapter and throughout the book helps reduce the risk of depression because you have the tools to become a successful lawyer. For example, proper time management, which incorporates exercise, vacation, and enough sleep, will lead to less stress, which has been proven to reduce the risk of depression.

Recharge

Everyone needs to recharge. The catch is that different people recharge in different ways. Some people need some alone time, others need exercise, and others need to spend time with their friends or family. In addition, some people can recharge in seconds while others take hours.

The number of ways people recharge is countless. From a firm management perspective, you need to encourage your team members, including yourself, to find what their most effective way to recharge is and to actually spend time recharging. Like sleep, many attorneys feel they can power through and do not recognize the need or value of recharging.

High-Stress Profession

Practicing law is a high-stress profession. Many of the issues we deal with require us to provide guidance in stressful situations or where there are big stakes involved for the parties. Tensions often run high for our clients, and those tensions translate into high demands on you to deliver.

Clients hold attorneys responsible for the outcome in their cases. Many attorneys already feel a great deal of pressure without the added pressure applied by their clients.

Impact on Your Firm

The wellness of your team members is critical in terms of your firm's efficiency and effectiveness. In simple terms, a healthier team can accomplish more and perform at a higher level. If you need a reason to invest in wellness beyond the well-being of your colleagues, the increased productivity is worth the investment.

Start with a Positive Focus

Starting with a positive focus seems generic and basic, but many attorneys do not understand the power of this simple concept and how it can center you even in the most stressful situations.

Starting each meeting on a positive note, whether it is with your team or with an existing client, can have a significant impact on the tone of the meeting. Approaching meetings in this manner can change the mood and tone by starting with positive momentum.

As attorneys, we are trained to find the strengths and weaknesses of our cases. As human resource managers, many attorneys focus on the weaknesses of team members and point them out regularly in their team members' reviews. We do not excel at pointing out the strengths and positives that a team member provides. Positive feedback, regardless of how insignificant it may feel to you as the owner or partner, can go a very long way in terms of team member morale and wellness.

Negative Analysis Paralysis

Taking the above concept one step further, the same principle can be applied to what is going on inside your mind as well as your team members'. It is not healthy to focus so much on the negative that you do not see the positives.

Dwelling on negative aspects of your firm and/or your well-being is not going to improve them. Simply stewing about negative issues will paralyze you and certainly will not help you turn a negative into a positive.

Ignoring a negative aspect is just as dangerous as dwelling on it. While you think you are ignoring it, that negative is in the back of your mind and the stress associated with it is building. You know that you are not doing anything to address the concern, and that sooner or later, it will blow up in your face. As difficult as it may be, it will be better to tackle the negative issue head on than to allow it to fester.

Paralysis by analysis can be counteracted by action. The key is to identify the issue and then use a simple framework to convert the obstacle into action. A simple strategy that can be used is to utilize your talent to *write things down*!

It is amazing how attorneys can write such persuasive and detailed briefs that take hours, days, or weeks to draft. However, when it comes to their own personal issues, they do not take the time to write them down. The same legal technical writing tools we have all been taught for legal issues can be used for our personal issues as well.

Utilizing a daily journal can be helpful, but it is not essential. At a minimum, we encourage you to write down the issue/challenge you are facing. Then write down the positive result you are looking to achieve. Now that you have a starting point and an end point, write down all the obstacles to achieving your result. Finally, write down the strategies you think could be implemented to achieve the positive result.

Wellness Section of Your Business Plan

We anticipate that your answers to the questions below will serve as an outline for the wellness section of your business plan. These answers will form the foundation for how your firm takes care of its team members.

1. What does your work/life balance look like?
2. How are you managing your time?
   a. Does your time management system include personal time?
3. What you are doing to maintain your physical well-being?
   a. What are you doing to ensure that you get enough rest?
   b. What is your exercise routine?
4. Have you designed your workspace to suit your needs?
5. What are you doing to maintain your mental well-being?
   a. Do you have any programs in place to prevent substance abuse?
   b. Do you have any programs in place to address mental health issues?
6. What attitude and atmosphere do you want to foster in your firm?
   a. What steps will you take to create this attitude in yourself and/or others?

23

Conclusion: You Are Ready to Run Your Own Firm.

We are confident that you have the tools to run a successful law firm.

Use the concepts and tips throughout this book to draft your own business plan. The answers to the questions at the end of each chapter will form a strong foundation for your business plan.

As you encounter day-to-day challenges of the business world, learn to embrace each challenge. You will learn that many of the challenges will become predictable (e.g., getting clients, cash flow), and to be successful you will need to develop an efficient way to respond to and overcome each challenge.

Creating a successful law firm and having a great personal life go hand in hand. Remember to strive for balance in your work and personal life from day one.

This book is designed to provide you with the key tools and strategies to help you respond effectively and build a successful law firm. It will not happen overnight, and there probably will be times when you are frustrated. Just understand that ups and downs are ordinary in all businesses.

Let your business plan serve as your guide whether you are opening your own firm or managing one with partners. Review and revise your plans regularly to minimize the downturns and maximize your successes.

We wish you the best!

Appendix

Sample Documents

1. Partnership/Operating Agreement
2. Job Offer Form Letter
3. Job Description Form
4. Office Manual
5. Review Forms
6. Intake Form for Potential New Client (PNC)
7. Client Closing Letter
8. Retainer Agreements
    a. Flat Fee
    b. Hourly Fee
9. Client Billing Invoice
10. Budget Spreadsheet
11. Training Guide
12. Procedure Examples

The sample materials included in this section can also be downloaded as editable files at http://ambar.org/successful-law-firms.

1. Partnership/Operating Agreement

PARTNERSHIP/OPERATING AGREEMENT

OF

ABC LAW FIRM, PLLC

THIS OPERATING AGREEMENT of ABC Law Firm, PLLC, a Virginia professional limited liability company (the "Company"), is made as of the ___ day of ___________, 20____, by and between its Members, whose names and addresses are set forth on Exhibit A attached hereto.

WITNESSETH:

WHEREAS, the parties hereto do desire to form a professional limited liability company for the sole purpose of providing professional legal services; and

NOW, THEREFORE, in consideration of the mutual covenants contained in this Agreement and other good and valuable consideration, the receipt and sufficiency of which are acknowledged, the parties agree as follows:

ARTICLE I

FORMATION

1.01 The parties have formed the Company as a professional limited liability company pursuant to the Virginia Limited Liability Company Act (the "Act") by filing Articles of Organization with the Virginia State Corporation Commission. The rights and liabilities of the Members shall be as provided in the Act, except as otherwise provided herein.

1.02 The term of the Company shall be perpetual, unless sooner terminated in accordance with this Agreement.

1.03 The Members hereby acknowledge their intention and agreement that the

Company shall be treated as a partnership for purposes of the IRC and Regulations, but for all other purposes the rights and liabilities of the Members and the Company shall be as set forth in the Act, except as otherwise provided herein.

ARTICLE II

DEFINITIONS

As used in this Agreement:

2.01 "Articles of Organization" means all documents constituting, at any particular time, the Articles of Organization of the Company. It includes the original Articles of Organization, the original certificate of organization issued by the Commission, and all amendments to the Articles of Organization.

2.02 "Bankruptcy" means, with respect to any person, being the subject of an order for relief under Title 11 of the United States Code.

2.03 "Capital Account" means, as of any date, the capital account maintained for each Member under Article IX.

2.04 "Capital Contribution" means any cash, property or services rendered, or a promissory note or other binding obligation to contribute cash or property or to perform services, which a Member contributes to the Company in its capacity as a Member.

2.05 "Code" means the Code of Virginia (1950), as amended.

2.06 "Commission" means the State Corporation Commission of Virginia.

2.07 "Company" means ABC Law Firm, PLLC, a Virginia professional limited liability company. "Company" may also be referred to herein as "the Firm."

2.08 "Distribution" means a direct or indirect transfer of money or other property, or incurrence of indebtedness by the Company, to or for the benefit of the Members in respect of their interests.

2.09 "Electronic Transmission" means any form of communication, not directly involving the physical transmission of paper, that creates a record that may be retained, retrieved and reviewed by a recipient thereof, and that may be directly reproduced in paper form by such a recipient through an automated process. Any term used in this definition that is also defined in Code § 59.1-480 shall have the meaning set forth in such section.

2.10 "IRC" means the Internal Revenue Code of 1986, as amended.

2.11 "Majority in Interest" means a majority of the Interests of the Company.

2.12 "Manager" or "Managers" means a Person or Persons designated by the Members of the Company to manage the Company as provided in the Articles of Organization or this Agreement. The Managers may hereinafter collectively be referred to as the "Manager."

2.13 "Member" means a Person whose name is set forth on Exhibit A or that has been admitted to membership in the Company as provided in this Agreement and that has not ceased to be a Member.

2.14 "Membership Interest" or "Interest" means a Member's entire interest as a Member of the Company expressed in terms of such Member's ownership units ("shares").

2.15 "Net Gain or Net Loss from Sale" means the net gains or net losses (including, without limitation, any interest on principal in the event of an installment sale) realized by the Company as a result of a sale, exchange or other disposition of any assets of the Company and any other transactions (such as casualty insurance recoveries) that are attributable to the capital of the Company and not in the ordinary course of business.

2.16 "Net Income or Net Loss" means the income or loss, as the case may be, of the Company for a period as determined in accordance with IRC Section 703(a)(1), including each item of income, gain, loss or deduction required to be separately stated, other than Net Gain or Net Loss from Sale described in Section 2.15.

2.17 "Person" means any individual, partnership, corporation, limited liability company, joint venture, trust, business trust, cooperative or association, and the heirs, executors, personal representatives, administrators, successors and assigns thereof, if applicable in the context.

2.18 "Principal Office" means the office, in or out of this Commonwealth, where the principal executive offices of the Company are located.

2.19 "Founding Member" means ________________.

2.20 "Equity Member" means a person who holds a share of ownership in the Company. An Equity Member may also be referred to herein as a "Member."

2.21 "Non-founding Member" means __________________. A Non-founding member may also be referred to herein as a "Member."

ARTICLE III

OPERATING AGREEMENT

3.01 The Members of the Company by this Agreement desire to regulate or establish the affairs of the Company, the conduct of its business, and the relations of the Members.

3.02 The Members owning one hundred percent (100%) of the Interests must agree to the original of this Agreement. Any Amendment to this Agreement requires unanimous consent of the Founding Members, and two-thirds (2/3) majority of all other Members.

ARTICLE IV

ADMINISTRATIVE PROVISIONS AND MANAGEMENT

4.01 Management of the Company shall be vested in the Members.

4.02 Each Member shall devote his or her full professional time and attention to Company activities and shall not directly or indirectly compete with the practice or business of the Company.

4.03 Each Member shall have an equal voice in the management of Company business except as set forth below.

4.03.01 All Members shall have one vote in Firm decisions.

4.03.02 Firm liabilities and/or expenses shall be apportioned among all members in proportion to the balance of his/her capital account.

4.03.03 The following Firm matters shall not be modified without the unanimous consent of the Founding Members:

a. Firm name;

b. Management Committee: Each Founding Member shall be a member of the Firm's Management Committee. The Management Committee shall consist of up to _____ additional Members, who shall be chosen by vote of all firm Members.

4.03.04 The following Firm matters may be modified over objection of a Founding Member by a 2/3 majority of voting Members:

a. Addition of a practice area to the Firm other than __________________ cases;

b. Hiring of first Member in a new practice area;

c. Decisions regarding office space including but not limited to expansion, relocation, satellite offices, real estate purchases, leases, and the like.

d. Obligations requiring personal guarantees and/or the approval of any loans/borrowing resulting in outstanding debt equal to or exceeding 20% of Firm profit during the preceding 12 month period.

e. Hiring and firing non-Members;

f. Income and equity distribution except "Partners/Members" Level of Compensation as referenced above in 4.03.03(b);

g. Advertising and marketing;

h. Substantial expenditures (more than $5,000 per expenditure).

4.03.05 The admission of a new Member or the removal of a Member from the Firm shall require a two-thirds (2/3) majority of voting Members except as set forth in Paragraph 12 of this Agreement.

4.03.06 Firm matters not denoted above or expressly stated otherwise elsewhere in this Agreement shall be decided by a majority vote of all voting Members. If any vote results in a tie, the Members shall continue to discuss the matter until a majority or compromise is reached.

4.04 One or more company bank accounts shall be established. All monies received by the Company shall be deposited in such account or accounts. Checks shall be drawn for Company purposes only. No more than three Members shall have authority to sign checks at any given time. The Members shall vote annually to determine which Members shall have authority to sign checks. In addition to the three Members, other employees (non-Members) may be given the authority to sign checks by a majority vote of all voting Members.

4.05 No Member shall, without the written consent of the other Members (which consent shall not be unreasonably withheld), do any of the following:

(a) Assign the Company property in trust for creditors or on the assignee's promise to pay the debts of the Company.

(b) Confess a judgment.

(c) Submit a Company claim or liability to arbitration or legal action.

(d) Make, execute, or deliver any Company bond, mortgage, deed of trust, guarantee, indemnity bond, surety bond, or accommodation endorsement.

(e) Borrow money in the Company name or use company property as collateral.

(f) Assign, transfer, pledge, compromise, or release any claim of or debt greater than $500 owing to the Company, except upon full payment.

(g) Convey any Company real property.

(h) Pledge or transfer in any manner an interest in the Company or its assets or profits, except to the other Members in equal proportions.

(i) Do any other act that would make it impossible to carry on the ordinary business of the Company.

G) Enter into contracts for the rendering of Partnership services for less than the current billing rates.

(k) Open vendor accounts, supplier, charge or credit card accounts.

4.06 The Members may take any action permitted or required to be taken by the Members without a meeting, either:

(a) Without prior notice and with consent, in writing or by Electronic Transmission, of all of the Members; or

(b) With ten (10) days prior written notice to all Members of a proposed action and thereafter without an in-person vote, the action can be taken if consent is provided in writing by at least the minimum number of votes that would be necessary to authorize or take such action at a meeting. A consent transmitted by a Member by Electronic Transmission shall be deemed to be signed for the purposes of this section. Copies of such consents shall promptly be sent to each

Member not signing such.

4.07 On any matter that is to be voted on by Members, the Members may vote in-person or by proxy.

4.08 The Members may delegate responsibility for some aspect of the business of the Company to one or more Members. By way of illustration and not limitation, the Members may delegate to a Member (as Manager) the right, power and authority on behalf of the Company and in its name to execute documents or other instruments.

4.09 The Members shall be entitled to charge to the Company, or to be reimbursed by the Company for all reasonable and necessary expenses incurred by them in connection with Company business, subject to provision of documentation of such expenses as may be deemed necessary by the Members.

4.10 Each Member shall be an agent of the Company for the purpose of its business. An act of a Member, including the signing of an instrument in the Company name, for apparently carrying on in the ordinary course the Company business, shall bind the Company, unless the Member had no authority to act for the Company in the particular matter and the person with whom the Member was dealing knew or had notice before such transaction that the Member lacked authority.

4.11 Any Member acting as Manager for a particular purpose, having followed procedures herein for approval of transactions, may sign and deliver any instrument transferring or affecting the Company's interest in property, which instrument shall be conclusive in favor of a person who gives value without knowledge of the lack of authority of the person signing and delivering the instrument.

ARTICLE V

LIMITATION OF LIABILITY

5.01 In any proceeding brought with respect to the Company or one or more Members of the Company, the Members shall, except to the extent indicated otherwise by the Act, be indemnified and held harmless from any damages arising out of any transaction, occurrence, or course of conduct.

5.02 The liability of a Member shall not be limited as provided in this section if the Member engaged in gross negligence, breach of fiduciary duty, willful misconduct, or a knowing violation of criminal law.

5.03 Except as otherwise provided by the Act, the liability of any Member for the losses, debts, liabilities and obligations of the Company shall be limited to paying the Member's Capital Contributions when due under this Agreement; the Member's share of any undistributed assets of the Company, and (only to the extent required by the Act) any amounts previously distributed to the Member from the Company.

ARTICLE VI

PROFESSIONAL LIABILITY INSURANCE

6.01 The Company shall, within a reasonable amount of time, procure and maintain a professional liability insurance policy with terms, conditions, limits of coverage, and deductible appropriate for its practice. The insurance policy shall not be cancelled or terminated without the unanimous consent of the Members. If a Member retires from the Company and any remaining Member chooses to continue to practice and maintain the professional liability insurance coverage, the retiring Member shall have the option of continuing to be named as an insured on the professional liability policy for all services rendered while a member of the Company at his or her own expense. A Member who retires and elects to be continued as a named insured shall be given notice and an opportunity to procure his or her own insurance coverage if the remaining Members at any time thereafter decide to cancel or terminate the insurance coverage.

ARTICLE VII

CONTRIBUTIONS

7.01 The Founding Members each contributed $__________ of capital to the Company. Non-founding Members shall make a capital contribution to the Company in the amount of $___________ ("Capital Contribution"). The Capital Contribution shall be made as follows: ____________________________.

Subsequent Non-founding members shall make a Capital Contribution in an amount and by terms decided by existing Members, amounts and terms requiring unanimous consent of the Founding Members and a majority vote of all other existing Members.

ARTICLE VIII

INFORMATION AND RECORDS

8.01 The Company shall keep at its principal office the following:

(a) A list of the names and addresses of each Member;

(b) A copy of the Articles of Organization and the Certificate of Organization, and all articles of amendment and certificates of amendment thereto;

(c) Copies of the Company's federal, state and local income tax returns and reports, if any, for the three most recent years;

(d) Copies of this Agreement and of any financial statements of the Company for the three most recent years; and

(e) Unless contained in this Agreement, a writing setting out:

(i) The amount of cash and a description and statement of the agreed value of the other property or services contributed by each Member and which each Member has agreed to contribute;

(ii) The times at which or events on the happening of which any additional contributions agreed to be made by each Member are to be made;

(iii) Any right of a Member to receive, or of the Company to make, distributions to a Member, which include a return of all or any part of the Member's contribution; and

(iv) Any events upon the happening of which the Company is to be dissolved and its affairs wound up.

8.02 Each Member has the right, upon reasonable request, to:

(a) Inspect and copy any of the Company records required to be maintained by this Article; and

(b) Obtain from any Member or other person with access to such information, from time to time, upon reasonable request (i) true and full information regarding the state of the business and financial condition of the Company, (ii) promptly after becoming available, a copy of the Company's federal, state and local income tax returns for each year, and (iii) other information regarding the affairs of the Company, except to the extent the information demanded is unreasonable or otherwise improper under the circumstances.

ARTICLE IX

CAPITAL ACCOUNTS

9.01 A Capital Account shall be established and maintained for each Member as described in Article VII herein. A Member shall have a single Capital Account, regardless of the time or manner in which any portion of such Member's Interest was acquired.

9.02 As of any date, a Member's Capital Account shall consist of: (i) the sum of (A) the amount of money contributed by such Member to the Company, (B) the agreed upon fair market value of property contributed by such Member to the Company, (C) allocations to such Member of Net Income and Net Gain from Sale (or items thereof), including income and gain exempt from tax, and (D) the amount of any Company liabilities assumed by such Member or that are secured by any Company assets distributed to such Member; minus (ii) the sum of (A) the amount of money distributed to such Member by the Company, (B) the fair market value of property distributed to such Member by the Company, (C) allocations to such Member of Net Loss and Net Loss from Sale (or items thereof), (D) the amount of any liabilities of such Member assumed by the Company or secured by any property contributed by such Member to the Company other than those taken into account in calculating Capital Contributions, and (E) allocations to such Member of expenditures of the Company, if any, that are not deductible in computing taxable income and not chargeable to capital accounts, as described in IRC Section 70S(a)(2)(B) or treated as such expenditures under the regulations thereunder.

9.03 The Capital Account maintenance requirements specified in Treas. Reg. Section 1.704-l(b), which generally mandate that partnership distributions must have substantial economic effect, may result in a special allocations to meet these Capital Account maintenance requirements.

9.04 If there is any basis adjustment pursuant to an election under IRC Section 754, then the Capital Accounts shall be adjusted to the extent required by the IRC regulations.

9.05 No Member shall be paid interest on his or her Capital Account.

ARTICLE X

DISTRIBUTIONS AND ALLOCATIONS

10.01 Subject to Article XIII ("Restrictions on Making Distributions"), all funds available for distribution shall be allocated and distributed among the Members as set forth on Exhibit B—COMPENSATION. The Company shall retain such funds as may be appropriate or needed in carrying out the business purposes of the Company. The Members may periodically revise and amend Exhibit B without requiring revision or amendment of this Operating Agreement. Revision or amendment of Exhibit B shall require unanimous consent of Founding Members and a two-thirds (2/3) majority of all other Members.

10.02 All allocations of net income and net loss for Federal income tax purposes shall be consistent with IRC Section 704 and regulations promulgated thereunder, which rules generally require that such allocations have substantial economic effect. The Members of the Firm shall cooperate to ensure that each Member's taxable income or losses are determined as follows: (1) income or losses shall correspond as closely as possible to actual distributions, compensation, and non-cash benefits (e.g., memberships, paid expenses) received by each Member; and (2) income or losses resulting from retention or payment of such funds as may be appropriate or needed in carrying out the business purposes of the Company shall be allocated to each Member as part of the Compensation allocation set forth on Exhibit B.

ARTICLE XI

ACCOUNTING AND TAXES

11.01 The Company shall keep its accounting records and shall report its income for income tax purposes using the cash method of accounting. Books and records shall be maintained at the Company's principal place of business. The Members shall provide to the Company full financial information on matters affecting the Company. All property acquired with Company funds will be Company property. The Company's fiscal year shall be the calendar year.

11.02 The Members shall use their best efforts to cause the Company to deliver to each Member as soon as possible after the end of each taxable year the information relating to the Company necessary for the preparation of the Members' federal income tax returns.

11.03 The Members shall designate a Member to make all elections necessary for federal income tax purposes.

ARTICLE XII

ADMISSION OF NEW MEMBERS

12.01 The Founding Members shall have complete decision-making authority as regarding the admission of Stephanie J. Smith. The admission of any of this individual requires unanimous consent of the Founding Members. Other Members shall not have a vote regarding the admission of any of this individual as a Member.

12.02 Other than the admission of Stephanie J. Smith, any qualified person may be admitted as a new Member at any time by a two-thirds (2/3) written consent by all voting Members.

12.03 The new Member shall be subject to this Agreement as modified at the time of admission. An admission of a new Member shall be evidenced by an Addendum to this Agreement that shall be signed by all of the Members (including the new Member), and shall state:

a. The date of execution of the Addendum;

b. The effective date of this Agreement as to the new Member;

c. The shares of Company profits and losses to be allocated among the Members;

d. The capital contribution of the new Member, if any;

e. Any amendments to this Agreement; and

f. Any other provisions that may be deemed appropriate.

ARTICLE XIII

RESTRICTIONS ON MAKING DISTRIBUTIONS

13.01 No distribution may be made by the Company if, after giving effect to the distribution:

(a) The Company would not be able to pay its debts as they became due in the usual course of business; or

(b) The Company's total assets would be less than the sum of its total liabilities plus the amount that would be needed, if the Company were to be dissolved at the time of the distribution, to satisfy the preferential rights upon dissolution of Members whose preferential rights are superior to the rights of Members receiving the distribution.

13.02 The Company may base a determination that a distribution is not prohibited under Section 13.01 either on:

(a) Financial statements prepared on the basis of accounting practices and principles that are reasonable in the circumstances; or

(b) A fair valuation or other method that is reasonable in the circumstances.

13.03 For the purposes of this section, the term "distribution" shall not include amounts constituting reasonable compensation for present or past services or reasonable payments made in the ordinary course of business.

ARTICLE XIV

FIRM COMPENSATION

14.01 Matters of compensation shall be controlled by Exhibit B—Compensation, as such Exhibit is amended or revised from time to time.

14.02 Draw. Beginning on May 1, 2018 and continuing on each May 1 thereafter, the Firm's Members shall establish their annual draw for the calendar year. The Draw shall be determined as follows: ____.

14.03 Profit Distribution. The profit remaining after the Draw described above shall be distributed as set forth on Exhibit B, as revised and amended from time to time.

ARTICLE XIV

EVENTS CAUSING A MEMBER'S DISSOCIATION

15.01 A Member shall be dissociated from the Company if at any time the Member fails to maintain his or her status as a member of the Virginia state bar or if the Member becomes a debtor in Bankruptcy or executes an assignment for the benefit of creditors.

15.02 Except as noted above in 14.02 of this Agreement, upon dissociation, a Member shall have no further rights as a member, except the right to receive a payment of an amount representing his or her capital account, determined on a cash basis.

15.03 The dissociation of a Member shall not cause the Company to be dissolved or its affairs to be wound up, and, upon the occurrence of any such event, the Company shall be continued without dissolution.

ARTICLE XV

PAYMENTS TO WITHDRAWING MEMBERS

16.01 Partner Election. A Member may withdraw from the Company upon three (3) months' notice in writing. A Withdrawing Member shall be entitled to the balance of his or her share of monies collected and accounts receivable existing on the date that the Withdrawing

Member provides notice of withdrawal, and the fair market value of net investment assets. A Withdrawing Member's "share" of such assets shall be determined by reference to Article XIV and Exhibit B. Net investment assets shall be defined as any investment assets minus any liabilities outstanding at the time that notice of withdrawal is given. The Withdrawing Member's share of monies collected, accounts receivable, and net investment assets shall be paid out either in a lump sum, or, at the discretion of the non-withdrawing Members, ratably over a period of up to twelve (12) months following actual receipt of payment for outstanding accounts receivable and within twelve (12) months of obtaining access to any investment asset. For example, if an account receivable is not collected until six months after the Withdrawing Member leaves the Company, the non-withdrawing Members may decide to pay the Withdrawing Member's share of the account receivable over the twelve (12) month period beginning on the date of collection, and if the Company invests in a Certificate of Deposit, the non-withdrawing Members may elect to pay the Withdrawing Member's share of this investment asset over twelve (12) months after the expiration of the Certificate of Deposit. Said payment shall not include a share of key man life insurance proceeds.

16.02 Retirement, Death, or Permanent Disability. A Member who dies or retires shall be treated as withdrawing from the Company on the date of death or retirement, as the case may be. Retirement for this purpose is the withdrawal from the Company with the intention to no longer practice law. In the event a Member becomes permanently disabled and remains permanently disabled for six (6) months or more, either the permanently disabled Member or the remaining Members may elect to treat the permanently disabled Member as withdrawing from the Company as of the date six (6) months after the date of the commencement of the permanent disability. Permanent disability will be deemed to have occurred when the disabled Member's attending physician determines that the nature of the injuries or affliction are such that the Member is no longer able to meet the performance requirements of his or her occupation. In the event of the death, retirement, or the permanent disability of a Partner for which an election is made to treat the event as a withdrawal, payment of the Member's share of the Company, which shall be defined as the Member's share of the accrual basis net book value of the Partnership, shall be made to the deceased, retired, or permanently disabled Partner ratably over a period of twelve (12) months.

16.03 Goodwill. Goodwill shall not be considered in valuing the Company for purposes of making payments to a withdrawing Member.

ARTICLE XVI

DISSOLUTION AND WINDING UP

17.01 The Company shall be dissolved and its affairs shall be wound up upon the happening of the first to occur of the following events:

(a) Upon the unanimous consent of the Members;

(b) The entry of a decree of judicial dissolution under § 13.1-1047 of the Code; or

(c) Automatic cancellation of its certificate pursuant to § 13.1-1064.

17.02 Upon dissolution of the Company, the Members agree to make a true account of all things related to the Company, and to duly and equitably adjust such accounting, if necessary. For this purpose, the Company will use an accrual method of accounting, so that, for example, net collectible client billings and accounts payable shall be taken into account and shall be reflected by the Members' respective capital accounts, and any investment assets shall be taken into account at their fair market value.

17.03 Upon dissolution and the winding up of the Company, the assets of the Company shall be distributed as follows:

(a) To creditors, not including Members who are creditors;

(b) To Members who are creditors to the extent permitted by law;

(c) To Members and former Members in satisfaction of liabilities for distributions; and

(d) To the Members in proportion to their respective Capital Accounts.

17.04 Goodwill shall not be considered in valuing the Company for purposes of dissolution.

ARTICLE XVII

NON-COMPETE

18.01 During a Member's association with the Company, the Member shall not practice law or mediation for him- or herself or any other entity whether for profit or pro bono without the written agreement of the other Members.

18.02 For so long as a member is obligated for a share of Company liabilities and/or expenses, as set forth in paragraph 4.03.02 herein, such Member shall not be permitted to practice law for him- or herself or any other entity for profit or pro bono in the Washington, D.C., metropolitan area until that Member has paid his or her share of such Company liability and/or expense.

ARTICLE XVIII

MISCELLANEOUS PROVISIONS

19.01 This Agreement and the rights and liabilities of the parties shall be determined in accordance with the laws of Virginia.

19.02 Captions contained in this Agreement are inserted only as a matter of convenience and in no way define, limit, extend or describe the scope of this Agreement or the intent of any provision hereof. Any parenthetical references to the Code contained in the captions are also inserted only as a matter of convenience. The fact that a caption references a Code section that may have been amended or repealed shall have no effect on the terms of this Agreement.

19.03 Whenever the context may require, any pronouns used herein shall include the corresponding masculine, feminine or neuter forms, and the singular form of nouns and pronouns shall include the plural and vice versa.

19.04 All representations and warranties herein shall survive until the termination of the Company, except to the extent that a representation or warranty expressly provides otherwise.

19.05 Every provision of this Agreement is intended to be severable. If any term or provision hereof is illegal or invalid for any reason whatsoever, such illegality or invalidity shall not affect the validity of the remainder of the terms or provisions within this Agreement.

19.06 This Agreement and any amendments maybe executed in multiple counterparts, each of which shall be deemed an original and all of which together shall constitute one agreement. In addition, this Agreement and any amendments may be executed through the use of counterpart signature pages. The signature of any party on any counterpart agreement or counterpart signature page shall be deemed to be a signature to, and may be appended to, one document.

19.07 This Agreement embodies the entire agreement and understanding between the Members with respect to the subject matter hereof, and supersedes all prior agreements and understandings between such Members relating to the subject matter hereof.

19.08 Any notice, payment, demand, consent, or communication required or permitted to be given by this Agreement shall be in writing and shall be deemed to have been sufficiently given or served for all purposes if delivered personally to the party or to an officer of the party to whom it is directed or if sent by registered or certified mail, postage and charges prepaid, addressed to the address contained in the records of the Company. Any consent or vote relating to any action required or permitted hereunder may be made in writing, including a facsimile copy thereof, signed and dated by the respective Member.

19.09 Any such notice shall be deemed to be given on the date on which it was delivered personally or deposited in a regularly maintained receptacle for the deposit of United States mail, addressed as set forth above. Any Member may change the address of that party for purposes of this Agreement by giving the other Members notice of such change in the manner set forth above.

19.10 By his or her signature, each Member verifies that he or she is in full compliance with the terms of the Firm Office Manual. Each Member further verifies:

(a) That he or she has engaged in no past romantic relationships with any person then employed by the Firm not previously disclosed in writing;

(b) That he or she is not currently engaged in any romantic relationships with any person currently employed by the Firm; and

(c) That he or she shall not engage in future romantic relationships with any person then employed by the Firm.

ARTICLE XVIII

ALTERNATIVE DISPUTE RESOLUTION

20.01 (a) If a controversy should arise under or out of this Agreement, the parties involved in such controversy or their respective successors or designees shall attempt in good faith to resolve the dispute informally through discussions, exchange of documents, or meetings following any such party's written notice to the Members and all other parties to such controversy of the existence and nature of the dispute ("Dispute Notice").

(b) If the parties are unable to resolve the dispute within thirty (30) days after the date of the Dispute Notice, they shall, while continuing to attempt to resolve the dispute, also establish a procedure for mediation of the dispute in the event it is not resolved.

(c) If the dispute has not been resolved and if the parties have not agreed to a procedure of mediation of the dispute within sixty (60) days after the date of the Dispute Notice, the dispute shall be submitted to mediation, initiated by written notice from any party to the dispute, in accordance with the commercial mediation rules of the American Arbitration Association. The parties shall share the cost of the Mediation.

(d) If the dispute has not been resolved pursuant to the aforesaid procedures within 120 days after date of the Dispute Notice, then, upon written request by either party, the dispute shall be submitted to binding arbitration, by a single arbitrator selected by the American Arbitration Association, and otherwise subject to the then-current commercial arbitration rules of the American Arbitration Association.

(e) The arbitrator shall promptly obtain such information regarding the matter as it deems advisable and shall decide with dispatch the matter and render a written award, which shall be delivered to the Company. Any such award shall be a conclusive determination of the matter and shall be binding upon each Member and each party to the dispute, and shall not be contested by any party. At the time of rendering the award, the arbitrator shall establish its fees and expenses in connection therewith. Such fees and expenses shall be allocable by the arbitrator in its award. Judgment upon any arbitration award may be entered and enforced in any court of competent jurisdiction. No dissolution or termination of the Company shall effect or impair any party's rights to arbitrate a dispute under this Article.

20.02 Notwithstanding the provisions of Section 19.01 to the contrary, any party may apply to the local Circuit Court for Fairfax County, Virginia, for injunctive relief and other interim measures to prevent or stop irreparable harm to such party's rights or property during the pendency of any mediation or arbitration proceeding.

ARTICLE IXX

CONFIDENTIALITY

21.01 The terms of this Operating Agreement and any Addenda or Exhibits are to be kept confidential and shall only be shared by and between the signatories and their counsel, if any. The financial information related to the Firm including, but not limited to, compensation, revenue, expenses, financial records, etc. shall be deemed confidential, and no such confidential information shall be shared with a non-Member without the unanimous consent of all voting Members unless required by law. The signatories hereto may vote to share the terms hereof with any person, and the vote shall be unanimous among the signatories.

IN WITNESS WHEREOF, the undersigned have executed this Agreement as of the day and year first above written.

MEMBERS:

Printed member name

Printed member name

Printed member name

Printed member name

Printed member name

EXHIBIT A

MEMBER NAMES AND ADDRESSES

EXHIBIT B—COMPENSATION

2. Job Offer Form Letter

DATE

William Sample

123 Victory Lane

Fairfax, VA 12345

Dear Mr. Sample:

On behalf of all of us at FIRM NAME, I am pleased to offer you the position of ________________________ with our firm. The following letter confirms the details of the offer.

Start Date

Monday, (Date)—full-time/part time status (XXXX hours, XXXX days per week)

Salary

This position is classified as a full-time/part-time, non-exempt status employee starting on ______________. The hourly rate is $_________ per hour. (Alternate for salaried: The annual salary is $____________ per year.)

Work Schedule

Your full-time schedule is _____ AM to _____ PM Monday through Friday. (Optional: There is some flexibility in the work hours, and from time to time you may need to work additional hours.)

Attire

Business

Paid Time Off (PTO)

When your position becomes full-time active status, you will receive 15 days of paid time off during the first year of employment for personal, sick, or other use. Participation in PTO begins after completion of the first 90 days of employment. We request advance notice for scheduling time off per our company policy. Emergencies are an exception to this. Time off cannot be carried forward from year to year. After completion of two years of employment, Paid Time Off beyond what is described will be determined per company policy.

[Consider breaking PTO into two categories: vacation and sick leave. There are a number of variables to consider when creating this policy, such as whether your policy will encourage sick people to still come to work and whether the policy may be viewed as having a disproportionately negative impact on a certain category of team members, such as working mothers.]

Holidays

FIRM NAME offers 7 paid holidays per calendar year as described in the Employee Handbook you will be receiving.

Performance Review

The standard for FIRM NAME employees is that your performance is reviewed upon completion of 90 days. In accordance with your offer of employment, we will formally review your performance at the 6-month anniversary of your employment, at which time a salary increase will be considered based upon your performance.

Your formal, annual performance review will take place beginning in December, __________, consistent with the firm's the annual review schedule.

401K/Profit Sharing

Upon completion of 12 months of satisfactory employment, employees are eligible to participate in FIRM NAME 401K Plan. Your eligible enrollment dates after the 12-month period are January 1 and July 1. The plan allows an employer's match of 3–4% on the contribution made by the employee. Details of the plan will be provided to you.

Medical and Dental Insurance

Employees have the option to participate in our medical insurance plan. FIRM NAME will contribute 50% of the premium cost for the employee. Information regarding the insurance plan will be provided to you. Eligibility for participation begins after completion of 60 days of active employment.

By accepting this offer of employment, you are confirming you understand that your employment will be on an at-will basis, and neither you nor any FIRM NAME representative has entered into a contract regarding the terms or the duration of your employment.

As an at-will employee, you will be free to terminate your employment with FIRM NAME at any time, with or without cause or advance notice. Likewise, FIRM NAME will have the right to reassign you, to change your compensation, or to terminate your employment at any time, with or without cause or advance notice.

Employment at FIRM NAME is contingent upon verification of all the information provided by you for the purpose of employment and completion of all employment documentation.

Acknowledgment

This employment offer letter represents the entire agreement between you and FIRM NAME, and no verbal or written agreements, promises, or representations that are not specifically stated in this employment offer letter are or will be binding upon FIRM NAME.

If you are in agreement with the above employment offer details, please sign below and return this employment offer to ___________________ by DATE.

Acknowledgment and acceptance of offer

______________________________ WILLIAM SAMPLE ________________ Date

I anticipate that you will play an important role in our Company and obtain personal and professional satisfaction. I look forward to working with you.

Sincerely,

FIRM PARTNER,

President

3. Job Description Form

Legal Assistant Responsibilities

New Clients

- Scan Personal Information Form (PIF) and save to server file. Original stays in hanging file until engaged.
- Once engaged, create client asset binder. Move PIF and any asset documents to the asset binder.
- If not engaged, follow instructions whether to return PIF/funding docs to prospect or shred.
- Input PIF into database.
- Generate Asset Report.
- Update database after Strategy Meeting. Consult attorney on any questions immediately following Strategy Meeting.
- Schedule meeting with clients.
- Prepare meeting packet.
- Attend meeting.
- Enter data into database.
    - Finish any remaining tasks in Counselling matter and close.
    - Create matter for client.
    - Record notes from meeting in matter.
    - Activate portal if they signed up.
- Agreements
    - Engagement Agreement: scan and save in Agreements folder. File original in

client agreements binder.

- Record notes in database under each asset.
    - Internal Law Firm notes: our tracking purposes, e.g., mailed form, waiting on confirm from client, etc.
    - Historical Client Comments: action items to client to do/follow up on.
- Scan and submit all signed forms.
- Follow up with clients and advisor on getting verifications about every 30, 60, and 90 days.
- Scan and file verifications as they come in.

4. Office Manual

INTRODUCTION

Firm Biography

LAW FIRM, PLLC ("the Firm") was established by ___________, ____________, and ___________ in 20____.

Purpose and Use of This Office Manual

The manual is designed to inform all employees of the Firm's policies in general and should be consulted and used on a frequent basis. The policies and procedures outlined in this manual are not to be considered conditions of employment. The manual is not intended to create, nor is it construed to be, a contract of employment between any employee and the Firm. The employment relationship between the Firm and its employees is "at-will," such that it may be terminated by either the Firm or the employee.

Establishment of New or Revised Procedures

This manual is intended to be a dynamic tool for implementing office procedures. The Firm reserves the right to modify, revoke, suspend, terminate, or change any or all of the policies set forth herein, at any time. All employees are encouraged to submit suggestions for revisions and additions.

RECEIPT

I, ______________________, acknowledge receipt of the _______ Manual. I have read the _____________ Manual and agree to be bound by the rules, regulations, and policies contained in the Manual, as well as by any changes in the rules, regulations, and policies that may be established in the future.

I understand and agree that nothing contained herein should be interpreted or construed as an employment contract. I further understand and agree that my employment is terminable at will and that both the Firm and I each have the right to discontinue the employment relationship at any time and for any reason.

I further understand that it is my responsibility to familiarize myself with all information in this Manual. I also understand that I should ask a partner or the Office Manager to clarify any information in this Manual that I do not understand. I acknowledge that any oral or written statements or promises made to me that are contrary to this Manual are disavowed and not binding on the Firm.

____

Printed Name of Employee

____

Signature of Employee

____

Date

General Policies and Procedures

Equal Opportunity Employer

The Firm is an equal opportunity employer. No employee will be discriminated against because of the race, color, religion, sex, national origin, ancestry, citizenship, creed, marital status, veteran status, age, sexual orientation, or disability with respect to hiring, promotion, firing, compensation, or other terms, conditions, or privileges of employment.

Sexual Harassment

The Firm has a "zero tolerance" policy of, and will maintain a work environment free from, sexual harassment. Anyone who claims that he/she has been the victim of harassment should report the harassment to a partner or the Firm's Office Manager. A prompt, thorough, and confidential investigation of the complaint shall be conducted, and appropriate disciplinary measures shall be taken against the offending party. All complaints of harassment, and any information developed during the course of the investigation of these complaints, will be kept strictly confidential unless required to be divulged as part of the investigation or pursuant to a legal proceeding. There will be no retaliation against any person pursuing his/her rights under the law or this policy, except that any person who willfully, knowingly, or intentionally files a false complaint under this policy can be subject to disciplinary action up to and including termination.

Personal and Professional Conduct

Clients are the main focus of the Firm's work. All clients and visitors should be treated courteously, their business given prompt attention, and their stay in the office made pleasant. The Firm also expects each employee to treat his/her coworkers with respect and courtesy. Each employee should respect the workspace of another and refrain from interrupting other employees when they are conducting the Firm's business. Conversations in the hallways and break room should not be so loud that others cannot conduct business without disruption.

Dress Policy

Absent special circumstances, professional attire shall be worn at all times.

Confidential Nature of Client Matters

All matters relating to any clients or office matters are completely confidential. A client often provides highly personal information to the lawyer or paralegal, whether during conversation or by providing documentation. Accordingly, the following policies should be adhered to at all times:

No confidential documents should be left in open or public areas, nor should computer monitors be left on in places where they can be easily seen by passersby or other clients.

All client boxes should be labeled with the client's initials only (not full or last names) and the last name of the lead attorney.

Any employee meeting with a client in his/her workspace should ensure that all documents and other information pertaining to other clients are appropriately and confidentially stored out of sight.

No client meetings should take place in the lounge area in the hallway nearest the file cabinets, the reception area, the kitchen, or in the hallways in general.

The door to any meeting area (such as an office or conference room) should be closed during meetings with clients.

No employee should allow a non-employee access to the office of a lawyer, paralegal, or Office Manager without that employee's prior consent.

Other than service calls prearranged by the Firm, no non-employee shall be permitted to use the Firm's computers, copiers, or other Firm equipment of any kind without direct and continuous supervision by a Firm employee.

Whenever possible, all information to be left for a lawyer, paralegal, or Office Manager should be placed in his/her chair.

Confidential Nature of Employee Information

No personal information about an employee (home address, cell and/or home telephone number, personal e-mail address, marital status, travel plans, etc.) shall be given out without the employee's prior approval. When in doubt, refer all such inquiries to the Office Manager.

Hours, Holidays, Office Closures, and Leave

Office Hours

The Firm's office hours are 8:30 AM to 5:30 PM, Monday through Friday, except for those days when the office is closed (see sections below related to holidays and other closures).

Work Hours

Employees are expected to work between 8:30 AM and 5:30 PM. Non-exempt employees are not required to work outside of 8:30 AM to 5:30 PM except in prearranged circumstances. Non-exempt employees shall not be required to work more than 40 hours per week.

Holidays

The following are paid holidays during which the office will normally be closed:

New Year's Day

Martin Luther King, Jr., Day

Presidents' Day

Memorial Day

4th of July

Labor Day

Columbus Day

Veterans Day

Thanksgiving Day

Day after Thanksgiving

Christmas Day

At the discretion of the Firm, there may be additional days upon which the office will be closed or will close early (such as before a three-day holiday weekend). If one of the above-referenced holidays falls on a Saturday, the office will be closed on Friday. If one of the above-referenced holidays falls on a Sunday, the office will be closed on Monday.

Inclement Weather

During inclement weather,* the Firm shall follow the schedule set forth by the ___________ County Circuit Court. Employees may monitor (LOCAL NEWS), or call the ___________ County Employee Inclement Weather Line at ____-____-SNOW (7669). In the event that an employee believes that his/her commute would not be safe given the weather conditions, but the __________ County Circuit Court is open, the employee should telephone/text/e-mail the Office Manager (or a Partner if unable to reach the Office Manager) to notify him/her of the conditions and the employee may take a personal day.

*The Firm only follows the __________ County Circuit Court for inclement weather. The Firm does not follow __________ County Circuit Court for other non-weather-related emergencies (power outages, bomb threats, etc.). In the case of a non-weather-related emergency, the Firm will be open, unless you hear otherwise from the Office Manager.

Paid Time Off (PTO)

Regular full-time staff members will be given paid time off on January 1 of each year, pursuant to the terms of employment set forth in an acceptance letter and/or review. This paid time off may be used for vacations, sick leave, personal time off, etc.

Paid time off cannot be carried over to another calendar year without the advance approval of the Office Manager. Prior to submitting a request for PTO unrelated to illness or emergency, each employee is asked to consult with the lawyer(s) to whom he/she is primarily responsible to determine a mutually acceptable time. PTO requests should be submitted at least two weeks in advance, in writing or e-mail, to the Office Manager. Any conflicts in PTO requests shall be resolved by the Office Manager.

If a staff member is ill and unable to report for work, he/she should call or e-mail the Office Manager before 9:00 AM to report his/her illness. If a staff member has used all of his/her PTO, he/she will not be paid for the absence.

Bereavement Leave

Any employee experiencing a death in his/her immediate family shall be granted three (3) days off with pay. Immediate family includes a parent, spouse or significant other, child, brother, or sister. Employees who experience a death of a grandparent, parent-in-law, aunt, uncle, nephew, or niece shall be granted two (2) days off with pay to attend the funeral or memorial service.

Pregnancy/Maternity Leave

Paid medical leave for reasons of pregnancy, childbirth, or complications arising there from will be allowed for up to a total of six (6) weeks. Pregnant employees should advise the Office Manager how far into their pregnancy they expect to work absent unforeseen circumstances.

Before departure, if possible, a pregnant lawyer should personally meet with each lawyer taking over one of her cases or matters. In addition, the lawyer should contact all clients to make them aware of the lawyer's absence and to introduce the client to replacement. In addition, each of the lawyer's case files should contain a "Case Status Memorandum" in the first section, outlining the client's name, the assigned back-up attorney, the opposing counsel, a synopsis of the background of, and issues in, the case, all scheduled hearing/trial dates, an outline of upcoming deadlines/tasks (with specific due dates where applicable), and any other important or special matters relevant to the case.

Paternity Leave

Every Firm employee is entitled to two (2) weeks of paid parental/paternity leave in the following situations:

- The employee's spouse or significant other giving birth to a child
- The adoption of a child by the employee

The paternity leave must be taken prior to the child reaching six months of age. Employees must notify the Office Manager before starting parental/paternity leave.

Leave of Absence—Military Reserves or National Guard

Any employees called to active duty in a National Guard or Military Reserve Unit will, upon their return from military service, be reinstated to their former position with the Firm in accordance with the Uniformed Services Employment and Reemployment Rights Act of 1994 (USERRA), and any amendments to that statute. Salary will end when the individual reports for active duty. A copy of the military active duty orders will be provided to the Office Manager at the time leave is requested.

Jury Duty

Employees will be given leave for jury service. Employees should notify the Office Manager as soon as they receive their jury service notification. Employees will be paid full salary for up to one (1) week of jury service. If an employee on jury service is dismissed before 1:00 PM on any day, he/she should return to the office for the balance of the workday.

Leave of Absence—Other

Under special circumstances, an unpaid leave of absence may be granted at the discretion of the Firm. Any employee desiring a leave of absence should submit the request in writing to the partners and Office Manager as early as possible. Such written request should set forth the reason for, and desired length of, the leave.

Election Service—Voting

The Firm encourages employees to vote in all elections. Up to four (4) hours may be taken during the workday to vote in national, state, or local elections.

OFFICE SECURITY AND EMERGENCY PROCEDURES

Doors

The door to the reception area should be locked prior to 8:30 AM and after 5:30 PM. The back door to the office space shall be locked at all times. Only employees shall be permitted to maintain keys to the office space. In no circumstance shall an employee provide a key to the office space to a non-employee.

Admission of Visitors and Strangers

At no time shall persons other than employees of the Firm be allowed to roam at will, unescorted, through the Firm's offices. It is a matter of courtesy to accompany clients and visitors to and from the exits or other office areas to which they may be going. If you encounter strangers in our offices who are unescorted and do not satisfactorily identify themselves, please advise the receptionist or Office Manager. Contact the police if such persons refuse to identify themselves or leave.

Fireproof Safe

The Firm has a locked fireproof safe located in the Office Manager's office for use in storing valuable original documents such as wills and stock certificates, or evidence such as tape recorders, etc. See the Office Manager regarding placement and/or removal of items from the safe.

Data Protection

All legal work should be downloaded and saved on the network for purposes of data protection. Employees are not permitted to maintain legal documents in any other location. Employees are required to protect all devices used to access client files, Firm e-mail accounts, or any other Firm-related materials with a password.

Personal Property

Personal items and property of value should be safeguarded. Purses, wallets, and valuable jewelry should not be left unattended in the office. Money (even small change) should not be left in the office overnight. The Firm is not responsible for loss of an employee's money or other valuables.

Fire/Emergency Alarms

In case of fire or emergency, employees should exit via the stairway outside the front door to the Firm's suite. In the alternative, employees may exit the back of the suite, take a right down the hallway (toward the entrance of the space), and take the stairway near the front door. DO NOT USE ELEVATORS.

The Firm's meeting point is the "No Parking Area," which is located near the hedges between Fairfax Boulevard and Captain Pell's on the most northeastern portion of the property. Exit the building in the rear, go around the building to the left, and walk toward Fairfax Boulevard on the Captain Pell's side.

Designated Fire Marshall:

1. Robert Kotwicki

2. Joanne Randa (if Robert is out)

This person will make sure all of the offices are empty before leaving. He/she will take a key to the office, ensure the front door is locked, and make sure that all of the Firm's employees are accounted for at the Firm's meeting point.

Earthquake Procedure

The following procedures are advised in the event of an earthquake:

- Drop to the ground, take cover by getting under a sturdy table or other piece of furniture, and hold on until the shaking stops. If there is not a table or desk near you, cover your face and head with your arms and crouch in an inside corner of the building.

- Stay away from glass, windows, outside doors and walls, and anything that could fall, such as lighting fixtures or furniture.
- Use a doorway for shelter only if it is in close proximity to you and if you know it is a strongly supported, load-bearing doorway.
- Stay inside until the shaking stops and it is safe to go outside. Research has shown that most injuries occur when people inside buildings attempt to move to a different location inside the building or try to leave.
- Be aware that the electricity may go out or the sprinkler systems or fire alarms may turn on.
- DO NOT use the elevators.

Power Outage Procedure

If a power outage occurs, turn off all electrical equipment to lessen the electrical load on the circuits. Open all shades to allow natural light to filter through the office. The building management will determine the cause and possible duration of the blackout, and any information will be communicated to the Firm.

First Aid

Bandages, aspirin, and first-aid supplies are available in the kitchen.

TERMINATION

The Firm hopes that each employee will remain with the Firm for a long period of time. However, this may not always be possible. Employment at the Firm is "at-will" and can be terminated, with or without cause, and with or without notice, by an employee or by the Firm, at any time, for reasons that either may consider sufficient.

Employee Notice of Termination

Before an employee makes a decision to resign, he/she is encouraged to discuss the matter with a Partner(s) and/or the Office Manager. If the employee wishes to terminate employment, notice should be given to the Partners and Office Manager at least two (2) weeks in advance of the intended date of termination.

Employer Notice of Termination, Including "For Cause"

If the Firm elects to terminate an employee, he/she will be provided, at the election of the Firm, with two (2) weeks' notice or two (2) weeks' pay in lieu of two (2) weeks' notice. No severance pay will be provided to any terminated employee.

Any employee terminated "for cause" will not be entitled to two (2) weeks' notice or two (2) weeks' pay. The phrase "for cause" includes, without limitation, acts of dishonesty, gross breach of professional ethics, gross negligence, and other acts of similar nature.

Property of the Firm upon Employee's Departure

No employee shall be permitted to remove anything other than personal belongings from the Firm upon his/her departure. Note that all materials saved electronically on the Firm server and/or individual computers are the property of the Firm and may not be removed from the Firm's server and/or computers at any time or for any purpose.

Letters of Recommendation/References

Letters of recommendation for departing employees are not a matter of right. Requests for such letters should be directed to the Office Manager.

All requests for a reference by a former employee should be referred to the Office Manager for response. Unless the Firm receives a written authorization or a release signed by the former employee, the Firm's response will only include dates of employment, salary, and job title.

TECHNOLOGY

Use of the Firm's Electronic Media

The computers, electronic media, and services provided by the Firm are primarily for business use to assist lawyers and staff members in the performance of their work. Limited, occasional, or incidental use of electronic media (sending or receiving) for personal, non-Firm business purposes is understandable, but this privilege should not be abused. All such use should be done in a manner that does not negatively affect the systems' use for their business purposes. All staff members are expected to demonstrate a sense of responsibility and not abuse this privilege.

Electronic media may not be used for knowingly transmitting, retrieving, or storing any communication that is:

1. Discriminatory or harassing;
2. Derogatory to any individual or group;
3. Obscene, sexually explicit, or pornographic;
4. Defamatory or threatening;
5. In violation of any license governing the use of software; or
6. Engaged in for any purpose that is illegal or contrary to the Firm's business interests or this policy.

Firm Review of Employee Communications

Generally, electronic information created and/or communicated by an employee using e-mail, word processing, utility programs, spreadsheets, voicemail, telephones, Internet, bulletin board system access, and similar electronic media is reviewable by the Firm. The following conditions, however, should be noted:

- The Firm reserves the right, at its discretion, to review any employee's electronic files and messages.
- No employee should assume that electronic communications are private. Accordingly, if an employee has highly confidential information to transmit, other means should be sought.

Software Usage

To prevent computer viruses, worms, spyware, and other malicious code from being transmitted through the Firm's computer system, unauthorized downloading of any unauthorized software is strictly prohibited. Only software registered through and approved by the Firm's Office Manager may be downloaded. Any questions with respect to this policy should be directed to the Office Manager.

Use of Encryption Software

Lawyers and staff may use encryption software supplied to them by the Firm for purposes of safeguarding sensitive or confidential client or Firm information. When using encryption for case files or other Firm matters that are stored on a Firm computer, employees must provide the Office Manager with a sealed hard-copy record to be stored in a secure location of all of the passwords and/or encryption keys necessary to access the files or other materials.

MISCELLANEOUS

Housekeeping

Each employee is urged to keep his/her workspace net, clean, and free of items not being used. Malfunction of any equipment should be reported to the Office Manager.

Use of Lunchroom/Coffee Station

The lunchroom is available to all Firm employees. The lunchroom has a refrigerator, microwave oven, and toaster oven for the convenience of the staff. Those who use the lunchroom should keep it clean by washing and putting away all utensils after use. All refuse should be placed in the trash, and an employee's eating area should be wiped down before leaving the lunchroom. Employees should also respect the property of others who keep food in the refrigerator. The refrigerator will generally be cleaned out on Friday afternoon, every other week. Any items not specifically labeled as to name of employee and date will be discarded.

The coffee station located outside of the lunchroom has a ready supply of coffee and tea for all personnel and office guests. Please immediately remove and discard used "K-cups" from the coffee machine.

Suggestions

Employee suggestions for the better and more efficient operation of the office are always welcome. All suggestions should be typed in memo form to the Office Manager, copied to the Partners, and may be made anonymously if desired.

Personal Use of Office Equipment

The Firm's supplies, copy machines, and postage meter are for the Firm's business only and may not be used for personal needs. Personal telephone calls during business hours, both incoming and outgoing, should be kept to a minimum and placed during an employee's lunch hour or break, when possible. Employees are expected to report, and pay for, any personal long-distance telephone calls.

COMPENSATION POLICIES

It is the Firm's desire to pay wages or salaries that are competitive with other employers in the marketplace and in a way that will be motivational, fair, and equitable. Compensation may vary based on roles and responsibility, individual and company performance, and in compliance with all applicable laws.

Salary: Each employee's initial salary is established by the Firm on the basis of the complexity and responsibility of the position he/she fills and that particular employee's experience. Salaries are subject to change at the discretion of the Firm.

Merit Increases, Decreases in Salary: Changes to salary are discretionary and will be decided by the Firm based on merit and the economic condition of the Firm. Merit includes accomplishment, ability, productivity, attitude, effort, initiative, and overall value to the Firm. Seniority may play a factor but does not, by itself, justify a salary increase.

Annual Performance and Salary Review: Toward the end of each calendar year, the Firm will undertake a comprehensive review of each employee's performance. Decisions regarding salary level and/or bonuses will be made by the Firm at that time and communicated to the employee in an in-person interview, attended by the Office Manager and a Partner at the Firm. If requested, the employee will also receive feedback in written form. Non-attorney employees will typically receive their review shortly before the Thanksgiving holiday. Attorney employees will typically receive their review shortly before the Christmas holiday.

Pay Period: Firm employees are paid 24 times each year on the 15th and the last day of each month. If these days fall on a weekend or holiday, the pay is issued on the last business day prior to the scheduled payday. Paychecks are processed through payroll service and shall be directly deposited to an account denoted by the employee.

Performance Bonuses: Performance bonuses may be given to Firm employees at the discretion of the Firm. There are two factors that typically determine bonus availability and amounts: (1) Firm performance and profits and (2) personal performance.

Overtime Pay: Overtime compensation is paid to non-exempt employees in accordance with federal and state wage and hour restrictions. All overtime work performed must receive a Partner's or Office Manager's prior authorization.

Benefits: The Firm sponsors a comprehensive benefits program for eligible employees, and each benefit plan has specific eligibility conditions. The benefits are summarized in separate booklets called "summary plan descriptions," which are provided to all eligible employees. The details of each benefit are contained in separate legal documents known as the "plan documents," which take precedence over anything contradictory in the summaries.

INSURANCE COVERAGE

Health Insurance: All eligible employees may participate in the group health insurance coverage provided by the Firm. In such event, the Firm will contribute to an employee's premium in an amount of up to one-half of the health insurance coverage cost for an individual employee.

Disability Insurance: The Firm makes disability insurance available to its employees. The Firm pays for short-term coverage, and the employee pays for long-term coverage. Each employee shall be responsible for the costs associated with disability insurance should the employee sign up for disability insurance.

Workers Compensation: All employees are entitled to Workers' Compensation benefits paid by the Firm. This coverage is automatic and immediate and protects employees from work-related injury or illness. If an employee cannot work due to a work-related injury or illness, Workers' Compensation insurance pays his/her medical bills and provides a portion of his/her income until he/she can return to work.

Unemployment Compensation: Unemployment Compensation is designed to provide a temporary income for those who are out of work through no fault of their own. Depending upon the circumstances, employees may be eligible for Unemployment Compensation upon termination of employment with the Firm. The Division of Unemployment Insurance of each state's Department of Labor determines eligibility for Unemployment Compensation. The Firm pays the entire cost of this insurance program.

Social Security: The United States Government operates a system of mandated insurance known as Social Security. As wage earners, employees are required by law to contribute a set amount of weekly wages to the trust fund from which benefits are paid. As an employer, the Firm is required to deduct this amount from each paycheck an employee receives. In addition, the Firm matches employee contributions dollar for dollar, thereby paying one-half of the cost of employee Social Security benefits.

RETIREMENT

Retirement Plan: The Firm supports employee retirement preparation and investment by providing a 401(k) plan. The details regarding participation, contributions, vesting, administration, and investments are provided in the summary plan description.

Presently, employees are eligible to participate in the 401(k) after one year of full-time employment (e.g., more than 1,000 hours of work in the previous calendar year), and the Firm matches employee contributions up to 4 percent of an employee's salary.

OTHER BENEFITS

Training and Professional Development: The Firm encourages all of its employees to participate in training and professional development courses, and it will pay for such courses so long as the employee obtains advance approval of the course from a Partner or the Office Manager.

Health Club: The Firm will provide a gym membership at the Fairfax Racquet Club to interested employees, at no charge. However, the firm is required to report the provision of the membership as compensation, and employees are therefore taxed on the value of the membership.

BILLING POLICIES

The Firm's billing policies begin with the initial contact with a potential client (PNC) and remain in effect throughout our relationship with our clients.

Initial Contact

- PNC calls: PNCs who telephone our office and ask for a specific attorney should be told the attorney's hourly rate.
- PNC meetings: All PNCs should be provided with a copy of the Firm's billing policies. If the attorney is willing to take the PNC's case, the PNC should be provided with a retainer agreement that discloses all of the hourly rates of the attorneys and paralegals.
- Representation: The Firm does not begin representing a PNC until a retainer agreement has been signed and a retainer fee has been paid. Under no circumstances, even a pro bono case, will the Firm represent anyone who has not signed a retainer agreement. It is the attorney's responsibility to inform the PNC that the Firm will not represent the PNC until the retainer agreement has been executed.

Each client receives a bill/invoice from the Firm every month whether or not any work has been performed in the client's case. Our invoices are the most consistent means of communication that we have with our clients. We must keep in mind that our clients are not likely to be pleased when they receive our bills. They are going through a very difficult time in their lives, and at the same time, they are paying a substantial fee for a service that they would prefer not to need.

For these reasons, and ethical and other reasons, it is critical that our bills are absolutely accurate and that they explain to the client what work has been done. It is important that the explanations of the work be detailed enough that clients, even the least sophisticated ones, understand that they are receiving something valuable for their payment.

This applies to every client regardless of wealth. Even the clients of limited means are often paying $500 or more in a given month. Please keep in mind that this is frequently a significant hit to our clients' budgets. Imagine that you were receiving a bill for $500, and keep in mind that you would like to see something in return for your hard-earned money.

Drafting Billing Entries

- Detail: Each entry you make must explain what you have done on the client's behalf with enough specificity that the client understands what you have done AND that the work done justifies the payment we are requesting. Also, the entries should be made with an eye toward the possibility that a Judge may eventually look at the bills in an attorney fee claim and need to determine if the fee charged was reasonable for the work performed.
- Consistency: We strive to use consistent language for all of our clients. Even though there are many different employees with different personal styles, particularly in cases that involves multiple billers, it is helpful to draft the billing entries consistently so it appears to the client that we are one team rather than several individuals working on a case. To the extent possible, please use the abbreviations that have been prepared to help maintain consistency in the billing entries. Attached please find a list of abbreviations that are programmed into Timeslips.
- No Charges: Even if you know that you plan to "no charge" time spent by you or another employee assisting you, it is important that the time spent on the case appear on the client's bill. We want the clients to recognize that more time was spent on their

case than what we are requesting in payment.

General Billing Rules

- Hourly Rates: We do not accept cases on a flat-fee basis. All of our clients are billed pursuant to our hourly rates in six-minute increments.
- Initial Consultation: We charge for our initial consultations at our hourly rate. There are two circumstances in which the individual attorney may decide not to charge a PNC. First, if the PNC is a close connection to a good referral source or other contact, the attorney may decide not to charge for the consultation. Second, if the attorney decides that he/she will not take the case even if the PNC wants to retain the firm, the attorney may opt not to charge the PNC.
- Retainers: We expect our clients to provide a retainer fee and that we will bill against the retainer fee. Attorneys may not accept cases without a retainer or continue to represent clients who do not have funds in their retainer accounts without the approval of a Partner.
- Pro Bono: Attorneys may not take on pro bono cases without the approval of a Partner.
- Write Offs: No attorney may write off more than the equivalent of two hours of time per billing cycle without the approval of a Partner. As a general rule, we do not agree to discount our fees in exchange for or as an incentive to get a client to accept a settlement offer.
- Travel Time: Clients are billed for our travel time to and from court and/or other locations related to the case. If you are leaving directly from home, the time billed to the client should start from the time that you pass the office. If it takes less time to

drive from your home to court, etc. than it would to get from the office to court, etc., the client can only be billed for the actual time that you spent driving from your home to the court, etc.

- Multiple Attorneys and/or Paralegals at Meeting/Phone Call: The lead attorney on the case will make a judgment call as to whether or not the others' time will be billed or "no charged."
- Office Conferences Regarding a Case: These "conferences" may be in the form of meetings, intercom, e-mails, etc. The lead attorney on the case will make a judgment call as to whether or not the time spent discussing a case, assigning a portion of a case, etc. will be billed to the client. The time spent in the associate and/or paralegal meetings discussing a case shall not be billed to clients.
- Copies of E-mails, Letters, etc.: No one will bill clients for reviewing a copy of a letter, e-mail, fax, etc. if another employee is simply forwarding the correspondence to keep the other employee in the loop on a case. If the correspondence is forwarded and action is required by the person who receives the forwarded correspondence, the employee may bill for the time to review the correspondence and the action going forward.
- Court Appearances for More Than One Client: The total amount billed to both clients cannot exceed the total amount of time that you spent traveling and at the courthouse. The attorney should do his/her best to determine how much of his/her time at the courthouse was spent on each individual case and should divide the travel time equally between the clients.
- Filing Fees: No checks will be written for clients who do not have enough funds in

their retainer accounts to cover the filing fees unless a Partner approves the check.

- Third-Party Bills: Notice of all third-party bills will be provided to the Office Manager so that the bills can be forwarded again to the client as part of the billing cycle/process.

5. Review Forms

You can provide your employees this Self-Evaluation Form before the Performance Review.

SELF-EVALUATION FORM

1) What do you feel you are doing well at the firm?

2) What do you feel you need to improve on and/or need more training in?

3) What aren't you doing that you feel you should be doing?

4) What does the firm do particularly well?

5) What does the firm need to improve on?

6) What isn't the firm doing that the firm should be doing?

Employee Review (Employer Form)

Performance Review

A. Meeting expectations of the job description?

B. Exceeding expectations?

C. Training—Grade____. Needs more training? What areas?

D. Technology Proficiency—Software, hardware

E. Punctual—At work? Specific tasks? Absent?

F. Demeanor/Appearance—Professional?

G. Communication—With supervisor? With team? With clients?

H. Strengths

I. Weaknesses

J. Attitude—Positive? Complainer? Problem solver?

K. Overall view of team member

L. Compensation—Salary increase? Additional benefits?

M. Thoughts on how the firm can do better to help team member succeed?

Reviewer Initials _________ Date _________

Employee Initials _________ Date _________

6. **Intake Form for Potential New Client**

POTENTIAL NEW CLIENT INTAKE SHEET

Date: ____________________ **Time:** ______________**AM/PM** □□ **CONFLICT**

□□ **NO CONFLICT**

Phone or **E-mail** **Taken By:** _________________ **Date entered into Conflicts List:**

____

Atty. Requested (Specific): __________________ **Atty. Assigned:**

____

PNC FULL NAME:

____

SPOUSE FULL NAME:

____

_

PREFERRED TELEPHONE: **(Cell/Home/Work)** ____________________________

(Permission to leave VM _)

PERSONAL E-MAIL: ____

Referred By: □□ Internet □□ Former Client □□ Attorney □□ Friend □□ Therapist □□ Mediator □□ Financial □□ Other

Specific: ____

______

INITIAL ADMIN INFORMATON

County: ______________________ **Number of Children (Ages):**

____

Any Court Filings/Dates: ______________________ **Spouse's Attorney:**

____

____

____

____

ATTORNEY NOTES ONLY

____

____

____

____

____

____

____

____

____

____

____

____

Attorney/Initial Consultation Fee Notification (Circle Below)

Attorney A:

$__________

Attorney B:

$__________

CALL PUT DIRECTLY THROUGH?

□ **Call Taken Immediately** □ **E-mail** □ □□ Attorney Unavailable ~ Date/Time of Call Back: ____

APPOINTMENT MADE?

Date/Time of Appt.: ___________________________ □□ NO—Left VM/Waiting for Call Back □ □□ NO—Found Another Attorney □□ NO—Cost

□ NO—Just Gathering Info □ NO—We Didn't Want It □□ NO—Referred Out □□ NO—Other ____

APPOINTMENT KEPT?

□ **YES** □□ NO—Canceled □□ NO—Found Another Attorney □□ NO—Didn't Show □□ NO—Other ____________________________________

RETAINED?

□ **YES** □□ NO—Still Deciding □□ NO—Just Gathering Info □□ NO—We Didn't Want It□ □□ NO—Referred Out □□ □ NO—Cost □ □□ NO—Other

□ PNC Given Retainer Other Info____

Thank You Note Sent to Referral: _________

7. Client Closing Letter

DATE

PERSONAL & CONFIDENTIAL

Client Name

Client Address

RE: Closing of Your File

Dear _________:

Enclosed please find a certified copies of __________________ entered in your case on ____________, 20____. These are certified copies of your Orders, so please keep them in a safe place with your other important papers. Should you require additional *certified* copies of these documents, you may obtain them from the clerk's office at the ______________ County Court for a nominal fee.

I would like to reiterate that unless you secure a Court Order formalizing any future agreed change to the terms set forth in your current Orders, the Court is unlikely to take any notice of discussions, or even written documents, between you and ___________. Please remember that subsequent changes in the law may also have an effect on the terms of the Order. It is important that you verify the current state of the law with counsel when considering any change to the terms of your arrangements. I would, of course, be happy to discuss any future changes with you.

Please be sure that you have reviewed any insurance, retirement, or estate planning documents, to ensure that they accurately reflect your current wishes, and be aware that you must change the beneficiaries immediately if the designations do not reflect your current wishes. If you would like to revise your estate plans, I can refer you to an attorney who specializes in wills, trusts, and estate planning.

This letter will confirm that there are no unfulfilled promises or additional actions that you wish us to take on your behalf at this time. Per your retainer agreement, your file will be saved in electronic format for 10 years. Any further matters undertaken by the firm will be the subject of a new retainer agreement.

Enclosed please find my firm's most recent invoice and a refund check totaling $__________ for the funds remaining in your escrow account. (Alternate: Enclosed please find my firm's final invoice showing an outstanding balance of $___________. Please contact my firm's billing department at your earliest convenience to pay this balance.)

I have truly appreciated the opportunity to work with you and wish you the very best in the future. If you require legal assistance in the future, I do hope you will contact me so that we can work together again.

Very sincerely yours,

Attorney Name

Enclosures

8(a). Flat Fee Retainer Agreement

DATE

NAME

ADDRESS1

ADDRESS2

ADDRESS3

FLAT FEE ENGAGEMENT LETTER

Dear NAME:

I am pleased that you have asked this firm to provide legal services to COMPANY. We have prepared this letter to outline the terms and conditions of our representation, billing arrangements, and similar matters. If acceptable, please sign and date one copy of this Agreement and return it to our offices along with your check so that we may begin work.

A. SCOPE OF REPRESENTATION

Your fee covers the following services:

Our counseling and design fees will be: FEE

B. PAYMENT DUE PRIOR TO WORK BEGINNING (1/2 of the total amount above): 1/2 FEE

The flat fee is only for the services described above. One-half of the total fee is due and payable at the commencement of our services, and one-half of the fee is due upon delivery of the services described above. Should you request additional legal services, those will be subject to a separate engagement agreement.

C. EXPENSES

In addition to the flat fee, you are also responsible for the payment of all expenses incurred in connection with our representation. Examples include filing fees, corporate book expenses, photocopying, postage, and similar charges. As these expenses are incurred, we will either bill them to you or request that a third-party provider bill you directly.

D. BILLING PROCEDURES

Payment of the bill is expected in accordance with the payment schedule in Section B above unless additional work outside the scope of the original agreement is performed. If payment is not received within thirty (30) days of the date of the statement, the total sums due will incur interest at the rate of three percent (3%) per month from the date of the statement first showing the charge. Interest will be compounded monthly. Where interest is charged and payments are later received, those payments will be first applied against interest and then to the outstanding principal.

If there is a balance due on your account at any time, we reserve the right to cease all work on the matter until specific arrangements are made for payment of the outstanding balance. Additionally, if you fail to pay the outstanding balance, we have the right to retain your files until all outstanding fees and expenses are paid. If we are forced to seek the aid of a collection firm, the courts, or any other means to collect any past-due amount, you will be responsible for payment of all expenses, including attorneys' fees, incurred in collection.

Disputes or questions as to the amount of a statement shall be brought to the attention of the firm in writing within thirty (30) days of receipt of the bill.

E. DISCLOSURE (BUSINESS CLIENTS)

Each party, as evidenced by their signature on this agreement, expressly acknowledges that FIRM represents the Company regarding the outlined scope of representation listed above and does not represent the parties individually in this matter. Each party expressly acknowledges this Relationship and has been advised to seek independent counsel regarding their rights for this matter. As evidenced by each party's signature to this agreement, each party accepts FIRM as attorney for this matter and waives any potential conflict of interest.

F. TERMINATION

Our engagement may be terminated by either of us at any time by written notice to the other. We normally do not terminate our representation unless a client misrepresents or fails to disclose material facts, fails to pay fees or expenses, makes it unreasonably difficult or unethical to represent them, or other just cause exists. In the event of termination by us, you will remain obligated to pay for all time and other charges incurred on your behalf.

Once we have received full payment, we will turn over all files, if you so request.

If the above terms are acceptable, please sign and date one copy of this Agreement, send us the signed copy, and keep the other copy for your files. When this letter is signed by both of us, it is a contract. We look forward to working with you. If you have any questions, please call us before signing.

Sincerely,

FIRM

By: ________________

Partner

By: ___________________________ __________________

COMPANY, NAME Date

8(b). Hourly Rate Retainer Agreement

RETAINER AGREEMENT

Scope of Representation

I hereby retain and employ the law firm of ______________("the Firm"), with respect to ________________, and no other legal matters are the subject of this Agreement. I understand that no settlement of my case may be made without my consent. This agreement, which is governed by Virginia law, does not extend to any appeals or retrials that may become necessary, either of which would require a new and separate retainer agreement. I agree to cooperate with my attorneys, to provide them with all pertinent information in my possession that they may request, to keep them informed of my current residence and employment addresses, and to attend all scheduled appearances in my case. I agree to report to my attorneys all developments relevant to my case and to advise them of any communications made to me by my spouse or my spouse's attorney.

Compensation

a) **Hourly Rates:** I agree to compensate the Firm for time spent on my behalf by its attorneys, paralegals, and legal assistants at their respective hourly rates (see below). Hourly rates will be subject to modest increases in January of each year.

b) **Administrative Costs and Fees:** I agree to bear the actual costs of my case, including filing and service of process fees, expert witness fees, commissioners' and court reporters' charges, and the out-of-pocket expenditures incurred by the Firm, including, but not limited to: monochrome copies, scans, prints ($0.____ per page), color copies, prints ($0.____ per page), faxes ($_____ per page for outgoing faxes only), postage, courier services, and online legal research outside Virginia. I agree that the Firm may use the funds in my retainer account to pay costs and fees described in this paragraph.

c) **Billing:** Bills will be rendered on a monthly basis on or about the 15th of each month, and payment is due by the 10th of the following month. Amounts not paid by the next month's billing will incur a service charge of ___% per month, as I understand that the Firm does not extend credit. Any objection to a bill must be communicated by me to the Firm within thirty days, or the bill will be deemed correct and fair. I understand that I am responsible for payment of legal fees and costs regardless of any negotiated or court-ordered contribution by the opposing party, although any such payment made directly to the Firm will be credited to my account balance.

d) **Retainer Funds:** I agree to pay **$________** as a retainer, said sum to be applied to current bills as rendered. I understand that at the end of each billing cycle, funds are drawn from the retainer to cover the work performed during that cycle. I understand that after completion of all work on my case, any unused retainer funds will be refunded to me. I recognize that this retainer does not in any way represent an estimate of legal fees and/or costs for this matter and that the legal fees and costs may well exceed the amount of the retainer. I agree to replenish the retainer upon request so that sufficient funds remain to cover anticipated legal services and costs. I agree that 90 days prior to trial I will provide an additional retainer fee in an amount sufficient to cover the anticipated costs to prepare for and represent me at trial. I understand that my failure to replenish the retainer as requested will result in the Firm withdrawing as counsel in my case.

e) **Document Retention:** Upon the termination of the representation, all original, client-furnished documents and any originals of legal instruments or official documents accumulated by the Firm during the engagement will be returned to me. All remaining documents possessed by the Firm pertaining to this engagement will be saved electronically or archived for a period of ten years, at which time all materials will be destroyed.

Termination

I may terminate this agreement at my discretion by notifying the Firm in writing. Subject to our obligations to maintain proper standards of professional conduct, the Firm also reserves the right to terminate this agreement and to withdraw from my case. Should I fail to make timely payments of fees, costs, or retainers as required under this agreement, fail to cooperate with my attorneys, fail to inform my attorneys of all information pertinent to my case, or fail to keep them informed of my current address, the Firm may terminate its representation of me. In that event, I shall pay the balance of my account upon termination, and I agree to compensate the Firm for the legal procedures necessary to withdraw from any pending lawsuit, at the foregoing hourly rate. Should the Firm institute legal proceedings to recover fees and/or advanced costs, whether itself or through other counsel, I agree to pay court costs plus attorneys' fees of 25% of the amount owed.

Please check form of payment:

□ Credit Card □ Check □ Cash □ Cashier's Check/Money Order

Dated: ____________________ Client Signature: ________________

The above employment is accepted upon the terms stated. Receipt is acknowledged of $ retainer.

Dated: ____________________ LAW FIRM NAME

By: ____________________

Attorney printed name

Hourly Rates: Attorney A: $_____; Paralegal A: $__________; Legal Assistants: $_____

9. Client Billing Invoice

FIRM NAME

Invoice Date: __________

Billing Period: ________ to _________

Client Name

Client Address

Client Number

Professional Services

Date	Provider	Action Performed
5/12/20	Attorney A	Reviewed letter from opposing counsel
5/15/20	Paralegal A	Organized responses to discovery requests

	Time	Amount
For Professional Services Rendered		$______
6/15/20 Payment from Client Retainer		$______
Total Payments and Adjustments		$______
Previous Balance of Retainer Account		$______
6/15/20 Payment from Client Retainer		$______
New Balance of Retainer Account		$______
Balance Due		$______

10. Budget Spreadsheet

Note: Not all months are shown for formatting reasons.

			Projected Yearly		Projected Monthly		Dec. 2018	January	February	September	October	November	Monthly
			Dec. 1, 2018 to Nov. 30, 2019		Dec. 1, 2018 to Nov. 30, 2019								
			Fixed	Variable	Fixed	Variable							Averages
EXPENSES													
Marketing													
	Sponsorships/Contributions	SUBTOTAL											
		Continuing sponsorships											
		Other											
	Advertising (general)												
	Advertising (primary source #1)												
	Advertising (primary source #2)												
	Miscellaneous												
	Website - webhosting												
	Website - updates												
	Website - SEO												
	Misc (Pictures, Signs, etc)												
	Announcements												
	Gifts/Flowers												
	Events												
	Meals (networking)	SUBTOTAL											
		Partners											
		Associates											
		Support Staff											
	Meals (Mediations, Conferences, etc.)												
	Meals (Events, Fees, etc.)												
	Professional Associations (all but VSB) SUBTOTAL												
		FBA											
		Alexandria											
		Arlington											
		VTLA											
		VWAA											
		PW											
		Collaborative											
		AAML											
		VBA											
		ABA											
		ALA											
		PANV											
		Other - Notaries											
	Marketing Subtotal												

HR												
	Professional Associations (VSB)											
	Seminars & CLEs											
	Travel/Hotel for seminars											
	Job Advertising											
	Meals (within office)											
	New Attorney Dinner											
	Fun Committee											
	Gym/Tennis											
	Employee Goodwill - Gifts & events											
	Medical Insurance											
	Life Insurance - Principal - ALL											
	Life Insurance - Northwestern - Partners											
	STD - Principal - ALL											
	LTD - Northwestern - Partners											
	LTD - Principal - Only Partners Costs											
	Workmens Comp/Business Owners											
	Malpractice Insurance											
	Reimbursements (mileage, parking, tolls, etc)											
	Payroll Processing											
	Payroll Tax (Aprox 7.5%)											
	American Funds - 401K Match											
	401K Maintenance											
	Salary											
	Bonus											
	Draw											
	Human Resources Subtotal											
Technology												
	IT Service Provider											
	Computer Replacement											
	Minor - Computer purchases and upgrades											
	Computer - Fixed Monthly Fees (Spam, Duo, Backup, etc.)											
	Computer Software Maintenance - Worldbox & ShareFile											
	Software Upgrades											
	Copier Maintenance											
	Copier Lease											
	Postage Machine Lease											
	Toners (printers)											
	Internet/Phone service											
	LexisNexis online research											
	Online research (PWCC, Arlington, Loudoun)											
	Technology Subtotal											

Physical Space												
	Storage											
	Furniture											
	Outdoor Furniture											
	Outdoor Plants											
	Library											
	Supplies											
	Beverages											
	TrueShred											
	Rent											
	Misc New Employee											
	Cleaning/Janitorial											
	OT HVAC											
	Office Move (Total Costs)											
	Physical Space Subtotal											
COGS												
	Bank Service Charge											
	Credit Card Costs											
	Printing/Stationary											
	Postage											
	Delivery Expense (reimbursed) - FedEx & Laser											
	Reimbursable Expenses (Copy cards)											
	Client Advances											
	Non-Reimbursable Expenses - Not Charged to Client											
	COGS Subtotal											
Firm												
	Legal Fees											
	Accounting Fees											
	Consulting Fees											
	Business License											
	Taxes											
	Investment											
	Firm Subtotal											
Subtotal Expenses												
TOTAL EXPENSES												
TOTALS (Expenses + Distribution + Performance)												
INCOME												
Fee Income												
Misc Income												
TOTAL INCOME												
PROFIT												

11. Training Guide

Training Schedule

- Week 1: General Setup/Orientation (Responsible Team Member)
    - Computer: logins for e-mail & AS, Google calendar link
    - Greet & set up clients for meetings
    - Office layout: where everything goes
    - Printer/scanner/copier overview
- Week 1: Mail (Responsible Team Member)
    - USPS: regular, certified, return
    - FedEx
    - Refill postage
    - Tracking expenses: when necessary, where to document
- Week 2: Phones (Responsible Team Member)
    - Basic phone skills: Answer, transfer, hold, conference
    - Set up voicemail
- Week 2: Phones (Responsible Team Member)
    - Review phone scripts and/or process for the following types of calls and tips on identifying each kind:
        - Prospective client
        - Current client with question
- Week 3: Calendar (Responsible Team Member)
    - Idea of ideal week
    - General scheduling goals for client meetings, advisor meetings, and phone

appointments

- Week 4: Meeting Prep & Follow Up (Responsible Team Member)
    - Packets
    - Where files go
    - Post-delivery meeting follow up/tasks
- Weeks 4 & 5: CRM/Database (Responsible Team Member)
    - General overview
    - Linking e-mails
    - Creating file notes
    - Completing tasks
    - Linking calendar appointments to action step matters

12. Procedure Examples

The following procedure examples are designed to show you how we have written two procedures for our firms. As you will see in the examples, our procedures are written informally and intended to give step-by-step instruction. From our perspective, the critical points of any procedure are that it be written down and that it is written in a manner that the team members who will be implementing the procedure will understand and be able to follow it.

Procedure for New Client Set Up

New Clients

- Scan Personal Information Form (PIF) and save to server file: original stays in hanging file until engaged.
- Once engaged: create client asset binder. Move PIF and any asset documents to the asset binder.
- If not engaged: follow instructions whether to return PIF/funding docs to prospect or shred.
- Input PIF into database.
- Generate Asset Report.
- Update database after Strategy Meeting. Consult attorney on any questions immediately following Strategy Meeting.
- Schedule meeting with clients.
- Prepare meeting packet.
- Attend meeting.
- Enter data into database.
    - Finish any remaining tasks in Counselling matter and close.

    - Create matter for client.
    - Record notes from meeting in matter.
    - Activate portal if client signed up.
- Agreements
    - Engagement Agreement: scan and save in Agreements folder. File original in client agreements binder.
- Record notes in database under each asset.
    - Internal Law Firm notes: our tracking purposes, e.g., mailed form, waiting on confirm from client, etc.
    - Historical Client Comments: action items to client to do/follow up on.
- Scan and submit all signed forms.
- Follow up with clients and advisor on getting verifications: about every 30, 60, and 90 days.
- Scan and file verifications as they come in.

<u>Scanning Instructions:</u>

1. Ensure all documents are free of staples, paperclips, etc.
2. If screen is black > Energy Saver
3. Main Menu > Scan and Send button
    a. Choose 2 Sided Original option if applicable
4. Address Button > Select appropriate folder > Green start button
5. On computer, go to Computer > select Shared > Scans > Select appropriate folder
6. Right click on file > Rename –
    b. Proper Format: Date, Client Name, Name of Document

c. **Example: 2015-Oct-21 John Smith Wells Fargo Statement**

7. Drag to Appropriate Client File

Index

V